The University of Manitoba

AN ILLUSTRATED HISTORY

THE UNIVERSITY OF MANITOBA

AN ILLUSTRATED HISTORY

J.M. BUMSTED

THE UNIVERSITY OF MANITOBA PRESS

The University of Manitoba Press
Winnipeg, Manitoba Canada R3T 2N2
www.umanitoba.ca/uofmpress

Printed and bound in Canada by Friesens
for the University of Manitoba Press

Cover and interior design: Doowah Design Inc.

CANADIAN CATALOGUING IN PUBLICATION DATA
Bumsted, J.M., 1938–

    The University of Manitoba

    Includes bibliographical references.
    ISBN 0–88755–172–6 (bound). – ISBN 0–88755–653–1 (pbk.)

    1. University of Manitoba-History. 2. University of Manitoba-
    History-Pictorial works. I. Title.
    LE3.M3832B85 2001   378.7127'43   C2001–911398–6

The University of Manitoba Press gratefully acknowledges the financial
support provided to its publishing program by the Government of
Canada through the Book Publishing Industry Development Program
(BPIDP) and by the Canada Council for the Arts, the Manitoba
Department of Culture, Heritage and Tourism, and the Manitoba Arts
Council.

Photo Credits and Acknowledgements

The University of Manitoba Press would like to thank the many institutions and individuals who assisted in locating the photographs needed for this illustrated history, in particular the knowledgeable and patient staff at the University of Manitoba Libraries – Archives & Special Collections, especially Director Shelley Sweeney and Lewis Stubbs. We would also like to thank Peter James of the University of Winnipeg Library and Archives, and the staff of U of M Imaging Services.

Invaluable student scrapbooks and photographs were provided by Pamela LeBoldus, Rosemary Malaher (who also provided the scrapbook kept by her mother, Flora Stevens), Wendy Kennedy, and Claire Jewers. Photographs were also provided by Wolf Heck, Henry Kalen, Bob Talbot, and Paula Horeczy. We would like to thank Barney Charach, who has chronicled the history of the U of M for many years, for permission to reproduce many of his photographs.

Finally, we would like to thank the authors of the memoirs excerpted in this book for their permission to reprint their work, and also the University of Toronto Press for permission to reprint an excerpt from Watson Kirkconnell's memoir *A Slice of Canada*.

Photo Credit Abbreviations:

MWG	Manitoba Writers' Guild
PAM	Provincial Archives of Manitoba
UMA	University of Manitoba Archives & Special Collections
UMA/T	University of Manitoba Archives & Special Collections (Tribune Collection)
UML	University of Manitoba Library
UWA	University of Winnipeg Archives
WFP	Winnipeg Free Press

Dedication

This book is dedicated to the members of
my family—Wendy, Jonathan, Geraint, and Carla—and to
the thousands of others who also claim the proud status of
being alumni of the University of Manitoba.

TABLE OF CONTENTS

Preface

As an historian, I am keenly aware of the constantly expanding archives of the University of Manitoba, the repository for—among other things—mounds of paperwork from countless committees that have documented the life and history of the university. There is a great need for a multi-volume, official history of the university, based on all those archival records, but this book is not that. This book attempts chiefly to remind alumni and other readers of what it had been like to be involved with the University of Manitoba over the 125 years of its existence. It serves as a chronicle of the people and events that shaped the university, and attempts to capture its changing spirit over the many peregrinations and reinventions.

Finding a perspective from which to approach such a chronicle was no easy matter. As this book documents, the University of Manitoba never had a single student body or a single faculty. For its entire existence, it has consisted of many component parts, often geographically separated within the city of Winnipeg and, until 1967, within the province. From the beginning, therefore, I tried to develop an abstract and somewhat artificial overarching perspective, focussing on the undergraduate student experience over the years

while providing enough historical background to put that student experience into perspective. The narrative point of view thus hovers first over the colleges, then over the Broadway and downtown campuses, and, finally, chiefly over the Fort Garry campus. I have relied heavily on student publications, in particular the student newspapers. To some extent, this reliance, reflecting the publications themselves, slights the experiences of professional schools not located within the ambit of undergraduate action, including the School of Art, the early Law School, and, of course, the Medical College, although I have tried to refer to those institutions at critical points in their development. After 1920, it also tends to slight the smaller colleges. Another decision I made from the start was to regard the history of the various colleges that eventually became separate universities (United College and Brandon College) as a legitimate part of the University of Manitoba's history until the point of separation.

As I became more involved in the research and talked to more people around the university, it became increasingly clear to me that portraying the post-1977 period was going to be a problem. The difficulty was partly that more recent events are always difficult to put into proper historical focus, especially for an historian who is still living within the system. Many of the participants in the events of these years are still active, and hold strong views about their participation. Not only do they have their own interpretations of the university's history, but they have an understandable interest in seeing that their bailiwick—whatever it was or is—receives not only judicious treatment, but what they would regard as an appropriate amount of attention in the discussion. I eventually decided that the recent history of the University of Manitoba would have to be written later, or by someone completely outside it. Here, readers will find the post-centennial history treated only briefly in an epilogue.

I would not claim that the following history is seen through rose-coloured glasses. The University of Manitoba has had more than its share of trials and tribulations, most of which have shaped the experiences of its faculty and students. To eschew completely a discussion of the university's many travails would be doing the reader a considerable injustice. To celebrate is not to avoid. But what should become readily apparent is the indomitable and unconquerable nature of those involved with the University of Manitoba, and therefore of the institution itself.

Acknowledgements

The author is deeply indebted to the dozens of alumni, faculty members, ex-faculty members, staff members, and ex-staff members who provided information and background for the story and illustrations that follow. Some of these people were formally interviewed, some responded to our call for information, but many answered questions on the telephone or in person—probably never realizing that they thus were being informally "interviewed" for the book. The author is also deeply indebted to Laird Rankin, Sandy Gregor, and Dick Johnson—as well as the anonymous reviewers for the University of Manitoba Press—who read the manuscript more or less in entirety and offered useful comments and suggestions. Lisa Friesen and Siân Bumsted served as research assistants.

Many librarians and archivists were indispensable, but a particular thanks is due to Lewis Stubbs of the University of Manitoba Archives & Special Collections, whose knowledge of the records of the university is unrivalled and who provided material above and beyond the call of duty, without which this book would not have been possible. David Carr, of the U of M Press, was not only the original inspiration for this project, but throughout the writing and production process has been more of a collaborator than simply an editor. Patricia Sanders, the Press's Managing Editor, has helped keep my prose on the level, while the imaginative and lively design and lay-out by Steven Rosenberg of Doowah Design has helped to make this a truly "illustrated" history.

Chapter 1 ❧ 1877–1900

On 28 February 1877, An Act to Establish a Provincial University passed its third reading in the legislature of the province of Manitoba. Like so many establishments in Manitoba in those heady days, that of a university was at least extremely precipitate, if not positively premature. The province itself had only been created by the government of Canada in 1870 under pressure of armed rebellion, led by Métis who did not want to be placed in colonial tutelage. The city of Winnipeg had been incorporated three years later, when its population was about 3500 and it contained about 900 buildings. Historian George Bryce—one of the first professors at Manitoba College—later observed, "It showed a consciousness of its own importance when

Winnipeg was incorporated that it at once became a city. It did not go through the chrysalis stage of village or town." To a considerable extent, the early inhabitants of both province and city had an optimistic sense of their own destiny that partially justified this impatience.

The early establishment of a university in Manitoba has often been credited to the colleges for which the university would, for many years, act as the degree-granting body. But although the three founding colleges—St. John's College, Manitoba College, and St. Boniface College— were willing to become part of a university, they had not particularly initiated the process of creating one. That honour must go to the province's lieutenant-governor, Alexander

Opposite: St. John's College staff and some students, 1885 (UMA). In the top row, far left, is Samuel Matheson, later archbishop of Rupertsland and chancellor of the university. Among the students, the second from the right (middle row) is John Machray, later chair of the BoG. The gowns were worn in the college all day by both faculty and students.

THE ACT OF PARLIAMENT,

STATUTES

AND

CERTAIN REGULATIONS

OF THE

UNIVERSITY OF MANITOBA.

Morris, who, in his 1877 speech from the throne, had pressed for the creation of a university and dragged the government of the day along with him in his enthusiasm. Until there was a university in the province, of course, bright young men who wanted higher degrees had to travel hundreds, if not thousands, of miles to acquire them. Often such men did not return to Manitoba.

At the beginning, only the men were allowed to seek higher education in the province. The first woman was admitted to university examination in Manitoba in 1886, only a few years after women had first been admitted to eastern universities like Toronto and Queen's; this student, Miss Jessie Holmes, graduated in 1889. We have no recorded reaction of a Manitoba student to this innovation, although Winnipeg clergyman Charles W. Gordon (who

had been a student at Queen's) recorded in his autobiography: "While I personally voted for the extension of university privileges to women I was conscious of a secret feeling of which I was somewhat ashamed, that something of the lofty splendor of university had departed with the advent of women. It was a little like playing baseball with a soft ball." Such attitudes help explain why, until the twentieth century, few women could be found in the classrooms of the university or its colleges.

At the time of its establishment, the University of Manitoba joined about twenty other degree-granting institutions of higher learning in the Dominion of Canada. Most of them were small undergraduate operations with fewer than 100 students each. A majority was, like the founding colleges of the U of M, denominational in affiliation, designed mainly to train clergymen. The new university in

Alexandre-Antonin Taché

(1823–1894) was born in Quebec, and came to Red River in 1845. Made bishop of St. Boniface of 1853 (and archbishop in 1871), Taché was one of the main leaders of Manitoba's francophone community and its principal advocate in the years after the Red River Rebellion. After Manitoba entered confederation in 1870, Taché fought tirelessly for guarantees of bilingualism and biculturalism in the new province.

Opposite: Upper Fort Garry in the early 1870s, seen from the St. Boniface side of the Red River (PAM); the title page of the 1877 University of Manitoba Act (UMA). Above: St. Boniface College, with Bishop's Palace and Cathedral, in 1878, just after the establishment of the University of Manitoba (PAM).

Manitoba was the first degree-granting institution created west of southern Ontario. It was also the first in Canada to be strictly organized on a federative basis and the first

The original building of Manitoba College in the 1870s (PAM).

such university to survive for more than a few years. (The University of Toronto was quasi-federative, while the University of Halifax, designed to federate a number of Nova Scotia colleges, was founded in 1876, but lasted only a few years.) The early models for the new prairie university were Canadian, British, and—much less frequently—American.

The university was founded in some terminological confusion and controversy. The leader of the Roman Catholic Church and francophone community in Manitoba, Bishop Alexandre Taché, had made his support of a university conditional on its having no teaching establishment of its own. Concerned about the implications of a single, secular educational institution—likely to be dominated by Protestant anglophones—Taché sought to ensure that

higher education in the province would remain in the hands of the colleges, one of which was the francophone and Catholic St. Boniface College. The first university act was based largely on the Ontario University Act of 1853 and the model of the University of London, a degree-granting institution with no teaching function of its own. The confusion came over Section 10, which had different wording in the French version from that of the official version passed (in English) in the legislature. The printed statute, as translated into French, referred specifically to the University of London, and the official version had the phrase "at present" after the statement that the university would have no professors or teachers. Taché had been brought onside by assurances that the university would never teach, while the official act allowed for eventual teaching as well as examining. As a result, the bishop refused to sit on the University Council formed under the act, and was represented by a delegate.

The early meetings of the University Council were held in various rooms in the city of Winnipeg. Several students of St. John's College were ordered to report to the first registrar in order to register. The registrar, Major E.W. Jarvis, produced a half-sheet of writing paper and had the students inscribe their names on it. The minimal functions of the early university were financed by small legislative grants and by fees for examining students and for the conferring of degrees. At the beginning, all teaching was carried on in the colleges, which were basically secondary schools with a small university component added at the top. As well as the Catholic St. Boniface College, the early

An architect's drawings of a proposal for a greatly expanded St. John's College, 1883 (PAM). The intention to use an English model for the college is quite evident in this drawing; the spires suggest Cambridge rather than Oxford.

university was composed of St. John's College, which was Anglican in foundation, and Manitoba College, which was Presbyterian and had been moved in 1874 from Kildonan to Winnipeg, where it purchased a building on the northwest corner of Main and Henry streets. St. John's and St. Boniface had both been in existence, off and on, since the earliest days of the Red River Settlement. Much of the public money for early higher education came from the province's marriage licence fees, which in 1884 contributed $3756.49 to its support. The marriage licence fees, which were assigned to the university between 1884 and 1889, were distributed to each classical, affiliated college in proportion to the amounts paid by members of the religious denomination to which it belonged, with any surplus apportioned equally to the colleges.

In 1872 St. John's built a new building on St. Cross Street in what is now the North End, completing it in 1874. It was a rambling two-storey building with a veranda running its entire length. The building contained classrooms, a library, a dining hall, teaching rooms, and dormitories. St. John's moved to new quarters on Main Street at Church Avenue in 1884, but the college students were returned in 1885 to their old building. St. Boniface College laid the cornerstone for a new building just east of the cathedral in St. Boniface in 1880. The building was thirty-six metres by eighteen metres and had four storeys. It housed both classrooms and residence students. Manitoba College in 1882 erected a new building with flaring eaves and

A Final Examination in Philosophy from 1899.

UNIVERSITY OF MANITOBA EXAMINATIONS, MAY, 1899
MENTAL AND MORAL SCIENCE – SPECIAL COURSE
SCHWEGLER

1. What was the great problem of pre-Socratic Philosophy? Sketch in brief outline the successive attempts at its solution.
2. "But, while it is my thinking, it is my thinking that has to decide upon all these points." Consider the bearing of this remark upon the relation of Socrates and the Sophists.
3. State the part played by (a) Socrates, (b) Heraclitus, in the genesis of Platonic Idealism.
4. (a) Describe after Aristotle the nature of man.
   (b) Compare the views of Plato and Aristotle as to the true relations of the universal and the individual.
5. Exhibit the inter-connection of the three Critiques of the Kantian Philosophy.
6. Consider how far Fichte may be said to be the true successor of Kant.
7. Exhibit the connection between Schelling and Fichte.
8. Fully describe what is known as the logical or dialectic process of Hegel.
9. Outline briefly Hegel's philosophy of mind.

Candidates will take either question 7 or question 8.

twin turrets on Ellice Avenue at Vaughan. Initially "out in the country," as the city of Winnipeg expanded, Manitoba College had by far the best location of the three founding colleges. Wesley College, whose foundation was anticipated by the Manitoba legislature in 1877,

was finally affiliated with the university in October 1888. At the time it was located in rented quarters, but it was raising funds for a building on Portage Avenue.

The university component of teaching at the colleges was chiefly the traditional, classical one developed in both Britain and France, emphasizing ancient languages and mathematics, and designed chiefly to prepare students for Holy Orders. Textbooks were carefully prescribed. Teaching was done in the colleges by individuals who carried heavy loads, often up to forty hours in the classroom per week. They had little incentive for research. Many of the early teachers were long remembered as hard-working and harried men. Instruction emphasized rote memorization and recitation. Material learned had to be retained long enough for the end-of-year examinations administered by the university, but prepared by the teachers in the colleges.

The University of Manitoba's first examinations were held on 27 May 1878. Seven students, all from Manitoba College, wrote these examinations. The Bachelor of Arts degree of the university was based on a yearly examination system, with papers set and written in either English or French. Matriculation, or entrance examination, came after a Preliminary Examination, which could be attempted by anyone in the province, including women after 1886. Students needed 25 percent in every subject to pass the Preliminary Examination, and 66 2/3 percent in all subjects constituted a First. The Preliminary Examination was designed to weed out the unprepared, and preparation involved classical subjects. After the

first year, students sat the Previous Examination before proceeding to special honours or general courses. Subjects for the Previous Examination were Latin, Greek, modern languages (including English), and mathematics, for a total of thirteen separate papers.

The same percentages as for Preliminary Examinations applied. Special or honours courses required specialization in a subject with high academic standing. In both courses,

students wrote an examination after the second year, known as the Junior Examination, and after the third year wrote the Senior or Final Examination. These upper-level examinations required a 34 percent in each paper and a 40 percent average, with higher grades in some subjects. The emphasis in the examination results was on standings (first, second, third, pass), which were usually published in the local newspapers. Actual percentages were published after 1896. Examination results were a matter of considerable competition among the colleges in the early days, and the number of firsts and medal-winners collected by a college was a mark of its standing in the larger community.

While it could be argued that the perpetuation of an educational system based along classical lines was somewhat surprising in a province obviously in desperate need of skilled professionals, it must be remembered that the colleges were intended to be, in the first place, the training ground for clergymen, and, in the second place, to serve their denominations as undergraduate liberal arts institutions. In such institutions, the emphasis had always been upon building character and leadership, rather than on specific professional skills. The classical

Left: William Reginald Gunn, the university's first arts graduate, 1880 (PAM). Below: Both sides of the university silver medal, 1893. Medals, awarded at graduation, were an important competitive feature of early student life, valued by both individuals and the colleges (UMA).

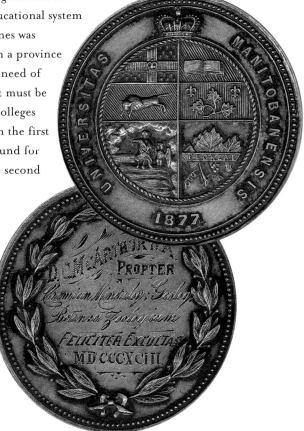

they were being required to shoulder the entire burden.

Almost from the creation of the university, pressure existed for the establishment of professional schools, the teaching of scientific and technical subjects, and a more practical, vocationally oriented course of study. Against the wishes of the Manitoba College of Physicians and Surgeons, for example, a private medical school was organized in 1882 and affiliated with the university in 1883. This affiliation made it impossible for the university to continue solely as an examining and degree-granting body. A year later, a reading course in law, providing three annual examinations leading to an LLB degree, was similarly accepted. At the same time, the denominational colleges were finding it increasingly difficult to stay afloat financially, and by the mid-1880s several colleges were talking about the total abandonment of arts instruction. Nevertheless, in 1885, when a land grant from the federal and provincial governments provided the first public financial support to the university beyond the marriage licence fees, the chancellor could still describe his institution as "a Republic of Colleges to which in conjunction with the Graduates of the University the State has practically committed the direction and government of the university."

By 1889 the question of university teaching was being seriously debated in the University

Archbishop Machray's letter to the council of St. John's College, nominating members to the council in 1886 (UMA).

curriculum of the colleges was never really designed to satisfy the pretensions of an up-and-coming young province, and it was the fault of the province—which had no money for higher education—rather than the colleges, that

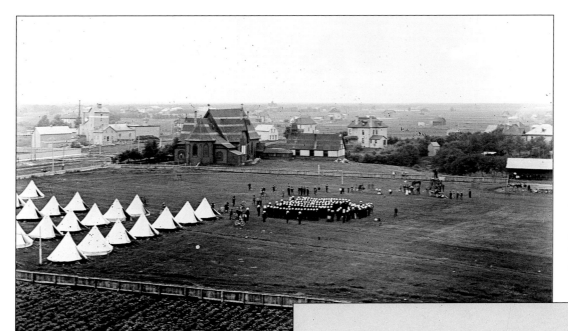

Left: The 90th Regiment in camp on the university's Broadway grounds, 1899 (UMA). Below: Downtown Winnipeg, as seen from the university's Arts Building, 1898 (UMA).

Council, with only St. Boniface really hostile to the idea. As a result of the debates, in November of 1889, a report of a committee on teaching called for the creation of chairs in natural science, mathematics, and modern languages, and the appointment of at least five university professors. The appointments were to be funded out of the land grants, but the federal government held up the grants and then the sale of lands until the larger university question was settled, thus providing a circular situation that prevailed until 1897. As an interim measure, the council decided to allow the three Protestant colleges to combine to teach science, and they did so in a flat rented in the McIntyre Block in the downtown area. By 1893 a committee of the University Council was appointed to consider available sites for a university building in Winnipeg. The province

refused to provide any funding until 1897, when it agreed to lend the university the sum of $60,000 to build and equip a science building, in return for a mortgage on its lands. The government also agreed to an annual grant of $6000 for teaching, with $5000 more to be charged against the lands.

In 1898 the government transferred to the university the Hudson's Bay Company lands on Broadway known as the "Old Driving Park," and after some objections from St. John's College and St. Boniface College, the Broadway site was approved by the University Council. Construction was begun on the science building in 1899, and it was completed in 1901. Meanwhile, the big discussion revolved around when the province would allow the university to take over teaching from the colleges. Almost everybody (except St. Boniface College) agreed that a single university on a single site was the goal, but there was disagreement over location, the method of administration, and the division of teaching faculties, all of which would hold matters up for years. During the protracted period of uncertainty, it was difficult for the colleges to plan anything.

While the system shuffled towards the creation of a teaching university, the students of the several colleges and schools began to manufacture what would gradually become an elaborate student life. Students of Manitoba College founded *The Manitoba College Journal* in 1885, the same year the *St. John's College Magazine* was established. The Manitoba College students also organized a football (rugby) club in 1885, which played two games against the provincial Normal School and captured the Provincial

Challenge Cup. The victory was celebrated with an oyster supper (fresh oysters were regularly available in Winnipeg from the early 1870s), which became a victory ritual for many years. In 1888 a five-team football league was organized, consisting of Manitoba College, St. John's College, the Medical College, the Normal School, and the Graduates. St. John's College won the first cup. A year later this league became an inter-collegiate football league, with the first members Manitoba College, Winnipeg Schools, St. John's College, the Medicals, and Wesley College. Track and field became inter-collegiate

Opposite: By the turn of the century, Winnipeg had grown into a thriving commercial centre. Every horse produced about fifty pounds of dung per day, much of it ending up on the extremely wide streets (PAM). Above: A student being "bounced" in front of Manitoba College, c. 1896. Although his colleagues do not wear gowns, they are formally dressed in suits and ties, standard garb for male students at the time (UMA).

An early benefactor of the university was Alexander Kennedy Isbister (1822-1883). The mixed-blood son of an HBC clerk, Isbister left Red River in 1842 to complete his education in Scotland and later became an important British educator. He was a long-time advocate for the rights of the mixed-blood population in Red River, and engaged in a long battle with the Hudson's Bay Company on their behalf. Although he never returned to Red River, Isbister established a substantial scholarship for U of M students and left his library of nearly 5000 volumes to the university (PAM).

in the late 1880s, and hockey, curling, and basketball were added in the early 1890s. Most athletic teams played in inter-collegiate competition, and not until after World War I were there university teams or games against schools outside Winnipeg.

As the roster of the football leagues suggests, the colleges were not the sole centres of student life, for the Normal School and the Medical College were also active intramurally and in other social ways as well. Athletic championships were added to university medals as ways of measuring the comparative achievement of the colleges. Some time around the turn of the century, the popular conception of a "college man" shifted from one of a near-sighted intellectual carrying an armload of books to what one observer called "a husky fellow in a padded suit with a rugby ball under his arm." The shift was part of the turn-of-the-century spread of the values of muscular Christianity, with its emphasis on the cultivation of character, fair play, and "honest, manly sport."

The college journals, to which Wesley College added *Vox Wesleyana* in 1897, reported an extraordinarily full student calendar by the 1890s. All colleges and schools had freshman hazing and a freshman reception, as well as regular athletic contests. Many of their students participated in an annual Halloween parade through the streets of Winnipeg, which often turned rough as students from the several institutions jostled with one another. There were regular college dinners, and regular meetings of literary societies, YMCA and YWCA societies, and various missionary groups (which probably drew best among the pre-theological students, of which all the denominational colleges had a good many). In addition, there were many informal activities, such as skating parties, bicycle parties, snowshoeing in the winter, and regular social gatherings in local homes. Dancing and dances were not yet being encouraged, however. St. Boniface had a music programme and a college orchestra, doubtless the successor to the brass band from the school that had played at the proclamation of the provisional government in Red River in 1869. St. Boniface also had four associations, canonically erected, to foster piety.

St. Boniface students were required to spend all day at the college and to attend games and sports as well as classes. Only those who lived nearby could go home for lunch. Other colleges expected similar attendance but did not demand it. Most colleges formally forbade the use of tobacco and strong stimulants, but everyone knew they were being used.

As the requirement to spend the full day at the college suggests, most students at the University of Manitoba lived at home or in lodgings near their colleges and schools. Thus, from the beginning, the university was a commuter school. All the colleges had some

Alexander Morris

(1826–1889) as Manitoba Lieutenant-Governor was an early advocate of the establishment of the University of Manitoba. A graduate of the University of Glasgow and McGill University, he had an active legal and political career in Ontario before coming to Manitoba in 1872. He was also responsible for negotiating treaties Three to Six, and later published an important book on these events. He returned to Ontario in 1878.

Manitoba Medical College,
c. 1894 (UMA).

Opposite far right: Robert Machray (1831-1904), Archbishop of Rupertsland and the U of M's first chancellor (UML). Opposite near right: Andrew Baird (1855-1940), professor of church history at Manitoba College (UMA). Right: Built as Manitoba College in 1882, this ornate structure would be the home of St. Paul's College from 1929 to 1958 (PAM).

limited residence space for male students from outside the city, although none could accommodate female students until the early years of the twentieth century. In 1904 Gordon Fahrni from Gladstone paid $10.00 per month for his room in Wesley College, and another $4.00 for a twenty-one-meal ticket at the college dining hall. Manitoba College was the largest and most active college before World War I, enrolling 200 students (140 in arts) in 1893, reaching a peak of 300 in 1910, and falling to 233 in 1912–13, when Wesley's enrolment began to advance. In 1893 Manitoba College claimed 128 of the 199 degrees awarded.

There was also a full roster of student pranks. On Halloween students regularly put buggies on the roofs of local barns. One group of Manitoba College students in the class of Professor Andrew Baird set off many alarm clocks to ring in succession in one of his classes.

At St. John's College, four students carried off and hid one instructor's bicycle, not once but twice. In all cases, students were required to apologize, but no further disciplinary action appears to have been taken. All in all, students at the constituent parts of the University of Manitoba led full and fulfilling lives. Many went off to successful careers elsewhere, but most remained in Manitoba, some joining the ranks of leaders of the province.

Chapter 2 ❧ 1900–1915

The fifteen years between the turn of the century and the start of the Great War saw the balance of power gradually tip at the University of Manitoba from the colleges to the university itself. While the university gradually increased its direct role in the educational structure, both with the addition of new professional and vocational faculties and with the creation of its own arts faculty, the major issue of debate was over the physical location of the new and enhanced university. After many years of chopping and changing, that debate was seemingly resolved with a decision in 1913 to develop the main campus at the university's present site in Fort Garry, ten kilometres south of downtown Winnipeg in the midst of open farmland. This decision proved

less than final, and working through the process of consolidation would require another forty-odd years. It would never be quite complete.

In 1900 amendments to the University Act allowed the university for the first time the power to appoint and dismiss professors, the beginning of the shift from an examining to a teaching institution. The University Council was allowed to appoint as the first three university professors the three academics from the colleges who had been cooperating since 1890 in the science department. Their half-time appointments were not to continue when the university finally appointed its own full-time professors. In the wake of the amendments, the council also adopted regulations governing the Faculty of Science and

Opposite: The graduating class of Manitoba College, 1912. By this time, a substantial minority of the undergraduate enrolment was composed of females (UMA).

The first faculty of the U of M, 1904. From left to right: Matthew Parker, Gordon Bell, A.H.R. Buller, Frank Allen, Swale Vincent, and R.R. Cochrane (UMA).

the establishment of a teaching university, as well as turning the arts curriculum of the four colleges into a four-year programme. Although the university arts faculty was not yet in existence, after 1900 most scholarships in arts were awarded by the university.

These changes at the university took place against the backdrop of a dramatically changing province. At the turn of the century, Manitoba seemed to be on the verge of a great leap forward. Its population had grown from around 15,000 in 1870 to about a quarter of a million. The rich farmland of the southern part of the province was now settled and cultivated; in 1901 the wheat crop exceeded 50 million bushels. Grain, and especially wheat, made the economy go. The period from 1900 to 1915 saw a massive immigration to Manitoba. A prosperity based on a wheat boom lasted until the year before the

opening of the Great War. The province, in the 1890s, had been the centre of national attention for its attempt to enforce an English-only educational policy designed to assimilate its linguistic minorities, including the French. Winnipeg was a bustling city of just over 100,000 people, often known as the "Chicago of the North," with a merchant class and an industrial working class. Like the province, the city was composed primarily of people of British origins, although in the North End there was a growing immigrant community of ethnic groups from all parts of Europe.

The early years of the century were years of growth for higher education in Manitoba, as they were for the province as a whole. Much of the growth occurred in the "practical arts" rather than in the traditional arts programmes. In 1900 the University Council approved a School of Domestic Science, funded by the Winnipeg Council of Women. In 1902 a royal commission recommended the establishment of a separate college of agriculture, but allowed for its affiliation to the university. The new college would have an agriculture department for men and a department of domestic science for women. For a province with as substantial an agricultural base as Manitoba, an agricultural college was hardly a luxury. As a result, the Manitoba government purchased a site of 117 acres on the south bank of the Assiniboine River in what was to become Tuxedo. This site later became Fort Osborne Barracks and is now the Asper Jewish Community Campus.

Also in 1902, the University Council offered to allow Brandon College to affiliate, but the college's Baptist religious principles would not

Chemistry lab, Broadway site, c. 1905 (UMA).

allow it to become associated with the state, and the city really wanted its own university and not a branch of one based in Winnipeg. Brandon eventually affiliated with McMaster University in 1912. And in 1902, the college of pharmacy established privately in 1899 became affiliated with the university, while, at Wesley College, a programme in Icelandic language and literature was begun. Two years later, in 1904, the university organized the Faculty of Science with six full-time professorships, financed by a gift from Lord Strathcona. As Donald A. Smith, Strathcona had helped bring Red River into Confederation and had been a key figure in the Hudson's Bay Company.

The first university professors, housed in the science building on Broadway, which was completed in 1901, were A.H.R. Buller (botany and geology), Frank Allen (physics and mineralogy), M.A. Parker (chemistry), R.R.

Cochrane (mathematics), Swale Vincent (physiology), and Gordon Bell (bacteriology). For the first time, teaching would be done by university appointees rather than by college appointees. Buller, a product of English and German universities, remained at the university until 1936; Allen, the author of 300 research papers, led the physics department until 1944; Parker led the chemistry department until 1936. Cochrane's tenure was much shorter: he was professor of mathematics and, later, chair of the University Faculty until his death in 1910. Vincent, who had studied medicine at Edinburgh, was chair of physiology until 1921, when he left to become professor of physiology at the University of London. As well as teaching at

the university, Gordon Bell also served as provincial bacteriologist and, later, chair of the provincial Board of Health. In those positions, he helped to make dramatic improvements to public sanitation throughout the province.

Also in 1901, Manitoba Agricultural College was created by statute. Its new buildings were completed at the Tuxedo site at a cost of $250,000 in 1906, and the first three staff members were appointed. In late 1905 and early 1906, Dr. Buller wrote a series of articles for the *Manitoba Free Press* advocating that the university expand and move from its Broadway location to a site in Tuxedo near the Agricultural College. These articles were the opening salvo in a reinvigorated debate over the future of the university.

Opposite: Military inspection at Broadway campus, c. 1900 (UMA/T). Above: The Tuxedo site of the Manitoba Agricultural College, 1911 (PAM).

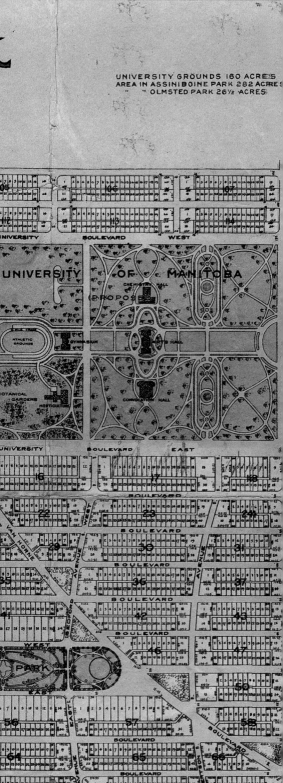

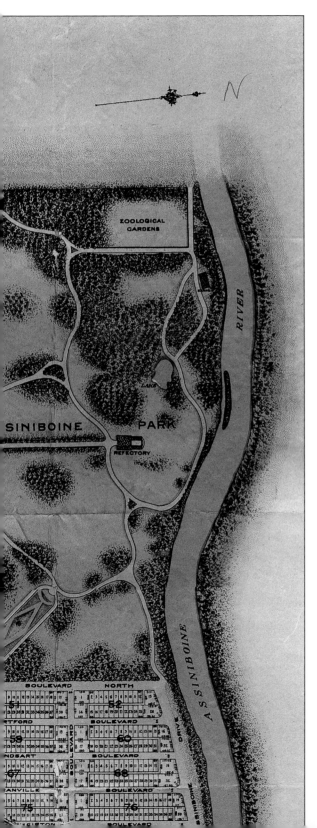

Early in 1907, a committee of the University Council reported on university expansion, recommending the establishment of departments of engineering with three chairs, plus the introduction of departments of history, political economy, law, and modern languages. These recommendations challenged the colleges by entering directly into liberal arts teaching for the first time. Not all the colleges were hostile. St. Boniface and Wesley wanted to retain the traditional structure of the "republic of colleges." St. John's College argued that the university needed a mix of colleges, denominational and secular, on a common site. Canon J.O. Murray of St. John's argued at a public banquet that "the right solution of the question was that the University should undertake a higher form of University work, and that the colleges should do tutorial and individual work." One Manitoba College alumnus responded to the proposals by observing, "When the university is prepared to take up teaching in all the Arts branches, then the colleges will gladly acquiese, and confine their attention solely to teaching Theology. But until that time the colleges will be inclined to remain where they are and continue the splendid work which they are doing."

As a result of the disagreements, another committee of the University Council reported that the government should appoint a commission of inquiry to examine the constitution and management of the university, its assets and finances, the connection between the university and its colleges, the scope of teaching at the university, and its site and buildings. This commission was chaired by

Left: The plan for a new Tuxedo site for the U of M, across from Assiniboine Park, prepared by the Olmsted Brothers firm, 1911. One of the Olmsted Brothers firm, who designed Assiniboine Park, was Frederick Law Olmsted, who was responsible for the original plan for Central Park in New York City. Note the square miles of suburban streets (some of them actually built) that surround the park and the campus (UMA). Below: George Bryce, pioneer Manitoba historian and a founder of Manitoba College (UMA).

J.A.M. (always known to his friends as "Jam") Aikins. It heard fourteen deputations and individual members visited the universities of Toronto, McGill, Laval, Minnesota, Northwestern, Michigan, and Illinois. While the commission was deliberating, the Tuxedo Park Company, through an open letter to the press, offered to donate 150 acres for the

THE FUTURE UNIVERSITY ACCORDING TO PROFESSOR SWALE VINCENT, 1906

The image of the ideal University of Manitoba.... I see in the not far distant future a generous tract of country with avenues of trees and swards of green, dotted with shining edifices of white marble and of classic outline. Here all departments of instruction and investigation find a cradle, a temple and a shrine. There are schools of literature, science, fine arts and music; colleges and engineering and agriculture. There is a school of medicine and a conveniently situated clinical hospital. The houses of the professors and lecturers and the residential halls for students ... a great students' club or union, with libraries, reading-rooms, smoking-rooms and an auditorium. And greatest vision of all, I see a vast University library with miles of shelving lined with the literature of the past and present and embracing all branches of knowledge....

I see a University moulding a race of men and women who have learned to take time to pause and ask themselves whether in eagerly pursuing the means of livelihood they are not forgetting that their function is to live—a University breathing the doctrines of sanity, repose, thoughtfulness, and humility, training men who do not fear to face the facts of the universe, but who nevertheless have a refinement, a breadth and serenity, a sweetness and magnanimity bred of a sound acquaintance with the best in science, literature, music and the fine arts.

Dr. Swale Vincent, Professor of Physiology, 6 December 1906, quoted in Alumni Journal

university on the southern boundary of Assiniboine Park, opposite the south entrance. The council liked the site, but held off a decision until the commission had finally reported. Late in 1907 an Order-in-Council affiliated the Manitoba Agricultural College with the university, and soon afterwards (March 1908) a student newspaper, *The M.A.C. Gazette*, joined the Literary Society, the YMCA, the Student Self-Government Organization, and the Athletic Association, as part of the student fabric of the institution.

Although there was still no report from the commission of inquiry, the university agreed in 1909 to appoint chairs in political economy, English, and history; teaching in these subjects was to be limited to third- and fourth-year arts students. When these appointments were actually made later in the year, a faculty of arts and science was, in effect, created, although the only faculty was called the University Faculty.

The report of the commission of inquiry was finally tabled in the legislature early in 1910. The seven commissioners could not agree, and as a result there were three reports. A minority report, signed by Aikins and Reverend A.A. Cherrier, wanted a traditional university dominated by the denominational colleges, with little government control. The other two reports wanted a full state-supported university managed by a board of governors on a large site, with a president, expanded teaching departments, and room for the colleges to teach what they wanted. The vital difference of opinion, said the commission, "was as to whether the denominational colleges should have representation upon any of the governing bodies

AGRICULTURAL COLLEGE AND FARM
ST VITAL.

Left: An artist's bird's-eye view of the new Manitoba Agricultural College campus at Fort Garry, 1912. Below: Another early proposal (1913) for expansion at the Fort Garry site, showing a new campus to the east of the Agricultural College (UMA).

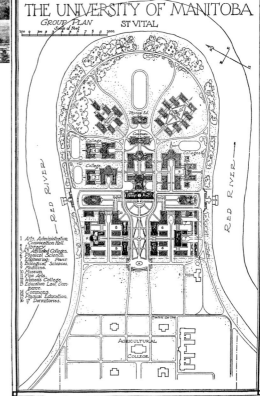

of the University and the extent and character of that representation." This was not quite true, for there was also a disagreement over the site, with the majority wanting a larger site away from downtown, and the minority desiring more land near Broadway.

While none of the reports was informed by any consistent philosophy of higher education beyond utilitarianism, all three reports wanted the financial and business administration of the university separated from the academic, and administered by "men of affairs" rather than by academics. Significantly, none of the reports had any vision of the colleges as integral parts of the university or any notion of colleges as liberal arts institutions. At best, the colleges were seen as interim institutions until the province could decide on its priorities. The commission argued, "The greater body of education lies and must ever lie outside of higher Arts courses. It is connected with the utilities and vocations.... Without such higher and special instruction

Canada will never take its place among the nations of the world as an industrial and commercial leader." All the parties to the commission thus favoured an American-style, provincial, full-service university as the ultimate choice for Manitoba, but did not offer either timetable or sequence of events for getting to the goal. Most importantly, the commission's report itself was not very clear about the nature of provincial financial support.

The commission's report obviously resolved very little. The Wesley College Board of

St. John's College, 1905, at its location in Winnipeg's North End (PAM). Compare this photograph with the right-hand side of the architect's 1883 plans for the college, shown in Chapter 1.

Governors found it so equivocal that they decided to press ahead with a new downtown building. The University Council voted in favour of the earlier proferred Tuxedo site at about the same time that the provincial government decided to purchase a new site for the Agricultural College. The argument for the Agricultural College's departure from Tuxedo was a lack of room for expansion. It eventually chose 570 acres on an oxbow of the Red River

James A. MacLean

(1865-1945), the university's first president, was a native of southern Ontario. Educated at the University of Toronto and Columbia University, he spent his early academic career in the U.S., first at Colorado University and then as president of Idaho State University. As president from 1913 to 1934, MacLean oversaw the university's first period of expansion.

An early science lecture room, Broadway campus, c. 1905 (UMA). Below: J.A.M. ("Jam") Aikins, chair of the commission of inquiry that reported in 1910 (PAM).

in the outer reaches of unincorporated territory, then part of St. Vital but which became Fort Garry in 1912. Within three decades, this site would become the university's main campus. Construction for the Manitoba Agricultural College at Fort Garry began in 1911, and its first buildings, Taché Hall, the Home Economics Building, and what is now known as the Administration Building, were opened in 1912. Taché Hall, the college's residence, could accommodate 500 students and contained two gymnasiums, a swimming pool, and auditorium. The college's main building contained classrooms, faculty offices, a library, and a museum. The move of the Agricultural College to Fort Garry, and the construction of these large and prominent buildings, would begin the process that ultimately drew the entire university away from downtown Winnipeg.

At the end of 1910, Professor Daniel Wilson published a little pamphlet entitled *The Case for Wesley College* in support of a petition for separate degree-granting powers for Wesley if such became necessary to guarantee the autonomy of the college. In his pamphlet, Wilson tried to develop a case for the liberal arts college, emphasizing small-group instruction, personal attention, and the development of social attitudes such as "a common bond of fellowship." Wesley was the only English-speaking college that sought to remain autonomous, and the

Girls' gym, Taché Hall, 1915, with female students (probably from Home Economics) dressed in their physical education uniforms (PAM).

public response to Wesley's initiative was one of opposition, on the grounds that separate degree-granting colleges would undermine a strong provincial university by spreading the finances too thin.

By 1912 it was clear that the University Council and the provincial government did not see eye to eye on the site business. The council continued to be keen for the Tuxedo site, while the government offered money for a new engineering building on Broadway. Alternatively, the province later offered to provide 137 acres between the Agricultural College and the university site, on which it would erect and equip an engineering building. That year, the government amended the Law Society Act (in which the word "person" had been held to refer to men only), and the first

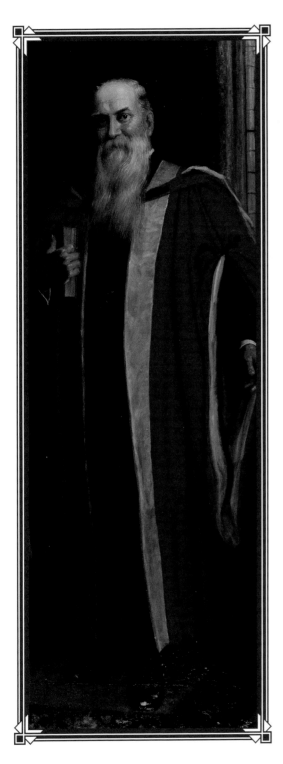

two women—Melrose Sissons and Winnifred M. Wilton—were admitted to the law school. Wilton won first prize in the final examinations.

In the midst of the uncertainty over the site for the university, several of the colleges had engaged in building programmes. Near the downtown, Wesley College constructed a building known as the Annex, which would accommodate sixty residential students and 200 in classrooms; in 1917 it became known as Sparling Hall, a residence for women. St. John's College decided not to build on Broadway, but to construct a three-storey building on college property at Church Avenue. It, too, was called the Annex, and had lecture rooms on the first floor and residences on the upper floors. Both these colleges understandably favoured a downtown location for the university. A year later, Manitoba College and Wesley College agreed to amalgamate as the United Colleges, a move that followed some years of teaching cooperation. Some idea of costs to students is available: in 1911, a student in residence at Manitoba Agricultural College paid $48.50 for the first term, including $25.00 board, $9.00 room rent, and $5.00 for tuition.

A number of major developments occurred in 1913, in addition to the creation of the United Colleges. On 1 January 1913, Dr. James Alexander MacLean—formerly of the University of Idaho—took office as the University of Manitoba's first president. A few days thereafter, the University Council agreed to talk with the government about the tract of land offered at Fort Garry. Premier Sir Rodmond Roblin replied that while the government still

Samuel Matheson (1852-1942), the university's second chancellor, was, like his predecessor Robert Machray, also Archbishop of Rupertsland (UML).

Paul Hiebert on the Class of 1916

I am always proud to say that I was a member of the first student body to ever graduate from this University as such. As I remember that class of 1916, the total number of graduates, not counting engineering and medicine, was about sixty or seventy students. As undergraduates we received much more individual attention than you can possibly receive today. We were known to each of the professors whether we took their classes or not. It was an age of much less efficiency than now and since efficiency is always the enemy of personality, we received much more personal attention.

The university was very definitely something of an ivory tower in those days. We were, in a sense, the elite. We entered a community of educated men, themselves the products of the British universities, and they were generally also what one might call characters. They were very eccentric, very opinionated, they rode their ideas to absurd lengths, but they were full of knowledge and our lives were enriched by associating with them. We picked up an education by osmotic pressure in addition to having to take their more or less rigorous courses. Two years of Latin were compulsory for all students as well as a year in Mathematics, and we always felt that after the first two years' hurdle we were well away and could not fail. But we acquired an outlook and an attitude which, I regret to say, was often supercilious with regard to those whom we regarded as not so fortunate, and a scale of values which we tended to assert in the face of those other assertions of wealth and social standing.

I said that we were treated very personally. When it came to convocations such as this, we were called individually from the front benches to the rostrum where the Chancellor of the University, in those days the very reverend Samuel Matheson, Archbishop of Rupertsland, shook our hand individually and by the authority vested in him as Chancellor admitted us to the Baccalaureatus in Artibus, or something like that. Our two years of Cicero, Virgil, Horace, Caesar, Ovid and things like that didn't always prepare us for the Latin we might meet. Unless of course it was cum laude, or magna cum laude, which meant that we were being presented with a medal or something. We always maintained about Archbishop Matheson, whom we affectionately called Sammy Rupertsland, that, because he was very tall and dignified in his robes and had a long white beard, he presented to a St. John's student a copy of the Holy Scriptures, suitably inscribed, "With the Compliments of the Author."

Paul Hiebert taught chemistry at the university for many years. Excerpt from Alumni Journal (1974).

Student theatrics, c. 1915. Note the students in blackface, still a popular ingredient of stage presentations (UMA).

Paul Hiebert

(1892–1987), a graduate of the class of 1916, taught chemistry at the university for many years. He is best known, however, as the author of the parodic poetry of Sarah Binks, "the sweet songstress of Saskatchewan," which has become one of the classics of Canadian humour. First published in 1947, "Sarah's" poetry was deliberately awful, and coupled a nostalgic view of the pre-Depression prairies with excruciating rhymes and images.

preferred the Broadway site, it would accept the Fort Garry one. The province and the university eventually agreed on Fort Garry. Meanwhile, the provincial legislature had created the Manitoba Association of Graduate Nurses and gave the University of Manitoba the power to conduct examinations in nursing. About the same time, the Agricultural College withdrew from affiliation with the university in preparation for its move to Fort Garry.

In the year immediately preceding the start of World War I, there were further developments. In February 1914, the university agreed to take over the pharmacy course begun

by the Pharmaceutical Association, and in May, the Manitoba Law School—organized by joint agreement of the university and the Law Society of Manitoba—affiliated with the university. In the same year, Manitoba College voted to discontinue its teaching in liberal arts, and turned over its entire student body in arts, plus professors and lecturers, to the university. It also turned its cheers—and its colours, yale blue on white—over to the new arts faculty of the university. For its part, the University Council agreed to begin teaching a number of subjects for arts degrees in the first and second year. As a result, in September of 1914, the university, for the first time, offered a full arts course. It was also rapidly moving toward a full-service role, with the addition of nursing, pharmacy, and law to its existing professional responsibilities.

At the beginning of the Great War, the main campus of the University of Manitoba was still downtown on Broadway, with each of the colleges and the Medical College established on their own sites somewhere else. Only St. Boniface College was far removed physically from Broadway, however. From 1911 onward, the university rented a terrace on University Place for the departments of history, political economy, and English. In 1915 the government allowed the university temporary use of parts of several other buildings, including the east wing of the old Deaf and Dumb Institute and the south wing of the old courthouse.

As for student life, like the physical plant it continued to grow and expand in fits and starts. Fierce rivalry continued among the colleges, especially Wesley and Manitoba before their

Home Economics classroom and students, Manitoba Agricultural College, 1915 (PAM).

merger. Wesley won most of the university academic medals, but it is difficult to establish the quality of the education offered. Libraries were small, laboratories were scarce, and most instruction was by lectures at which attendance was compulsory. A 90 percent attendance rule led to a student strike at Manitoba in 1906, in which classes ceased for a week. The faculty rejected the offer of a 75 percent rule from the students, telling the students to leave or knuckle under. The students gave way, and the rules were eased a year later.

Whether student life at the University of Manitoba was typical of student life in Canadian universities in this period is difficult to determine. In the first place, there was no such thing as a typical Canadian university. For students nationally, the two most important variables were probably the questions of residency and of regimentation, particularly by the religious colleges, which regarded themselves as generally acting "in loco parentis." The two variables were often combined. Student complaints about parietal regulation—especially in residences, which was usually both strict and strictly enforced—were endemic across Canada.

In the second place, there was no such thing as a typical Manitoba experience, either. Many students were enrolled in the denominational colleges—some of which had residences—but many were enrolled in the professional faculties and, after 1900, in the secular university itself, many of which did not have residences. The experience of a student living in residence in a denominational college—where strict rules of chapel attendance, the wearing of gowns,

prescribed meal hours, the performance of religious duties, and the hours of bedtime and waking were all carefully monitored—was quite different from that of a student living in a boarding house and looking after his or her own life. Certainly, the denominational colleges operated on a moral regimen that kept students busy literally from morning to night, offering little opportunity for unapproved extracurricular activity and probably precious little time for even approved events. Finally, we do not have very much student testimony from this early period. What there is suggests that most Manitoba students were carefully monitored, and usually accepted the regimentation. The colleges even experienced occasional upsurges of religious interest, often associated with enthusiasm about post-university missionary activities in the far corners of the world. Religious sensibilities undoubtedly explain the reluctance to allow social dancing. In 1909 Manitoba College held a dance for graduating students, the first such occasion recorded at any of the colleges.

Other major student developments had occurred in 1906. A student union was first organized among the various components of the university, suggesting that a university student body was coming into existence alongside that of the colleges. This first union did not flourish,

Below: The new residence (Taché Hall), 1912 (UMA).
Insert: The building of Taché Hall, 1911 (UMA).

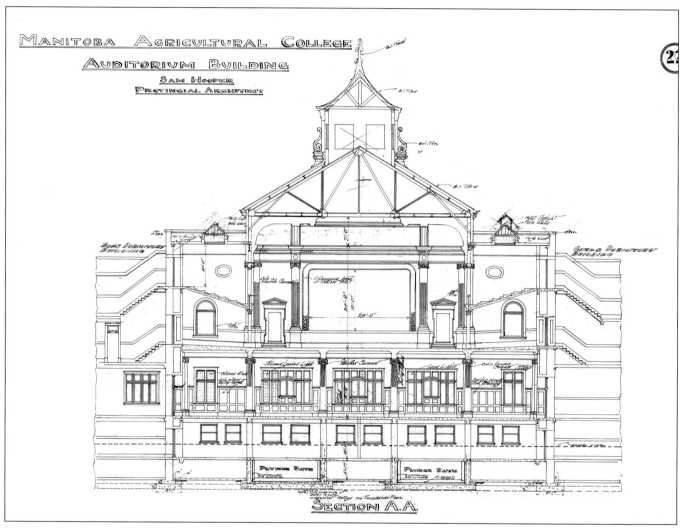

MANITOBA AGRICULTURAL COLLEGE
AUDITORIUM BUILDING
SAM HOOPER
PROVINCIAL ARCHITECT

SECTION A.A.

Original architect's drawings show cross-sections of the Taché Hall auditorium and main cafeteria (above), and the Administration Building (opposite) with its distinctive central staircase and cupola.

however. A debating society was also first organized in 1906, and debating quickly became one of the major extracurricular activities (and areas of competition) among the various colleges and schools. Over the years, any number of leading politicians and lawyers first honed their ambitions and rhetorical skills at debating; the first noted Manitoba debater was probably Jimmy Gardiner, later an important Saskatchewan and federal politician.

On Halloween of 1906, a great battle was fought between Wesley College students and about fifty medical students. One medical student was captured and taken to Convocation Hall, where he was "bounced" and forced to make a speech with an apple in his right hand. "Bouncing" involved being agitated up and down in a giant, rubber, inner tube. Then there were musical performances and refreshments. This sort of rowdy behaviour

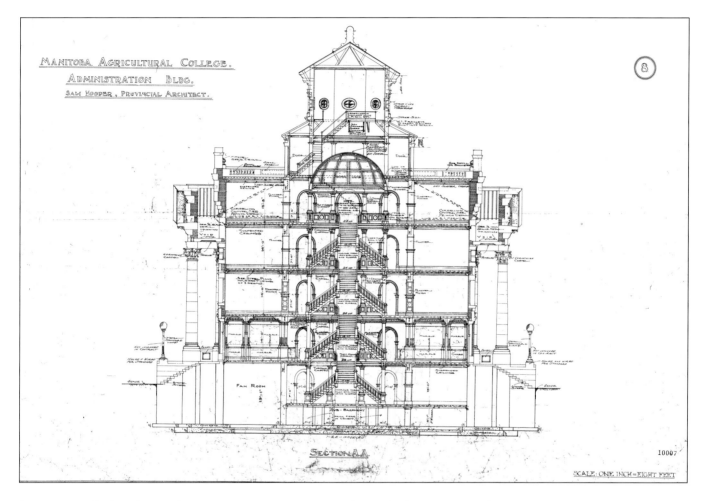

became typical of Halloween for many years. Residents of downtown Winnipeg dreaded the night. However, rowdy behaviour was not confined to Halloween. In 1913, at the beginning of the school year, the freshman class assembled on the outskirts of the grounds of Manitoba College and refused to enter to be initiated by the sophomores. A large supply of storage eggs was available to the freshmen, who ended up throwing them at a number of spectators standing around, observing the event.

A second round of important student developments occurred near the beginning of World War I, as the university continued to establish its own student institutions, particularly in the wake of the transfer of the Manitoba College students to the university and the establishment of the arts faculty. The first intra-university sporting contest, a track meet with the University of North Dakota, was held in September 1914 on the Winnipeg Exhibition Grounds. The university student body began the publication of a semi-monthly journal,

The first graduating class
from Manitoba Agricultural
College in 1911. Note that
there are no female
students (UMA).

called *The Manitoban,* on 5 November 1914. A
few weeks later, the University Dramatic Society
held its first University Theatre Night at the
Walker Theatre. It presented Bjornson's *The
Bankrupt,* under the direction of Mrs. Harriet
Walker (the actress wife of theatre impresario
C.P. Walker). The university orchestra played
for the occasion, as well. A few weeks later still,
the first international debate between the
University of Manitoba and the University of
North Dakota was held, with 500 people in
attendance. The colleges continued their own
student life.

The 1914–15 President's Report showed an
enrolment at the University of Manitoba of 496
in arts and science, 178 in medicine, 84 in
engineering and architecture, 126 in law, and
16 in pharmacy, with 44 special students, for a
total of 974 students. By year the breakdown
was:

    Year 1: 339
    Year 2: 276
    Year 3: 161
    Year 4: 125
    Year 5: 43

Of these students, 155 were women, with 142
in arts, six in medicine, six in law, and one in
pharmacy. The report further indicated that
900 student registration forms had been
tabulated, which showed that 427 of the
students were from Winnipeg, and 473 from
beyond the city, widely distributed, with 326
from rural Manitoba and 147 from outside the
province (but mainly from the adjacent
provinces of Ontario and Saskatchewan).
Whether these figures included students from
any of the colleges is not clear. This data

suggests that the university was not merely a
Winnipeg institution, but was indeed serving
the entire province. In any case, by the outbreak
of the First World War, the University of
Manitoba was clearly a going concern.

Manitoba Agricultural
College, Tuxedo site, c. 1912
(UMA).

(Sung to "He Is an Englishman," Gilbert & Sullivan)

For he is a Manitoban.
Yes, he is a Manitoban.
And if he himself can stand it,
To him we'll have to hand it
That he's still a Manitoban.
For he might have gone to Toronto
To Princeton, Yale or Chicago.
Or yet Saskatchewan!
But in spite of all temptation,
To acquire an education,
He remains a Manitoban.
Yes, he remai=ai=ai=ains a Manitoban.

(Charles Rittenhouse, 1928)

Chapter 3 ↷ 1915–1932

Although the Great War was a traumatic experience for the University of , its students, and its staff—as it was for all of Canada—life went on during the war years. The university continued to expand and change. The period from 1915 to 1932 was characterized by several developments other than the constant enrolment increases. Perhaps the most important was an ongoing redefinition of function of the university by both the province and the university governors themselves. In 1917 the province finally accepted financial responsibility for the university it had brought into existence some forty years earlier. Professor Chester Martin reported in the 1916–17 yearbook with obvious pleasure that the University of Manitoba had become a proper "Provincial Institution." Not all members of the university community, especially those in the colleges, were equally certain that the university's successes were necessarily a good thing, however.

A number of unresolved institutional questions persisted after 1915. One was how the university would survive the war. Another revolved around the relationships between the founding colleges and the university. A third was whether the university would be able to absorb academically all the new vocational facilities it kept having to incorporate into its ranks, without losing its sense of direction and educational purpose. And most important of all, where would the main site of the university ultimately be located? Underneath these overt

Opposite: Manitoba Premier Norris and John Bracken, then president of the Manitoba Agricultural College, in front of the college, 1922. The other individuals in this photo have not been identified. Shortly after this photo was taken, Norris's government was defeated in a provincial election, and he was replaced by Bracken, who would remain premier until 1943 (UMA).

Endowments of the University of Manitoba for Designated Purposes in 1924	
Isbister Trust Fund	$125,000.
Physiological Research	$1,000.
Doupe Medal Fund	$500.
Sir James Aikins Prize Fund	$5,000.
The Chown Prize Fund	$3,977.
Khaki University and YMCA Memorial Fund	$12,000.
Rockefeller Foundation Fund	$507,614.

questions were several less apparent but equally crucial ones. One was the question of finances. The university had been chronically underfunded before it had become part of the provincial educational portfolio, and its funding continued to be problematic, especially after the Depression cut badly into provincial revenue. Until 1932 nobody seemed very concerned about the extent of consolidation of financial responsibility in the hands of John Machray, who was simultaneously vice-chair of the Board of Governors and chair after 1926, honorary bursar, and head of the firm that handled the university's endowments and investments. Neither province nor Board of Governors saw fit to audit the books for many years. When the accountants finally went to work in 1932, the result was a shock for the entire province and a challenge to the earlier assumption that businessmen rather than academics were best able to administer the university's financial operations.

Despite the series of external and internal traumas—including the war and the onset of the Depression—over the years enrolment grew, teaching went on, and the student life of the university continued to become increasingly richer and more complex, as well as becoming better documented. In 1915 the first issue of *Varsity Year Book: Being a Resumé of Student Activities 1914–1915* appeared. In the introduction to this volume, Professor W.F. Osborne of the English department suggested the students should make freer use of the large existing body of college songs and yells. He also wanted the old academic names "Freshman, Sophomore, Junior, and Senior" revived, since they made better rallying cries than "First, Second, Third, and Fourth." The yearbook noted that the social life of the university in this year had been placed in the hands of the Literary Society. Sports in 1914–15 included football (soccer), basketball, tennis, hockey, curling, and ladies' athletics (tennis and basketball). Varsity teams, the yearbook added, were hampered by the loss of athletes to military drill during available practise hours. In the autumn of 1915, Paul Hiebert became editor of the *Manitoban*, becoming well known for his humorous and sometimes satiric column, "Drinking Hemlock with the Editor." Also in 1915, the University of Manitoba Students Association (UMSA) had been reorganized, representing four different faculties: engineering, pharmacy, medicine, and science and arts (under the name Varsity College).

Probably no class experienced more chopping and changing than did the Arts Class of 1916. A few members of this class attended St. John's

College from the beginning to the end of their undergraduate days, but most had begun their first years at Manitoba and Wesley colleges in 1912. They spent their second year at United Colleges (the result of the Manitoba-Wesley merger), and when the United Colleges ceased teaching arts a year later, they became third-year students at the university under the auspices of Varsity Arts. In their last year this class became part of the new University of Manitoba Students Association. Eighteen members of this class were killed in action or as the result of wounds in the Great War.

The response of the university community to the war had been swift and one of total commitment. A number of faculty and students had volunteered for service in 1914, and in March 1915 the Canadian Officers Training Corps (COTC) of the university was gazetted under Professor Fetherstonehaugh as captain and adjutant. Eight companies of sixty men of all ranks were formed, later reduced to four companies as some went on active service. The total enrolment in the university's COTC was 474, with 256 completing forty drills. By March of 1915, over 225 university people were in the military, and sixty-four students were taking special classes to qualify as officers. The 1918–19 yearbook noted with pride that university members had won one Victoria Cross, two CMGs, two Officer of the Order of the British Empire awards, twelve DSOs, sixty Military

Above: Canadian Officer Training Corps (COTC) troops at Camp Hughes, 1916 (UMA). Below: Home Economics class, 1914 (UMA).

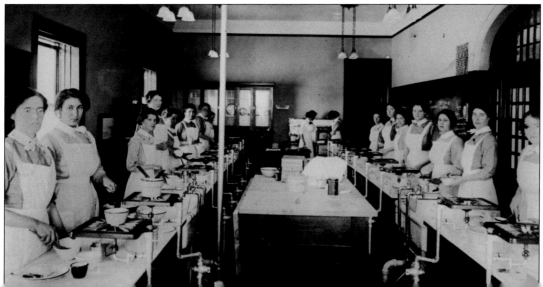

The Broadway Campus in the 1920s

Much of my time was spent in that ancient square building on the Broadway campus. In that square building Botany, Chemistry, and Physics were taught. During our first and second years we also journeyed over to the old Law Buildings where the Faculty of Arts was housed. No one I knew particularly liked that journey. The halls were full of laughing, giggling co-eds. They filled us with terror as we edged to our classroom. To be seen talking to a co-ed was a no-no. I never quite knew why, as some of them were most attractive and all appeared friendly.

Well remembered are the classes in French conducted by a Professor whose name is less well remembered. It escapes me! But, he was most interesting. One day I was amused by a large spider spinning a web in a corner. The professor spotted my inattention and carrying his chair he sat directly in front of me near a door leading outside. In French he said, "Ward, for your penalty you are appointed dog remover!" A friendly dog would enter the room sometimes through the open door, to the amusement of all. My task was to remove him. All conversation was conducted in French. I can still hear him. If I missed on the assignment . . . "Ward, le chien! Fermez la porte!"

We played intramural soccer. Science had difficulty finding eleven players as we were not numerous. Many times we cornered a male student and drafted him for the team. Anxious moments occurred at game time as we counted players. The intramural hockey team was easy to man. We only required six or seven players. We provided our own skates and sticks. The Student Fund provided green and gold sweaters and long stockings of similar color. Fortunately, we somehow obtained pads for our goalie. Defence men protected their shins with the Saturday Evening Post or the Ladies Home Journal magazines inside their long stockings. The rest of us were completely unprotected. Out of such players in all faculties came the University hockey team and they performed very well in the different leagues. One day I appeared without my skates. Couldn't find them! Eddie Johnson, the team captain, was aghast. Somehow he got into his brother's locker, who played junior hockey for the university, and borrowed his skates. The borrowed skates were like wings on my feet and I scored three goals for the glory of Science!

George Ward graduated from the university in 1926. Excerpt from Alumni Journal (1989).

Left: Enlistees in front of the Broadway campus, 1915 (PAM). Below: Dean Featherstonhaugh (Engineering) and the COTC troop, Broadway campus, 1915. The University of Manitoba contributed hundreds of soldiers to the Canadian Expeditionary Force in World War One (UMA).

virtually depopulated for the duration of the war. At St. John's College, by 1917 there was not a single able-bodied male student over the age of eighteen. An Overseas Correspondence Club had been organized in 1916 to write letters to students abroad to keep them in touch with university activities. This club was largely staffed by female students. The war cut deeply into enrolment, which fell to 662 in 1916–17.

In 1917 the provincial government, at the request of the University Council, amended the University Act to replace the old University Council (which had grown to seventy members and was quite unwieldy) with a Board of Governors of nine persons appointed by the

Crosses, a Distinguished Flying Cross, and twenty Military Medals. With sadness it reported that 120 members of the university community had been killed in action or had died in active service. Some parts of the university were

The First BoG in 1917

The university's first Board of Governors included representatives of the province's business and political elite.

Isaac Pitblado (1867–1964), chair. Born in Nova Scotia, Pitblado held a BA (1886) and MA (1893) from the U of M. A prominent lawyer, he would be a member of the Committee of 1,000, formed by the business community to oppose the 1919 Winnipeg General Strike.

John A. Machray (1865–1933), vice-chair, was also a U of M graduate (1884). A nephew of former chancellor Archbishop Machray, he was a prominent Winnipeg lawyer.

Robert Thomas Riley (1851–1944) was born in England, and educated at St. Thomas Charterhouse School. He came to Manitoba in 1881 and was the founder of a number of financial and insurance companies in Manitoba, including Great-West Life Assurance Company.

J. R. Little (1862–1951) of Brandon was a local insurance adjustor.

Sir Augustus Nanton (1860–1925) was born in Toronto and became a leading investment banker in Winnipeg after coming to the city in 1883. He was on the boards of dozens of corporations and was, like Pitblado, a member of the Committee of 1,000 in 1919.

Dr. Henry Havelock Chown (1857–1944) received his MD from Queen's University in 1880. He began practising in Winnipeg in 1883 and in 1898 he was named professor of clinical medicine. He served as dean of medicine from 1900–1917, when he resigned to join the BoG.

A.J. Cotton (1858–1942) from Swan River was one of early Manitoba's most successful farmers. He became famous as Manitoba's "Wheat King" because of the size and quality of his crops.

Lieutenant-Governor in Council (i.e., the cabinet). The BoG had substantial powers of management and control of the university and its policy. The University Council was retained with smaller numbers as the academic wing,

responsible for such matters as examinations and degree granting, admissions requirements, and the regulation of the standing of students. Departmental and faculty business passed through the council to the board, which was ultimately responsible for everything. A subsequent amendment made the government responsible for the finances of the university, which had very few financial resources of its own.

University assets at the time of reorganization consisted of $100,000 in buildings; a land endowment fund of $802,000, which yielded $37,000 income in 1917; unsold land from an endowment of 52,363 acres; and an Isbister bequest of $125,000, yielding $5850 per annum. The university was using old surplus government buildings, mainly downtown. The 1917 legislation

left the colleges in affiliation and with rights to teach, but they had no representation on the BoG. The denominational schools no longer had any power over the university. Instead, control had been vested in a small group of businessmen, drawn from the traditional élite of the province, and especially the city of Winnipeg. The separation of financial from academic administration was total and quite distinctive to Manitoba. Few other places had businessmen as confident that they knew best how to run academic institutions. The president of the university would not become its chief executive officer until 1921.

As the war drew to a close, the university responded to the hope of peace by agreeing that all men who had served in the Canadian forces would get full tuition remissions in arts and half-remissions in engineering, architecture, pharmacy, and medicine. In the spring of 1918, Wesley College was put into turmoil by the dismissal of popular faculty member Salem Bland, an active social gospeller and reformer. A student investigation decided that Bland had been dismissed for political reasons, "because he expressed his opinions and convictions on the issues of the day." A subsequent official enquiry by the Methodist Church concluded that the motives for the dismissal were purely financial.

The situation of the professional schools continued to be volatile. In October 1917, the Medical College faculty had handed over the school charter and land to the university, and

Opposite: Isaac Pitblado, who was associated with the University of Manitoba as registrar from 1893 to 1900 and later as member of the BoG from 1917 to 1933 (PAM). Above: University football team, 1927. Note the leather helmets (UMA).

would become a faculty of medicine of the university. A few weeks later the degree of Bachelor of Home Economics was approved. After several years of discussion, in 1920 the University Act was amended to turn management of the Agricultural College over to the university BoG. Pharmacy turned over its property to the university in return for faculty

status that same year. The question of siting the university also continued to be a live one. The BoG in 1919 insisted on a preference for the Tuxedo Park site earlier preferred by the University Council, which meant that the question of location had been reopened.

The return of the demobilized soldiers marked a new era for both the university and for its student life. The post-war period saw a marked increase in student organizations and in extramural competition with other universities. In April of 1919, the organization of the University of Manitoba Student Union (UMSU), a federation of college and university student bodies, was approved. The union was to control student societies and student publications of the university, including the Glee Club, the Dramatic Society, the Athletic Association, the yearbook (which in 1920 became the *Brown and Gold*), and *The Manitoban*, a monthly publication that soon briefly became weekly during the school year. In January 1920, the *Manitoban*, under editor Graham Spry (later one of the founders of the CBC), published on a daily basis while the other city newspapers were unable to print because of a paper strike. Spry used the occasion to argue for proper university buildings.

In 1921 the University Alumni Association (UAA) was founded, with branches in various cities and towns of the province. That same year, the first issue of *Brown and Gold* appeared. It observed with pride that teams and organizations no longer appeared under the name of UMSU but "have been sent forth under the name of University of Manitoba, or more fondly known as 'Toba'." The first varsity team to compete under this rubric was the Agricultural Students' Stock Judging Team, which became the first Canadian team in major competitions in Chicago and elsewhere in the United States. The Western Inter-University Athletic Union (WIAU) was also formed in 1920, to provide a venue for sports competition between universities in western Canada. While

Opposite: Lecture at the Medical College, 1915. Students still dressed formally for classes (UMA). Left: Caricature of a Manitoba medical student from the *Brown and Gold*, 1922 (UMA).

most student athletics continued to be "intercollegiate," there was an increase of teams competing on the "inter-university" or "varsity" level. The first UMSU co-ed track meet was held in 1920s; Wesley won.

Although internal sports rivalries were not quite as keen as during the college era before the war, they were still important. There was a constant if submerged rivalry between Wesley and Varsity (the university arts and sciences

The University in the 1920s

In 1927-28 the university was quite small. The student body numbered slightly more than 2,700 including those attending the affiliated colleges and a substantial number called "extramurals." In September 1927, 405 freshmen came through the portals, less than one-tenth the number who registered last autumn [1967] in the universities and colleges in Manitoba.

In the academic year when the university observed its 50th anniversary, student conditions were the same as they had been for years. The university was without a permanent home. The students were lacking a gymnasium, a rink, a stadium, a swimming pool, and a Union Building. On the Broadway site where most of the students were congregated there was neither commissary nor cafetorium nor common room. After the fashion of Caesar's Gaul, the university was divided into parts: the Broadway site, the Emily-Bannatyne location of the Faculty of Medicine, the Sherbrook-Portage habitat of the Engineers, and Fort Garry where the happy and boisterous members of the Faculty of Agriculture and Home Economics were the sole occupants. The affiliated colleges were also geographically dispersed. Brandon and St. Paul's had yet to become affiliated with the university.

Judging by today's standards, we ought to have suffered irreparable psychological damage as a result of impoverishment and deprivation. If we did, we were blissfully ignorant of the tragic nature of our condition. We did have some assets. First and foremost was a small but distinguished group of men and women who brought the full power of their enlightenment and personalities to bear upon the traditional challenge of stimulating and civilizing young minds.

We also had a library. In terms of acquisitions and holdings the library we knew would be considered less than adequate today. But books were read, the contents discussed and debated endlessly. Science students today might regard the laboratories and equipment of 1927-28 as rightfully belonging in the Smithsonian Institution. From those murky quarters, encased in a perpetual fall-out of nauseous fumes and odours which gravely offended the rest of us, there emerged a group of survivors whose performances continue to bring honour to themselves and renown to their Alma Mater.

All the essential ingredients for the educative process were then present--students, teachers and some material. Our astonishment should be not that the university was made to work at all, but that it worked so well.

Douglas Chevrier graduated from the university in 1929, and later would be its registrar from 1947 to 1967. Excerpt from Alumni Journal (1967).

faculty); the two were about the same size in student numbers. Agriculture and medicine were the dominant powers in sports in the '20s. Girls' sports became more important. The big team sports were football (i.e., soccer), hockey, and basketball. The girls did consistently better than the boys at Wesley College. United Colleges (after a 1926 merger, having a larger student pool) became more of a powerhouse, winning the football title for most of the '20s and '30s. In his memoirs, Hugh Saunderson recalled that "basketball, soccer, curling, hockey and track and field had regular teams and the games had many spectators too. Often we had to make up in enthusiasm what we lacked in skill, but most of us took some part."

Hugh Saunderson also observed in his memoirs, "In these days of colour television, the word 'University' conjures up a vision of ivy-covered buildings set in a beautifully treed park, with a carpet of green lawn around them. The University of Mantioba, when I entered it as a freshman in 1920, was noticeably different. We had no treed parkland, and no ivy, and most of the buildings in which our work was carried on were 'cast-offs' loaned to the University by a provincial government which had replaced them for its purposes by newer, larger, and better buildings." There were three arts buildings, including the old legislative offices and the old courthouse. The science complex was a fawn-coloured brick building erected in 1900 to accommodate science classes of the affiliated arts colleges, and expanded by a temporary annex put up in 1919–20 to house returning veterans. The buildings were close to the law courts, Legislative Building, the HBC store,

The Orpheum Theatre, a popular destination for students from the Broadway campus in the 1920s (PAM).

Eaton's, and to the Orpheum, where students could go on Monday afternoon to see the week's vaudeville acts before they were censored. Girls had rooms on the top floor of the main arts building (the Ek-O-Le-La Club Rooms), which overlooked the place where capital offenders were hanged. The library was on the second floor of one of the arts buildings, small in number of books and in study accommodations. One student ditty, sung to the tune of "The Road to Mandalay," went: "Between the jail and the court-house /And the Government garage / Stands our dear old Alma Mater / With her red-brick camouflage." In 1919 two large lecture theatres had been built on then Osborne Street

between Broadway and St. Mary's. Known as the "Cowsheds," lecture theatres A and B, joined later by Lecture Theatre C, were the sites of most of the large undergraduate courses at the university. Engineering and architecture were in the old Deaf and Dumb Institute building on Portage at Sherbrooke, and medicine was in decent buildings beside the general hospital.

Despite the limited facilities, there was a good deal of student activity. In 1921 the first report of the Dean of Women Students was published. It recounted the results of a survey on the living conditions of women students. Of 179 registered and surveyed female students, 149 were living at home. Of the thirty who were being accommodated outside their homes, nine were in residence at Manitoba College; of the remaining twenty-one, ten were boarding with friends or relatives and five were living in boarding houses scattered around the city. The report added that at Wesley College—where there were sixty women in arts—thirty-nine were in residence and only twenty-one lived in homes in the city. The dean observed without further comment that a women's residence at the university would doubtless increase the numbers living in residence. In 1922 a survey of 265 University of Manitoba students examined their financial arrangements for attending university. It disclosed that 110 were entirely responsible for their own support. Of the remainder, 100 earned more than 50 percent of the costs of their own maintenance, and only seventeen were totally dependent on others for their support.

These two reports suggested the extent to which the university was already both a commuter campus and an institution of higher learning in which most students supported their education at least in part through their own labour. These characteristics of the University of Manitoba student body went back a long way. A column in the *Manitoban* in early 1922 by Jack Russell claimed, "A large number of our undergraduates are at present self-supporting. Some of these support themselves as an exhibition of will power, others through force of circumstances, but the majority of students get their actual expenses paid for them and use their earnings as pocket money." No early survey broke down the ethnic composition of the student body, but there was a large enough number of Jewish students to support a very active Menorah Society—the principal Jewish university student organization of the time— which in 1922 beat out sixty-five other such societies at North American universities for the quality of its Menorah work.

In October of 1921, the great Halloween parade was resumed, sponsored by UMSU. The parade was to be led, wrote the *'Toban,* by the Faculty of Arts with a brass band. All 400 students would be decked out in blue and white clown suits. That same autumn, Wesley College held its first co-ed field day, and "stunt night" was reactivated in early November at the college. The custom began of stunt night in autumn and a theatre night in the spring. Stunt night quickly acquired the format of a skit from each segment

Opposite: Garden party, Manitoba College, 1923. Ladies obviously wore their hats to such events (PAM). Below: Jack Pickersgill at United College, c. 1927, modelling what the well-dressed college man wore in the 1920s (UWA).

of the college community: one from the collegiate, one from each year in arts and science, one from theology, and usually one from residence. In 1929 there were three skits on the site question. One was from the junior class: "Miss Una Varsity, living with her aunt, Moll Broadway, was compelled by her uncle, Mr. Tex Payer, to reject the proposal of marriage from Mr. Tuxy Dough. She later accepted the hand of another suitor, Mr. Agry Kulture, the marriage being conducted by Rev. J. Bracken. While the register was being signed everyone sang lustily that touching old ballad, 'How're you goin' to keep 'em down on the farm.'"

Hugh Saunderson's memoirs recalled pranks, especially "clean-ups" of other faculties or affiliated college groups, "using their firehoses on their students and their hallways." Charles Rittenhouse insisted, "We weren't violent or disruptive, though—just prankish." He recalled one successful stunt that involved breaking into the administration building after-hours and leading a cow up the stairs, where she was tethered outside the library. The 'Toban advocated as a student yell:

Iji ittiki, kiyi yip
Manitoba, Manitoba, rip, rip, rip.
Kanna, kenna, wawa, kanna keeka, tah
Go it, 'Toba! Go 'Toba! Rah, rah, rah.

It is insisted that these words, when rehearsed by larger bodies of students, "were found to be altogether satisfactory and like honey in the mouth." In 1922 UMSU abandoned the Halloween student parade because of the costs of presentation, although hijinks involving the medical students and those at United College continued throughout the '20s. Instead, UMSU held a dance and carnival at Minto Barracks, where an imported jazz band and "girl show" performed. According to the *Manitoban*, "many weary souls were rejuvenated at the bar and in the electrical show," and thousands of students and outsiders were let in at 25 cents admission to drink and dance.

On 24 November 1922, the St. Boniface College building, containing classrooms, chapel, assembly hall, and student residence, was totally destroyed by fire. Nine students and one brother died. The 20,000-volume library,

Freshettes dressed for hazing in front of Welsey Hall, United College, c. 1924 (UWA).

the laboratories, the seismograph, all were destroyed. The college had $140,000 in insurance, which paid its debts, but the total loss was calculated at $800,000. Arson was suspected, as several other Catholic buildings were also destroyed by fire during the same period. The college's classes were continued in

the Petite Séminaire. A rebuilding campaign, mounted largely in Quebec, raised only $73,000, despite an initial $25,000 grant from the province.

In June of 1923, a commission to examine the educational facilities of the province was appointed by the government, chaired by Walter

Murray, president of the University of Saskatchewan. The commission hired Dr. W.S. Learned of Carnegie Foundation to study the university and the Agricultural College. Learned did not much like the Guelph model of an independent agricultural college, and recommended against it. He also noted that

"the part played by the colleges in the life of the present University is relatively insignificant," recommending that the church colleges should be relocated on the new university campus to provide a proper "moral purpose" to intellectual affairs and to provide unity in citizenship and principle. The colleges, wrote Learned, could "maintain for its students an environment that fosters clean living, intimate and wholesale associations, and the growth of an intelligent and convincing moral purpose in intellectual affairs." He opposed the union of Manitoba and Wesley colleges, preferring instead "for each to retain its identity and

Left: Student F.F. Parkinson mugging for the camera in his room in Taché Hall, 1916 (UMA). Above: Female students at Manitoba Agricultural College doing the can-can, c. 1924 (UMA).

develop as a separate unit." He also saw the possibility of an anglophone Catholic college.

Learned wanted the new colleges to develop with professors, "who take a somewhat broader view of their responsibilities to their students than does the average university professor," what he described as "an intimate community of collegiate interests." Thus he wanted each college to maintain "on its own foundation a small group of recognized University teachers." He saw the need for certain "common standards of training, status, salary, and so forth, in collegiate faculties." He even saw that the university might well advise in which departments collegiate appointments should be made. Learned may have been influenced by the English model for colleges, but was probably thinking more of the American liberal arts college, which he imaginatively sought to combine with the multi-university.

A scene from the student
production of Gilbert and
Sullivan's *Princess Ida,* 1931
(UMA).

The commission ultimately reported that the Agricultural College should become a faculty of the university, which should build on the Fort Garry site. The commission itself had a vision of a large campus on which "affiliated colleges, playing fields, and buildings, serving the physical and social life of the students, can find ample room in close association with the centre of university life," and pointed out that a scattered campus destroyed "the sense of unity" and prevented "efficient and close co-operation." It emphasized that the affiliated colleges could and should come to the new campus.

In 1925 the University of Manitoba began a highly innovative five-year honours course, in which three years of general education would be succeeded by two years of specialized study in sixteen courses for two majors. Students enrolled in the programme would be listed

The Tywhoopus and the Red Herring

During the quinquennium 1925-30, I was to room on the top floor of the
men's residence at United College, Winnipeg. Although I was a member of
the professorial staff, I had no administrative responsibilities and simply
lived along with some sixty students in a sort of uneasy symbiosis. The
uneasiness sprang from the fact that I was working under terrific pressure
and published six books during that five-year period, while work of any
sort seemed the last thing in the world desired by some of these healthy
young animals. As my nerves rebelled more and more at their uproar, I
invented, for college journalism, a creature called the "Tywhoopus" and
published a list of Ten Commandments for him, based on actual daily
experience, for example: (2) When you wish to speak to a fellow tywhoopus,
never go to his burrow and look for him. Just stand in the corridor and
howl his name. (6) Soak your socks in the wash-bowls overnight. The
flavour lingers. (9) Telephone annunciations should always make the windows
rattle. If you can't do it alone, let ten men help.

It was during this period that intimacy with college and university
journalism made me the faculty representative on the Manitoban. The editor,
an intrepid and candid youth named Leonard L. Knott . . . ventured to
criticize his employers, the Students' Council, and was warned to 'lay off.'
Enraptured by this rebuff, he doubled the dose, and was sacked, along with
his staff. Nothing daunted, he launched a paper of his own, The Manitoba
Student. Then there was surreptitiously printed, by still another group, one
issue of a truly scandalous sheet called The Red Herring ('It smells but it
sells'), Case 1, Tin 1, Feb. 9, 1927. It was a four-age edition in black
ink on red paper, and almost every article was good for a libel suit. For a
wonder, President MacLean was awake, struck immediately, seized the edition
and burned it--but not before a few advance copies had reached United
College. The alleged editor was Herr Ring and the business manager, Jack
Fish. A feature column was entitled 'The Stewed Aunt.' A big boxed
advertisement declared that "The Red Herring Is All Backbone--Has 100 Eyes,
Is Read All Over, and Swishes A Mean Tale".

I recall this episode as one of the things that reassured me as to the
brilliance and potential industry of our Western students. One of the
chief Herring-trailers (later a distinguished theological professor at
Yale) tried eloquently but unsuccessfully three times to bluff his way
through my examination on the English Novel and flunked each time through
a dare-devil failure to read any of the prescribed fiction. One of a
University's problems--whether at Queen's, Oxford, or Manitoba--is how to
mobilize such gifts for academic service.

  Watson Kirkconnell taught English and Classics at United College from
  1920 to 1940, and would later become president of Acadia University.
  This excerpt is from his memoir A Slice of Canada (1967).

among the class of 1929 but would actually graduate in 1930. Unfortunately, most students were not interested in spending longer at the undergraduate level, and the university failed to provide instruction as innovative as the programme. Thus, when the first graduating class of this course reached its fifth year, it had its own cheer: "Look us over, / take your time; / we're all that's left / of '29."

Meanwhile, at the downtown campus, students were beginning to complain about hazing and were also starting to organize fraternities and sororities. Despite the muttering, some votes against initiations, and a few statements from the administration, hazing went on. A medical school initiation in October 1923 featured a boxing match between two pairs of blindfolded "freshettes" with boxing gloves dipped in molasses and covered with feathers. A report of a committee on initiation in 1924 insisted that members of the freshman class were within their rights to resist initiations, but objected to some of the rowdy methods of resistance. In 1925 the science students were marched through the downtown streets to local theatres, covered in green paint and other lurid colours. In the theatres they did university yells and songs. At the annual freshman's stunt night in 1925, pharmacy men were initiated when they were taken away "very scantily attired" to be subjected to "ancient rites," including paint and flypaper collars. In 1926, 165 freshettes were initiated in the evening. "Each donned the insignia of her rank, a nightie, a bonnet, green ribbons and a bib," and they were shown into Lecture Theatre A,

Left: Varsity students, c. 1920. Obviously, university students did wear raccoon coats in those days (R. Malaher). Above: "Old King Cole," the freshman "king," is paraded in front of United College, c. 1927 (UWA).

Students selling *The Manitoban*, 1920, undoubtedly during those few days early in the year when the newspaper was the only one in town (UMA).

where they sang "Hail Manitoba," followed by skits and stunts.

A major intramural athletic controversy sprung up in mid-decade over the issue of ringers—players who were not members of the colleges or faculties for which they were playing. Debates drew large crowds; in 1926, 1500 people flocked to the Walker Theatre to hear a British imperial debating team defeat the university debaters. The Manitoba debaters annually met a team from the University of North Dakota, usually winning, and annually met an imperial debating team, usually losing. The yearly performances by the Dramatic Society and the Glee Club (which did a Gilbert and Sullivan operetta beginning with *The Mikado* in 1928) were also extremely popular. The leading lady in many early university dramatic presentations was Evelyn Morris, later to achieve stardom on Broadway as Judith Evelyn. The first production of *The Mikado* had scenery painted by Phillip Surrey and LeMoine Fitzgerald, and was presented at Gordon Bell Auditorium. When Mrs. Harriet

Walker retired from producing the Dramatic Society plays at the end of the decade, the G&S performance became more important in the annual calendar than the Dramatic Society's dramas. Marshall McLuhan in 1931 was introduced to George Bernard Shaw by the Dramatic Society production of *Pygmalion*, which, he wrote to his mother, "didn't feel for an instant" like "an amateur performance." Before the Glee Club shifted to Broadway musicals in the 1950s, it had done *The Mikado* four times, *The Gondoliers* four times, *Iolanthe* three times, plus *HMS Pinafore*, *Yeoman of the Guard*, and *Ruddigore* twice, as well as *Patience*, *Princess Ida*, and *Utopia Limited* once each. In 1929 the production of *The Gondoliers* filled the auditorium for four nights.

Although they were far less visible, the colleges had not entirely disappeared. St.

Boniface rebuilt in 1924, adding a new four-storey wing to the Petite Séminaire. A new agreement between Wesley and Manitoba colleges took effect on 1 July 1926, by which each college would retain its own charter until a joint one could be formed. The joint name would be "United Colleges." Theology would be taught at Manitoba, and arts and religious knowledge at Wesley. On 10 August 1926, an agreement was signed between the Roman Catholic Archepiscopal Corporation of Winnipeg and the Oblate Fathers of Mary Immaculate of the St. Mary's Province to provide teaching staff for an English-language Catholic college, to be called St. Paul's College. On 15 September of that year, St. Paul's opened its doors with a staff of six in the former YMCA Building on Selkirk Avenue. The colleges also clearly had a different culture from that of the professional schools and the secular campus. In 1931 one successful UMSU president running from the Medical College was so jeered in United College because of his participation in university military training that he did not receive a single vote from that college.

In early 1927, one of the earliest of many confrontations between UMSU and the *Manitoban* produced a legendary hoax, which was talked about on campus for many years thereafter. A newspaper entitled *The Red Herring: It Smells but it Sells* was printed in red and distributed anonymously on the university campus. *The Red Herring* was published after a major hassle between Leonard Knott, editor of the *Manitoban*, and the UMSU council. Knott had been criticizing the council in the newspaper, was asked to resign, did so, and

decided to bring out his own newspaper, *The Manitoba Student*. A group of UMSU leaders, including J. Livy MacPherson, David A.

Freshettes at United College, c. 1927 (UWA).

MacLennan, Ralph C. Ham, J. Allen Davison, and H.H. "Dinty" Moore, decided to beat Knott to the punch. The idea "came out of a blue sky," said MacPherson later. The sheet kidded everybody on campus, including its authors. Mr. Ham (the *Manitoban* business manager) was accused of taking out girls on the free tickets he got through his office. Dramatic Society rehearsals were said to be sofa parties, with Mr. MacLennan (president of the society and usually its star actor) the chief sofa-er. The pranksters were caught when someone took down the licence number of a car distributing the paper—it belonged to MacPherson. The university president called the culprits to his office, was surprised to learn that student leaders had done such a thing, and forced them all to resign their UMSU positions.

A persistent growth in student enrolment in the 1920s (from 2161 in 1920–21, with 241 women, to 3939 in 1925–26, including 1511 in special courses, falling to 3231 plus 774 in summer school in 1927–28) continued to put heavy pressures on the physical plant of the university, most of which still consisted of downtown buildings that had been cast off by the province. Not only was there significant overcrowding, but there was much deterioration of the fabric of the buildings. A report on accommodation submitted to the BoG by the Faculty of Arts and Sciences in December 1927 showed that lecture-room accommodation was inadequate, having been designed for 900 students and now serving 1600, plus engineering students. Those in the Broadway building complained of noise. More lab space

Premier John Bracken, 1925 (PAM).

was needed. If more space was not provided within two years, the committee warned, "it will be difficult, if not impossible, to carry on." Women's quarters for 430 girls registered in arts and sciences were a particular disgrace, with only seven toilets and four wash-basins, inadequate locker room space in the new building, and three toilets and three wash-basins in the old building. Library accommodation was also inadequate. There was no place to study, since there were places for only 120 students.

The student newspaper editorialized every year, and students regularly demonstrated at the legislature, for new buildings and a downtown location. On the occasion of the university's fiftieth anniversary, the *Manitoban* insisted, "The people of Manitoba may with reason be ashamed of the conditions under which the University has been obliged to carry on its work, but they have some right to be proud of the work actually accomplished." The Manitoba legislature in May 1928 appropriated $1 million for new university construction, to be available only after the final decision had been made on the site to be developed. This stipulation annoyed the BoG. But it was true that the matter of site still remained unsettled. The Tuxedo Land Holdings

Company, earlier called the Tuxedo Park Company, had sued the university in 1927 in an attempt to force it to honour its earlier agreement to build at Tuxedo. In 1928 the university allowed the Tuxedo agreement to lapse, and it ultimately (1930) paid $62,000 to the Tuxedo company to settle claims.

In 1928 the first register of graduates of the university was compiled. It reported that the university had conferred approximately 5000 degrees on 4700 persons; 375 graduates were known to be deceased; and 88 percent of the graduates resided in Canada. No significant flow of graduates to the United States had occurred, except in engineering. At about the same time as the compilation of the list of graduates, a study was made of the racial origins of the present enrolment. It found that students of Anglo-Saxon and French stock provided 74 percent of enrolment, students of central European origin 18 percent, and others 8 percent. These figures demonstrated, to nobody's real surprise, that the student body over-represented the province's population of older ethnic groups and under-represented the new immigrant groups.

In her annual report in 1928, the Dean of Women Students noted that ten years earlier

Top: Baseball game in front of Taché Hall, 1930. Note the parked automobiles (UMA). Above: Faculty and students of the Manitoba Agricultural College, 1923 (UMA).

Students at the Manitoba Agricultural College, c. 1920 (UMA).

W.L. (William) Morton

(1908–1980) became one of Canada's best-known historians and educators. The son of a prominent southwestern Manitoba family, he graduated from the university in 1932 and went to Oxford as a Rhodes Scholar. He returned to teach history at the U of M from 1942 to 1964. During this period, he wrote his seminal history of Manitoba as well as important books on national history, such as *The Canadian Identity*. He founded University College in 1963.

there were many small parties held in the buildings, which required chaperonage. "Now the numbers are so great," she wrote, "that no parties are small enough to be held in one of our own rooms, the cost of renting a room is prohibitive, and there are very few functions except the regular and more formal dances." The dean went on to note that the percentage of women students from outside Winnipeg had risen from 20 to 35 percent. This report contained the first mention of sororities by the Dean of Women, who subsequently reported in 1929 that five sororities were duly affiliated with a national organization, and another local group expected affiliation soon. The dean also observed that women were in advance of men in giving up the old student initiations. "A reception is now held instead, and always takes the form of a children's party which affords such abundant scope for costumes and general fun that even the upper classmen prefer it to the old order of things."

Early in 1929, UMSU collected 1400 signatures on a petition for new buildings. On 15 February 1929, a large crowd, mainly students, paraded to the Legislative Building to demonstrate for new buildings. Premier John Bracken came out onto the steps to speak to the students, who gave him "three loud cheers and a whole jungle of hungry tigers." According to Charles Rittenhouse, student participation in such protests was motivated by a quest for "freedom from the sorry working conditions of the Broadway campus." Tommy Tweed—later a CBC personality—led many of the protests. In the wake of the mid-February effort, the government appointed yet another committee

Manitoba College Graduating Dinner. March 24th 1922.

to study the site question. The commission heard from the parties. St. John's College and St. Boniface College wanted the university to remain on Broadway, as did John Machray and President MacLean. Wesley College wrote that while it would follow the university wherever it went, in the short term, for financial reasons, it would "remain where it is."

Despite strong support for the Broadway site from various quarters, the committee recommended in November of 1929 "that the new University buildings be at the Agricultural College site and that it together with the facilities provided by the present buildings situated thereon be used for instruction in the Senior Years of the University and instruction in the Junior Years be continued in the buildings situated on the present Broadway site." The government indicated it would accept this recommendation. Thus, the campus of the University of Manitoba was to be split in half, a situation that would remain for another quarter-century. The *'Toban* subsequently reported the fears of John Glassco of Winnipeg Hydro that a university out of the city could have a bad moral effect on the students. Glassco visualized students going to university every morning in "flivvers," while carrying thermos bottles of liquor. "Our university," he opined, "would probably descend to the low moral level of the University of California at Berkeley." Nevertheless, the deed was done, and construction was announced of an arts and science building, to be designed by Arthur Stoughton of the Faculty of Architecture, on the new site. The building would be sixty-seven metres long and eighteen metres wide, with five storeys. One of the consequences of the move to

Graduation dinner, Manitoba College, 1922 (UMA). The bearded figure front left is Andrew Baird.

Student Activism in the 1920s

After my freshman year [1925-26] almost the only papers I ever wrote were final exams. Once I was sufficiently moved by Virgil's forsaken Dido to attempt a blank verse translation of her lament. I handed the lines to the grey professor after class. Startled, he glanced at them and said: "Do you want me to mark this?" "N-n-no," I stammered. "Just look it over . . . if you want to." In a week or so he returned them with no comment other than "It's all right, I guess." End of episode. Beginning and end of any creative writing for any course . . . or of any critical or expository writing for that matter.

After months of such unenthusiastic pedagogy, the chief academic concerns of most undergraduates were slogging for grades and trying to psyche the examiners. Of course, there were the gifted ones who didn't need to slog, whether they did or not. Such careerist students did not need to be motivated by a gracious campus, well-equipped building, or innovative progressive teachers. Neither, in fact, did most of us at Manitoba in the twenties. We had been brought up in a very young, sturdy city in a province only fifty-five years old. Those of us who weren't competitive WASPS were the thrusting sons and daughters of immigrants from Central Europe and Iceland. We provided our own motivations. Manitoba's cram-and-exam system offered a simple framework within which we could work, and we rather approved of work. Given the requirements of some stiff courses we were off and running.

In the twenties the term 'student activism' may not yet have been coined, but plain old student protest, an extracurricular activity, was quite common in Manitoba, if not so all-consuming as it became on the campuses of the sixties. We weren't violent or disruptive, though--just prankish. The only freedom we sought was freedom from the sorry working conditions of the Broadway campus. Our usual form of agitation was a straggly parade to some prominent downtown location, such as the steps of the Bank of Montreal at Portage and Main. Here a 'professor' in tattered gown and beat-up mortar board would lecture us and curious passers-by; his speech punctuated by trombone blasts and drum rolls and drowned out by boos whenever he mentioned the failure of the Bracken government to select a site and start building the long promised 'new' university.

   Charles Rittenhouse was a graduate of the class of 1930.

Fort Garry would be the loss for senior students of easy access to the Orpheum Theatre's weekly vaudeville shows. So many students attended Monday matinees—the first performance of the new bill—that it was impossible to do anything on campus during that afternoon.

Whatever its long-term economic and social impact, the arrival of the Depression in late 1929 had very little immediate effect on either enrolment or student life at the university. Hard economic times certainly made it difficult for the Alumni Association to raise funds for a $50,000 endowment fund for scholarships for needy students. By 1931 the fund had raised a mere $500. Nevertheless, several new chapters of fraternities and sororities were established in 1930, including Phi Delta Theta and Delta Delta Delta. By the end of the first year of the Depression, there were thirteen fraternities (including two medical ones), and six sororities at the university. Most of them were Manitoba branches of international organizations that had the majority of their chapters at American universities. Typically, they had rooms in downtown apartment blocks. The 'Toban

thundered editorially about the cost of the university rugby team, which had not won a game in two years. The newspaper also called for a chair of fine arts to coordinate dramatic productions and other performance activities. Four drama units—the Dramatic

Above: The No. 97 trolley car from downtown Winnipeg to the Fort Garry campus (UMA). Left: The 1923 Varsity Arts crest (R. Malaher).

Society, the Glee Club, the Menorah Society (the chief Jewish student organization on campus), and Delta Phi Epsilon sorority—met about this proposal. Delta Phi Epsilon achieved some notoriety in September of 1930 when it was forced to give up a production of Elmer Rice's *Street Scene* because the owner of the play's copyright refused to sanction its performance in Winnipeg while road companies were still itinerating in the United States. Later in the decade, the sorority was allowed to present the play.

One sign of the times was a debate in late November 1930 on the subject "Resolved that this House favours a Dictatorship." Two very successful debating teams of the early 1930s were those of W.L. Morton and Lloyd Stinson, and a pairing of Morton and Sam Freedman. A Dramatic Society production of Sudermann's *The Joy of Living* was cancelled in January 1931 because of unfavourable publicity the play had received in the press. It subsequently turned out that the professor at the University of Toronto who had criticized the play for its "immorality" had been confused and had been thinking of another play entirely. In 1931 the Glee Club produced *Princess Ida* and the Menorah Society presented Herschbein's *Green Pastures*.

Also in 1931, the University of Manitoba Grads hockey team travelled to the World Championships at Krynica. The team was financed by gate receipts, but it wore uniforms of brown and gold—the university colours—supplied by the Canada Cycle and Motor Company. The Grads played in Europe before the tournament and in the United Kingdom

Samuel Freedman

(1908–1993) graduated from the university Law School in 1932, and became of Canada's best-known and most respected jurists. The son of Russian immigrants in Winnipeg's North End, he was first appointed to the bench in 1952 and served as Manitoba chief justice from 1971 to 1983. Known for his compassion and learning, Freedman served as university chancellor from 1959 to 1968. Freedman's younger brother Max (1914–1980), who became a well-known journalist working for both the *Manchester Guardian* and the *Chicago Daily News*, was known as a "graduate" of the university's library. Because the Freedman family could only afford to send one of the brothers to university, Max never formally attended classes but spent four years in the campus library, reading as many books as he could.

Opposite: Ladies' hockey team, representing the science faculty, c. 1920s. They are obviously not in full uniform (UMA).

afterwards. In the championship, the Grads won all their games, were not scored upon, and received no penalties. Overall, the team played forty-one games, winning thirty-nine and drawing two. After every game the team gathered at centre ice and shouted "with all possible lung-power" the "Iji" and "Locomotive" cheers of the University of Manitoba. Whether they raised sufficient volume for the words to be like "honey in the mouth" is another matter.

The Fort Garry Campus in the 1920s

The Residence [Taché Hall] was the hub of the small campus shared by Agriculture and Home Economics students in the early years. It provided living quarters, dining facilities, swimming pools, gymnasia, and an auditorium under one roof. It was at the dining room (the Oak Room) that first contact was made with the "other" faculty (the opposite sex). Large oak tables, covered with sparkling white linen, seated eighty-four women and four men. Lists were posted each week assigning table number and personnel. These were checked with interest as they would indicate one's table-mates for the coming week. On weekends, tables and table companions were chosen.

There was great competition to secure one of the four tables for which a "good" waitress was responsible (a good waitress being one who could obtain a second bowl of the delicious, campus-made ice cream). Another of the kitchen's specialties were the hot rolls served on Sunday mornings. These rolls, dressed in honey, enticed the otherwise reluctant residents to Sunday breakfast. Many special events were celebrated in the dining room: sports trophies were presented here, with appropriate table decorations. And graduation dinners were held, with menus and decorations suitable to the occasion. The staff was served in a small separate dining room. But some members of the faculty sat in the Oak Room, at a table near the don, in an attempt, perhaps, to lend some decorum to the dinners. Once, when visitors were expected, we were admonished "to keep the soft pedal down."

The swimming pool in the basement was available either for swimming, or for chastising a student whose behaviour was deemed unsuitable. A "party" would be arranged, and the unsuspecting offender would be dumped into the pool. Scandalous! The residence gymnasium was the centre of sports activity; classes, basketball practice and games, folk dancing and the annual spring gym display. West Gym was off-limits to women, except during classes, games etc. Lady pianists for the folk dancing classes were met on the east side, and escorted, by the Gym instructors, to the gymnasium.

Though East and West Taché were officially separate, unofficial 'raids' were undertaken to both sides. One might find oneself suddenly tipped from one's bed and aroused from sleep, only to see a figure departing into the shadows. Or one might shake off sleep to stare into the eye of an odiferous goat (said livestock had then to be coaxed by the outraged residence dean and amused residents to make its way down the long hall, down the stairs, and to the outer doors--after which time, house coats could be observed "airing" from the windows of the girls' quarters).

Phyllis Rankin graduated from the university in 1929.

A *Report of the Student Commission of the University of Manitoba*, prepared in the early months of 1932, gives us some glimpse into both student life and student opinion in the early days of the Depression. The report was prepared by a group of ten students that included A.K. Dysart, Sam Freedman, Charles H.A. Walton, and W.L. Morton, not necessarily representative of the university as a whole but perhaps fairly reflective of its student élite. According to Walton's later memoirs, the student commission was chiefly intended to investigate the problem of racism at the university, although in the end it ranged much farther afield than simply that issue. Indeed, the racism problem was relatively downplayed, taking up only one page in a report of twenty-nine pages.

The report opened by observing that university officers had occasionally interfered in organized student affairs, thereby only stiffening student opinion in the opposite direction. It added that the absence of university residences except in agriculture and home economics meant that there was less need for tight administrative control. Not many women participated in student government, although the recent growth of sororities may have drawn women from the broader campus. Both fraternities and sororities had gained considerably in recent years, noted the commission, and in campus politics, undergraduate opinion tended to be hostile to the Greeks. Membership in Greek-letter organizations was expensive and potentially inequitable as well.

The commission thought that UMSU, rather than the university administration, should control student athletics, and it feared the "quest for college spirit through athletics—largely the result of American imitation," preferring an emphasis on intramural rather than inter-university athletic competition. It wanted a central board to coordinate the activities of the various student publications, chiefly to prevent overlapping and competition in advertising. While the commission liked musical and dramatic activities, it opposed a full-length production of a "quasi-professional" sort, since

Arts students, Broadway campus, c. 1925 (R.Malaher).

it involved great expenditures of time. The commission defended the student body from much of the adverse criticism levelled against its social life, noting that student dances were held downtown for want of suitable campus venues and that much of the trouble came from those outside the university who were admitted to these events. The commission's pious hope that student activities should not interfere with "the training of the intellect" suggests that in some cases extracurricular events did get in the way. A more serious problem, thought the commission, was the absence of a sharp demarcation between high school and university, which meant that many students did not give university as serious attention as it deserved.

The gold medal for French won by Elizabeth Dafoe in 1923. Dafoe, the daughter of editor John W. Dafoe, was the university's chief librarian from 1937 to 1960 (UMA).

Some of the views of the 1932 student commission represented discreet but real student complaints about the university. What this élite corps of students did not like about the academic side of their university is interesting, not least because it would appear that nothing much has changed between then and now. One complaint was an absence of study space at night on campus. The commission also devoted much attention to the pedagogical emphasis on lecturing and the resultant lack of good teaching,

emphasizing "it is not wise that ... research should be carried on at the expense of the interest of the elementary students." Classes needed to be smaller in general, it thought, and the introduction of seminars or tutorials might correct one of the problems of a non-residential campus, which was an absence of opportunity for personal contacts. The existing system of collecting credits, likened by some to "the accumulation of coupons to be exchanged at the end of a given time for a prize," was seldom criticized by students before the commission, which nonetheless thought some reform was in order to provide more coherence to the course of study.

The university might have responded that the five-year honours course, which been introduced in 1925 and had attempted to respond to these sorts of criticisms, had been a resounding failure at the box office.

The commission also wanted better first-year courses, particularly ones specially designed for students not planning to major in the subject. And it complained bitterly about an examination system that placed a premium upon memorization of notes and discouraged original thinking. "The Commission believes that it should be impossible for any student who limits his activities to the lecture notes and the

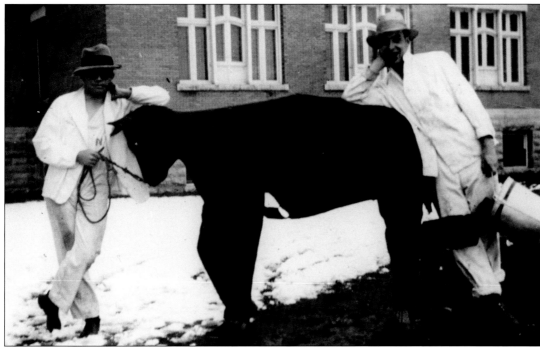

Students at the Manitoba Agricultural College, c. 1920s (UMA).

text-book, however thorough be his mastery of them, to obtain high marks." The commission's report emphasized that the responsibility for students who lost interest in their studies had to be shared by the students, the faculty, and the university administration. "Some means should be provided whereby the student is brought into closer relationship with the faculty and it is suggested that a spirit of co-operation on the part of the faculty would be more beneficial than the autocratic and dogmatic attitude which is often present today."

"The Racial Problem" was considered under a heading entitled "The Attitude of the Student in the University." The commission concluded that there was a problem, related chiefly to an anti-Semitism on the "part of the Anglo-Saxon majority." The students from racial minorities often worked much harder than those of the majority, argued the commission, for their education represented a "very real sacrifice" and their exclusion from many extracurricular activities forced them to find an outlet in study. The commission insisted that formal regulations by university administration or student council would do little good, but noted that it believed that the new environment at Fort Garry would "lead to a gradual abatement of the problem." It did not explain what Fort Garry would change, however.

The annual survey of education in Canada conducted by the Dominion Bureau of Statistics reported in 1932 that the University of Manitoba was the second largest university in Canada in terms of enrolment. Despite the Depression and threatened salary cuts for staff, the university still had much of which it could be proud.

Chapter 4 ✿ 1932–1945

Between 1932 and 1945, the University of Manitoba faced three major crises, external and internal. The first external crisis was, of course, the Great Depression of the 1930s, which provided for Manitoba a backdrop of farm disaster, industrial unemployment, and the loss of provincial revenue. The second external crisis was World War II, which, like the Great War, had an enormous impact on both the larger society and the university community. The third crisis was internal, and it was difficult to avoid the thought that it could, at least in part, have been prevented.

On 25 August 1932, the Winnipeg newspapers reported that John A. Machray, nephew of Archbishop Machray, honorary bursar of the university, and chair of the BoG, had been arrested and charged with embezzling from the university. Since 1903, Machray's prestigious law firm had overseen the investment of the university's endowments and its land grant. As bursar, he was also in charge of the university's financial books. In his dual role as bursar and chair of the BoG, and as a trusted member of the Winnipeg establishment, Machray had been able to stall attempts to audit the university's books for many years. The 1932 audit finally revealed that through a long series of bad investments and slipshod accounting, Machray had lost nearly all the university's endowment income.

The resultant financial losses, coupled with provincial budget cuts, ensured that the

Opposite: Downtown Winnipeg, 1928, looking south from Portage Avenue (PAM). The Broadway site is visible to the right of the Legislative Building.

university would have to operate through the 1930s under extraordinarily tight budget constraints. Like society generally, the University of Manitoba managed to stagger through the Depression. But due to the "defalcation," as the Machray business came to be known, the 1930s became increasingly a time of cheese-paring economies on the campus. The fabric was allowed to deteriorate, new initiatives were put on hold, and the campus remained physically divided for many years longer than had been originally intended.

The full implications of the Machray embezzlement were not understood for many years. Nearly $1.9 million in total was lost—$869,000 from the university itself (including revenue from the land grant), and $1 million lost by the Anglican church, St. John's College, and private clients. To put this into perspective, the total university budget in 1932 was $629,000. For many years Machray had

continued to pay interest to clients for investments, often in Winnipeg real estate, which had long since gone bust; the largest portion of the missing money ($782,000) had disappeared in this way. Another $300,000 was taken for Machray's personal use, $200,000 was paid in taxes and expenses on speculative real estate, and $400,000 was lost in bad investments. Machray, who was seriously ill when he was arrested, died in Stony Mountain penitentiary in 1933. Only $40,837.77 was ever recovered, and that from his insurance policies. Because of the number of variables involved, it is almost impossible to convert monetary figures from one era to another. But a modern equivalent of the total amount involved in the Machray business—almost $2 million in 1932 dollars—might be something of the order of $100 million.

A royal commission appointed by the province sat to determine the losses and the reasons for them, but there was nothing else to be done. The commission, headed by Saskatchewan judge W.F.A. Turgeon, held public hearings in the law courts from 29 September 1932 to 19 January 1933, sitting for fifty-four days, hearing forty-four witnesses, and filing 257 exhibitions. The commission avoided finger-pointing at individuals, largely because so many were involved in the failure to monitor the financial activities of the culprit over a protracted period of time. The Board of Governors was understandably shocked by the revelations of Machray's chicanery, and both it and the provincial government were directly responsible for the losses,

John Machray (c. 1912). Below: some of the new regulations implemented in response to the defalcation.

Marjorie Darragh

THE UNIVERSITY OF MANITOBA

REGULATIONS
RELATING TO
BUSINESS
MANAGEMENT

—

APRIL, 1935

—

PUBLISHED BY
THE OFFICE OF THE BURSAR

THE UNIVERSITY OF MANITOBA

FIRST SUPPLEMENT
TO
REGULATIONS RELATING TO
BUSINESS MANAGEMENT
ISSUED IN APRIL, 1935

APRIL, 1936

PUBLISHED BY
THE OFFICE OF THE BURSAR

since neither had insisted upon a proper audit for many years. The commission recommended reform, including a larger Board of Governors and a more administratively active president, but it was too late. Nevertheless, as Arthur Lower pointed out in his autobiography, *My First Seventy-Five Years*, the Machray business ended the Red River equivalent of the "Family Compact" in Upper Canada, in which the older families associated with the Hudson's Bay Company and the Anglican church had "held on in positions of influence long after the old colony had been submerged in the growing province."

Ironically, Machray's ultimate successor, Walter Crawford, who was hired to stabilize the university financial situation, became almost as powerful in his own way as his predecessor. Crawford, whom some observers called "The Boss," had absolute control over expenditures and resolutely refused to authorize any of which he did not approve. A no-nonsense man, Crawford once told President Sidney Smith, "Here are the facts you wanted for those letters you're going to send out, Sid. You put in the bullshit."

One of the chief effects of the Machray business was that the process of relocating the university from Broadway to Fort Garry was left incomplete. The university departments moved to the suburban campus were housed in 1932 in buildings completed as unemployment relief projects cost-shared between the province and the Dominion. Both the Arts Building (later the Tier Building) and the Science Building (later the Buller Building) were of collegiate Gothic design, constructed of Tyndall

United College, built as Wesley College in 1900 (UMA).

limestone. By themselves they were quite handsome, although their design and look were quite different from the buildings of the Agricultural College, which were adjacent to them. From the beginning of expansion, there was no attempt to ensure a congruity of architectural styles on the Fort Garry campus. The Arts (Tier) Building housed the arts faculty, the library, and the architecture faculty on the top floor. The Science (Buller) Building housed five science departments: botany, chemistry, geology, physics, and zoology. Senior and honours students attended classes taught at Fort Garry, while students in their first two years (the Junior Division) were taught downtown in the Broadway buildings. The first

A 1938 *Brown and Gold* cartoon about the streetcar ride on the number 97 tram to the Fort Garry campus.

administrative offices—registrar, comptroller, dean of arts—on each campus. Students moving from downtown to Fort Garry were struck by the newness and cleanliness of the buildings, by the availability of small classrooms as opposed to only large lecture theatres, and by the comfort of the segregated common rooms. Describing the university in 1935, Ernest Sirluck wrote in his autobiography, *First Generation*, that while first- and second-year students were spared the tram-ride to Fort Garry, "in every other respect they were disadvantaged: cut off from the society and influence of senior students, and most of the time, senior faculty, limited to a divisional library with few books, fewer journals, and almost no study space, and to laboratories capable at most of rudimentary demonstrations, with no local athletic or recreational facilities, and with literally no residential presence." Historian Arthur Lower, who taught at United College from 1929 to 1945 and who became one of the leading Canadian historians of his generation, subsequently wrote that the United buildings were shabby, but the Broadway buildings of the university were "shabbier and dirtier." Smoking in the corridors and gambling on the premises were forbidden on Broadway in 1937 in some attempt to make the place appear less seamy. In his memoir, *One Version of the Facts*, Harry Duckworth complains of being taught English by Fletcher Argue in a classroom of eighty students that was "poorly ventilated." The variations in heat from one part of the main building to another were legendary.

Despite the grime, heat (or absence thereof), and other problems, many of the students

downtown year was really grade twelve, offered because most rural high schools in the province went only through grade eleven.

Most university faculty taught in both locations. They commuted by streetcar (tram) or automobile between the two campuses. Library resources were divided, but most of the books were at Fort Garry. There were duplicate found their university experience a liberating one. Ernest Sirluck observed that whatever its limitations, the university was such an advance on life in his native Winkler, a small town south of Winnipeg, that he did not complain. He later wrote, "The university offered so many opportunities for activities for which I'd been starved that I threw myself into them without much regard for the effect on my grades." Sirluck became involved in debating, the Dramatic Society, a fraternity, the Menorah Society, and student politics. Marshall McLuhan, another U of M student in the same period, attended classes at the Broadway and Fort Garry campuses until he received his MA in 1934, but was somewhat less active. McLuhan turned down an opportunity to become an assistant editor of the *Manitoban,* offered to him by editor W.L. Morton, preferring to concentrate on his studies, although he did serve as editor of the literary supplement. But he debated in 1934 with partner Abram Fiskin against Saskatchewan in the first radio debating series, broadcast from coast to coast

During his time as an undergraduate, McLuhan was a regular contributor to both the *Manitoban* and to another student publication, *'Toba,* a short-lived "Manitoba arts quarterly." McLuhan's articles included philosophical musings with titles such as "Spiritism, Not Spiritualism" and "Heavens Above." A somewhat earthier contribution came from another undergraduate, Bill Mitchell, later better known to generations of Canadian readers as W.O. Mitchell. Mitchell's "Panacea for Panhandlers" was

Marshall McLuhan

(1911–1980) was one of the most influential thinkers of the last half of the twentieth century. Sometimes called the "Oracle of the Electronic Age," McLuhan changed the way we think about technology and communications with a series of influential books that included *The Gutenberg Galaxy* and *Understanding Media.* Throughout the 1960s and 1970s, he became a well-known public figure and many of his aphorisms, such as "the medium is the message," became part of popular culture. McLuhan attended the university from 1928 to 1934, graduating with an MA in English before leaving for studies at Cambridge. While at the university, he wrote frequently for the *Manitoban* and other student publications.

'toba

heavens above!

By MARSHALL McLUHAN

THERE is one compensation which the daily trip to the Manitoba union offers to everyone, and it has been disreg plumes. These No one accustomed to see of cloud and sl buil

t have been called ches' brooms." But art, in the midst of pression of organic eir freedom. One that is often to erfect likeness to maple.

'toba

panacea for panhandlers

By BILL MITCHELL, Arts '34 U.

WHICH would you prefer, "Rocked In the Cradle of the Deep" or "Locked in the Hold With Johnny the Greek"? So went the motto of the English sailors on board the Greek tramp steamer, "Onassapinellopi," with her crew composed mostly of Greeks, a sprinkling of English, two Frenchmen, a Dutch oiler, an Italian donkeyman, a German fireman and an old Turk going to Morroco—not to mention the nine stupid-looking sheep serving as meat

truck and hay cart, footloose and care-free in the Old World, drifting whimsically, seeing a new pattern of familiar things—this is the panacea of the hitchhiking panhandler in Europe.

* * *

anchored in quebec may 4th, 1933

Every man on board feels his job is the most demanding, while in reality that of galley boy is the most tiring and thankless.

I helped the Old Turk peel potatoes

William Boyd, professor of pathology, and some of the textbooks that made the Medical College famous in the 1930s and 1940s (UMA).

AN INTRODUCTION TO THE STUDY
OF
SECRETION

BY
SWAL
LL.D., D.Sc., M.D., F.R.S. (Ed
Professor of Physiology, Univer
School); formerly Profess
Manitoba; Assistant
College, London,
Birmingham
Lecture

Author of "Interna

Churchill's Empire Series
THE BIOCHEMISTRY
OF MEDICINE

A. T. CAM   BY   C. R. GILMOUR
M.A., D.Sc., F.I.C.   F.R.C.P. (C.)
Professor of Biochemistry
Biochemistry, University
Biochem.; Winnipeg G

ED

A TEXT-BOOK
OF
PATHOLOGY
AN INTRODUCTION TO MEDICINE

BY
WILLIAM BOYD
M.D., M.R.C.P. Ed., F.R.C.P. Lond.; Dipl. Psych., F.R.S.C.
PROFESSOR OF PATHOLOGY IN THE UNIVERSITY OF MANITOBA; PATHOLOGIST TO THE
WINNIPEG GENERAL HOSPITAL, WINNIPEG, CANADA
ILLUSTRATED WITH 267 ENGRAVINGS AND A COLORED PLATE

LEA & FEBIGER
PHILADELPHIA
1932

carried in instalments over three issues of 'Toba. "Panacea" was a diary of Mitchell's travels throughout Europe in the summer of 1933, and included observations such as his account of an evening in Paris: "Well, I've been to the Folies Bergere and can truthfully say that a leg now means no more to me than a shoe-tree."

The normal teaching load at both the university and the colleges was sixteen contact hours of lectures per week, plus papers and any additional seminars or tutorials. Most faculty ranged widely in their teaching, which was often done in courses on subjects well beyond their specialties. Many were also active as advisors to various student extracurricular organizations. A number of faculty established reputations as exceptional teachers. Arthur Lower at United and Rupert Lodge at the Fort Garry campus were two of the most respected because of their knowledge and enthusiasm. Both treated students as adults. Lodge once explained that he asked students to "write a large number of essays upon the moral and intellectual problems arising out of their own development to maturity," adding that "these essays are discussed in class and in connection with these discussions an outline of systematic thinking on ethnics, logic, theory of knowledge, and metaphysics is presented in such a way as to show the students how to make practical application (both to life-problems and to their problems as students of arts and science)."

Given the faculty workloads, the remarkable thing was that many faculty—including Lower and Lodge—did carry on research and publish fairly regularly, their scholarly activities proudly reported in the president's annual report. A handful of faculty, mainly in the sciences and medical school, even achieved international reputations. Textbooks written in the 1930s by the Faculty of Medicine's Swale Vincent, A.T. Cameron, and William Boyd remained in use in their respective fields for many years. In courses taught simultaneously at both the university and the colleges, a single final examination was marked cooperatively. Optional questions made it possible for all students to write a common examination. The marking was usually done at Fort Garry, much to the unhappiness of the college instructors. Faculty took several salary cuts in the course of the 1930s, and pension arrangements were primitive at best. But the cost of living in Winnipeg was low, and most senior faculty could afford a servant or two if they chose to employ them.

Despite the economic problems caused by the Depression and the defalcation, student life went on. *The Manitoban* was forced to undertake a circulation campaign because of the decrease in the payment of student dues to UMSU, and in 1932 the literary supplement was cancelled because of the expense. But the newspaper kept publishing, simultaneously affording its staff an opportunity at journalism and its readership contact with the world of the campus and of the mind in a new semi-weekly format. In early 1933, an editorial complained of a lack of discussion of national and international issues on the campus because there were few organizations to provide a forum. The newspaper insisted that part of the problem was the physical division of the university, reflecting a common student opinion that the university really belonged downtown.

Theatre and other amusements continued to be of significant student interest throughout the 1930s. In 1932 Oscar Wilde's *The Importance of Being Ernest* was selected for UMDS production over several plays of George Bernard Shaw, and

early in 1933, Delta Phi Epsilon finally got the production rights of Elmer Rice's *Street Scene*, which had earlier been denied. In the autumn of 1933, *A Well Remembered Voice*, a play by Sir James M. Barrie, was produced by the UMDS and presented at the Civic Auditorium. It starred Frank W. Jones (the university's Rhodes Scholar for 1934), while supporting roles were filled by Brian Dickson, later the Chief Justice of Canada, and Duff Roblin, who twenty-five years later would become premier of Manitoba. In 1936 a "Variety Night" held at the civic auditorium on Vaughan Street drew an audience of 1800. Most departments had student clubs that met regularly. The English club, designed for selected senior students, was called "the Morons," and assembled each month to listen to scholarly papers and literary readings. An UMSU dance in 1933 cost $1.00 per couple for tickets. The first inter-faculty rugby game, between St. Paul's College and the Medicals, was played on 28 October 1932.

The early 1930s also seemed to witness a revival of the hazing of freshmen and other earlier traditions. In September 1932 the *Manitoban* spoke of pajama-clad Science freshies being paraded down Main Street, urged on by

Following page: Map of the university, showing its scattering components, from a 1930 *Brown and Gold*.

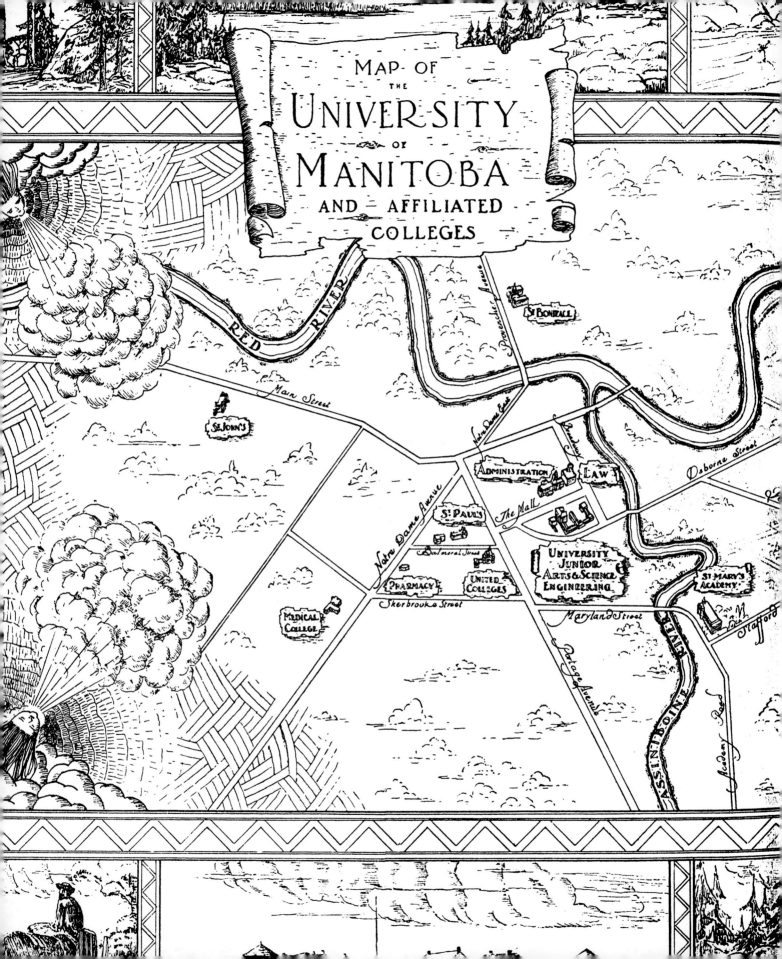

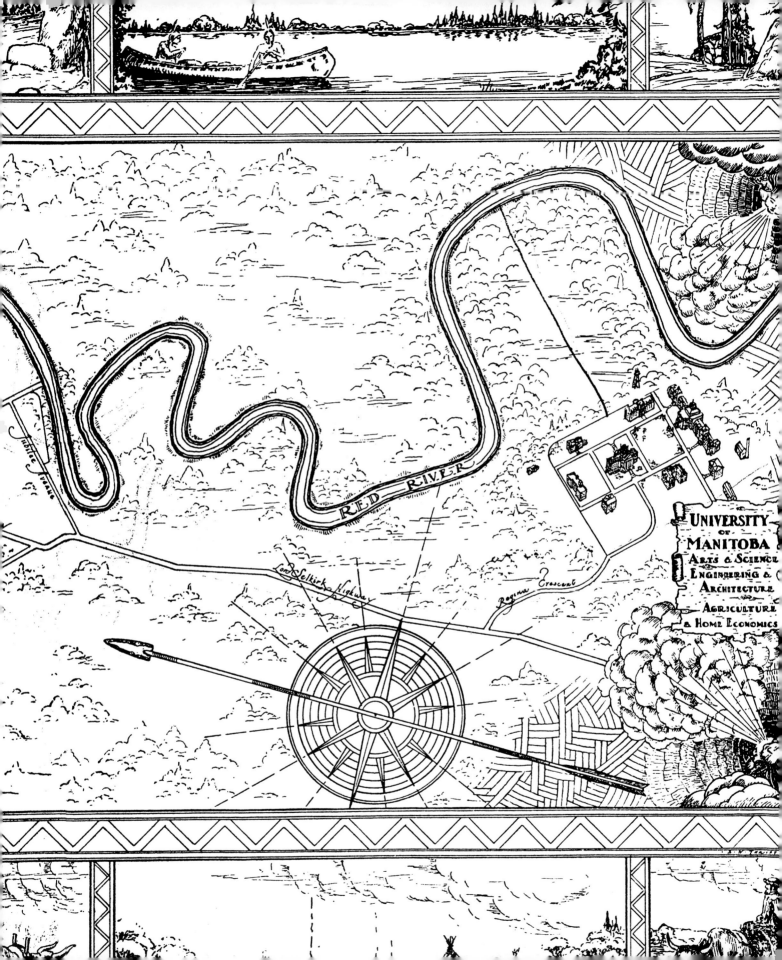

UNIVERSITY
OF
MANITOBA
ARTS & SCIENCE
ENGINEERING &
ARCHITECTURE
AGRICULTURE
& HOME ECONOMICS

RED RIVER

Lord Selkirk Highway

Regina Crescent

John Dafoe, editor of the *Winnipeg Free Press*, was chancellor of the university from 1932 to 1942. Dafoe was probably the most influential Canadian journalist of his time (PAM).

sophomores swinging wooden paddles. Fraternity and sorority life continued despite the economic climate and the move to the suburbs. Many of the Greek chapters had their own apartments or houses, which continued to be located downtown. Legend reports that the university administration refused to allow the Greeks to move to the Fort Garry campus. Alpha Kappa Fraternity, organized in 1929, was affiliated in 1932 with the international Tau Delta Fraternity, and that same year Beta Phi Sigma became Beta Gamma chapter of Sigma Kappa Sorority. Greek "rushing" occurred mainly in September among freshmen, who were probationary members for some months before initiation as full members. Much hazing went on in the fraternities and sororities. In 1936 the sororities recruited forty-two members in University Arts and Sciences, twenty-five in Wesley College, two in St. John's College, four in St. Mary's College, thirty-six in Home Economics, and one in Architecture, for a total of 110 "probies." That same year, five of the sororities banded together to have their chapter rooms under one downtown roof. The 1932 student commission complained that many of the student body who regarded the university as a "social finishing school" were active in the Greek world, particularly that of the sororities.

In 1935 the Dean of Women Students reported such a rich social life at the university that careful scheduling was necessary to coordinate the activities of the affiliated

colleges, the medical faculty, and the university itself, all of which were asked to accept UMSU dates for their freshmen receptions and grad farewells, and to give no more than one dance a year for which tickets were on sale to non-faculty members. The outsiders were universally held responsible for most of the rowdyism blamed on the students. Large events open to all students included freshmen's receptions, various dances and balls—including the "tea dance"—the major dramatic production, inter-provincial debating, the Glee Club, minor dramatic productions, and grad farewells.

The university attempted to maintain an active athletic programme, although the limited athletic facilities of the student union at Fort Garry were taxed to their utmost. Varsity teams competed in women's track and field, swimming, junior and senior basketball, and hockey. Men competed in swimming, rugby, basketball, and junior hockey. The Dean of Junior Men reported that the downtown Broadway campus was much handicapped by its lack of athletic facilities, although arrangements had been made for membership with the YMCA, partly paid for by student organizations and partly by the university. In 1936, 1000 students participated in athletic activities. A small track team (four men and four women) won a track championship in competition with the universities of Alberta and Saskatchewan. The varsity hockey team won both games with the University of Minnesota. On the negative

Convocation in the mid-1930s (UMA).

W.O. Mitchell

(1911–1998), author of classics
such as *Who Has Seen the
Wind,* was one of the best-
loved and most-celebrated
Canadian writers of his
time. He attended the
university from 1931 to
1934, where he was
known as "Bill" Mitchell. A
native of Weyburn,
Saskatchewan, Mitchell came
to the university to study arts,
and majored in philosophy and
psychology. His many extracurricular activities
included writing (along with Marshall McLuhan) for a
student arts magazine, as well as cheerleading and
acting. The caption next to Mitchell's picture in one
student publication asks cryptically: "Bill Mitchell—
does he ever pay?" Ill health forced Mitchell to leave
the university before graduation, but he eventually
continued his studies at the University of Alberta.

side, most varsity athletics and virtually all
intra-university competition was cancelled for
the entire duration of the Depression, a lacuna
that carried over into the war. Moreover, many
observers agreed with Ernest Sirluck that
"everybody left the campus as soon as their
assignments for the day were over, and the
professors fastest of all." Despite the obvious
availability of a rich social and extracurricular
life, many students of the '30s found the
university's atmosphere "impersonal," especially
in the classroom, and preferred the closer life
of the colleges (if one enjoyed religious
regimentation) or the Greek World.

Not quite everyone went home at day's end.
By the mid-1930s, there were several hundred

Intramural football, 1936
(UMA).

students in residence in Taché Hall at Fort Garry. The men lived in the west end and the women in the east end. Each half had, in the basement, a gym, a small swimming pool, and a small lounge. Students came from all faculties, although the men's side was dominated by agriculture, engineering, and arts and science, and the women's side by home economics. There were occasional raids by men on the girls' side, including some "panty raids," and sometimes the fire hoses would be turned on. In 1936 there were protests against meals in the residence dining room, chiefly complaining about the institutional sequence of meals.

At the University of Manitoba, as elsewhere in Canada, the student body was relatively unpolitical throughout most of a decade that saw many attempts to transform the political and social order in Canadian society. The 1932 student commission divided the undergraduate student body into four distinct groups. The smallest consisted of talented students who sought to satisfy a craving for knowledge. A second, medium-sized, group wanted professional advancement and "has no undue enthusiasm for learning." A third larger group wanted to avoid "a life of manual labor or lowly positions in business." A fourth and medium-large group attended the university with neither interest in learning nor ambition, "being sent there by their parents on account of the social and financial standing of their families." According to one student at Fort Garry, "the students doing political things were just a minority. The bulk of students didn't give a damn." A University Society for Social Reconstruction (the USSR, a conceit appreciated by its members) formed at United College, but never attracted a large membership. U of M students had organized a chapter of the Student Christian Movement (SCM) in 1930, which was active in sponsoring speakers with controversial ideas and advocating social justice. A national student conference in

Winnipeg in December 1937, sponsored by the SCM, led to the 1938 organization of the Canadian Student Assembly, which had a local branch. The *'Toban* applauded the national conference as "the greatest student intellectual marathon" of all times. Students listened to Reinhold Niebuhr (regarded as the greatest American theologian of his time) and discussed public issues among themselves from a largely left-of-centre perspective.

One of the most surprising features of the 1930s for contemporaries was that although enrolment had fallen off a bit in the early part of the decade, it held up surprisingly well through the Depression. Two features of the enrolment picture were an increased number of women, particularly in arts, and a general resurgence of student numbers in the colleges. The larger number of women was part of a continental trend. The gains for the colleges were local phenomena. The move to Fort Garry had virtually coincided with the start of the Depression, and many students chose to remain downtown by transferring to the colleges, which often had lower fees. The fee differential became more marked after the Machray business forced the university to raise tuition substantially. Moreover, although special tramfares for students were

available, transportation to the suburbs was an additional cost. In 1934 the Dean of Arts and Sciences at Fort Garry complained of the "unethical underbidding in fees," which he described as "a pistol pointed at the University Faculty of Arts and Science." An article in the 9 June 1934 issue of the Canadian magazine *Saturday Review* commented that fee differentials and the remoteness of the site had affected the distribution of student numbers. Totals were not down at the U of M, said the magazine, but enrolment in the affiliated colleges had risen substantially. There were 170 arts graduates in both 1928 and 1935. In the former year, 14 percent of these came from Wesley College, while in 1935 the Wesley contribution was 54 percent.

One of the less attractive features of the university was a strong current of anti-Semitism, both informal and informal. The 1932 student commission report emphasized that racism, especially in the form of anti-Semitism, was rampant at the University of Manitoba, and it called upon the university to "correct any attitude of antipathy or condescension on the part of the Anglo-Saxon majority," although it advocated no specific course of action. There was a quota for Jews at the medical school, not publicly admitted until the end of the Second World War, and it was reputedly difficult for Jews to enter engineering. They were admitted to the law school, but on graduation were

A Depression era "rider of the rails" (NAC).

expected to article only with a Jewish firm. No Jews were members of the university faculty, apart from the medical and law schools, both of which employed many part-time faculty. Fraternities and sororities were strictly segregated, and there was at least one Jewish fraternity, Sigma Alpha Mu. Ernest Sirluck commented in his autobiography that, socially, Jews were set apart. Others who were students in the 1930s agree, although some have noted that the U of M merely reflected the larger society of Winnipeg in the 1930s, and was probably more open generally than was that society. Nevertheless, Jewish students, many of whom made the long streetcar ride each day from Winnipeg's polyglot North End, often did play prominent roles in the university's life. These include Monte Halparin, a pre-med student who became UMSU president in 1943, and who later became known to generations of North Americans as Monty Hall, host of TV's *Let's Make a Deal*. Not until 1939 did the university attempt to ascertain the number of students of Jewish origin it registered; at that time it was 310, or 11.1 percent of the total student body, perhaps the highest percentage anywhere in a Canadian university.

Sidney Earle Smith

(1897–1959), the university's second president, was educated at King's College and Dalhousie, and, after teaching several years at Osgoode Hall, returned to Dalhousie as dean of its law school. After ten years as president of the university (1934 to 1944), Smith left Manitoba for the University of Toronto, where he became president in 1945. He later became Minister of External Affairs in the first Diefenbaker government.

Ethnic Composition of Student Body, 1938–39

English	1026
Scottish	616
Irish	350
Hebrew	310
French	123
German	96
Ukrainian	75
Icelandic	57
Dutch	37
Polish	34
Russian	21
Welsh	16
Norwegian	13
Swiss	11
American	11
Belgian	9
Swedish	8
Austrian	5
Hungarian	4
Ruthenian	3
Czechoslovakian	3
Mennonite	2
Italian	2
Syrian	2
Chinese	2
Manx	1
Total	2839

[source: University Bulletin, 3 January 1939]

Opposite: United College staff and students in the annual freshie march through downtown Winnipeg, c. 1934 (UWA).

President MacLean had resigned in 1934, and was replaced by Sidney Earle Smith, who had been Dean of Law at Dalhousie University. The new prexy was one of those men who could remember your name and something about you for months after having briefly met you. He said of himself that he was a pillar of brass by day and a bag of gas by night. Mixing (or perhaps continuing) the metaphors, Smith brought a breath of fresh air into the administration of the university, supporting innovation and insisting on positive thinking. In his inaugural address as president in October 1934, Smith declared a commitment to the importance of the liberal spirit in education and to the liberal arts, and he later became known as a strong advocate for the arts and humanities. He also believed that the university's task went beyond developing

· SOUTH · ELEVATION ·

This 1932 architect's drawing shows plans for a new St. John's College, intended for the Fort Garry site. These new buildings were never begun, one of the many victims of the financial difficulties after the defalcation (UMA).

intellectual capacity, emphasizing the need to improve students' "physical, social and moral qualities." Smith was even willing to admit that too much of the work of student evaluation tested rote memorization instead of "original work," although he did little about this problem. From the outset, he also emphasized the need for improved salaries for faculty and for outreach into the community. In his 1937 presidential report, he argued, "The University owes a duty to its shareholders, the tax-payers of Manitoba, to minister directly to their needs." The Smith era would see increased programming for the community, sponsored by the university. In 1936 a new University Act was approved, which replaced the old University Council with a Senate, while leaving the dual system of administration of finance and academics in place. A comptroller of finance had replaced the old bursar, but the system's finances were still outside the hands of the academics.

Despite—and in some cases because of—the economic climate, both the colleges and the faculties continued to experience substantial

change over the Depression years. For example, the Society of Jesus of Upper Canada in 1933 legally assumed all the assets and liabilities of St. Paul's College, which was more than $140,000 in debt, and took over the administration of the college. St. Paul's prospered under the Jesuits, and by 1939 the teaching staff had increased to eighteen Jesuits, one diocesan priest, and one layman. Most students were in the high school, many remaining for grade twelve before entering university with senior matriculation. However, enrolment increased in years one and two of the university course. St. Joseph's College (the women's department of St. Boniface for francophone students wishing to follow a bilingual university course) affiliated with the university in 1936, and St. Mary's had a strong university programme throughout the decade. In October of 1936, labour unrest hit the campus as part of the *Manitoban* staff walked out over working conditions and low wages in the print shop that printed the paper. Three non-striking staffers reported the strike with an extra.

BROWN AND GOLD
HURRY – ORDER NOW

In 1938 several important college developments occurred. The United Colleges formally became United College (UC). William Creighton, the new principal of UC, was installed in October of that year. In his inaugural address he found advantage in the distinctive Canadian pattern of higher education, in which church colleges cooperated with the state and were not left to fend for themselves. Despite the pattern, United was in serious financial difficulty, with a mortgage of $100,000 and a bank overdraft of $74,000 to set against assets of less than $100,000. The college operated at an annual deficit, and had depleted its 1914 endowment fund of $218,486 to $50,000. The United experience suggests that had Machray not embezzled endowment funds, they would have been spent during the lean days of the 1930s anyway, perhaps providing a slightly more affluent experience but certainly not accumulating as capital to provide a large endowment. In August of 1938, a Committee of Arts and Sciences from the university discussed with Brandon College the principle of affiliation. It initially recommended affiliation as a liberal arts college only, expressing concern about the quality of the laboratory facilities. At this time, Brandon was easily the best-funded of the colleges, having received considerable private support from the A.E. McKenzie Foundation. The first Brandon representative to the university Senate was welcomed in December 1938.

As for faculties, while the Depression was not exactly prime time for expansion, in 1936 the university agreed to offer examinations in all grades of music, and it established a diploma programme. Eva Clare was appointed the first Director of Music. In 1937 the Bachelor of Commerce degree was introduced. Like the University of Toronto, the University of Manitoba attempted to involve businessmen in the planning and implementation of the commerce programme.

In 1933 the Alumni Association, which had fallen on very hard times, was reinvigorated and reorganized. Such an organization was certainly needed to create links between the graduates of the university—who by 1934 numbered just over 7000—and the university itself, as it was undergoing many problems. The 1932 student commission was scathing in its comments about

Eva Clare, founder of the School of Music. A native Manitoban, Clare had studied in New York and Germany, and would lead the school until she retired in 1949 to devote more time to her own teaching.

the attitude of the alumni to the university, obliquely commenting, no doubt, on the response to the Machray affair. The commission noted, "At a time when loyalty and co-operation were most needed, nothing but apathy and indifference were to be found." The commission worked hard to uncover the reasons for the almost total lack of graduate support. The historical growth of the university, it pointed out, left loyalties with colleges and faculties rather than with the university itself. But the commission also pointed the finger at those in the general arts courses in the university or at the colleges, who found that their years of higher learning were "years of

fruitless effort," producing "little that is commensurate with the time and money spent." And it felt that political interference, lack of government leadership, and the "startling disclosures" of financial mismanagement had helped bring the university into disrepute. The student commission called for efforts to awaken "the long-dormant loyalty of the entire graduate body to spring into life," but did not specify from whence the leadership was to come.

As if to emphasize the point of the lack of alumni support in the early years of the Depression, in 1934 only about 4 percent of all graduates were fee-paying members of the association. In that same year, the *Alumni Quarterly* was replaced by the *Alumni Journal*, which combined news of the university with news of its graduates. The new journal was mailed at considerable cost to as many of the graduates as possible, but the gamble did not work and memberships continued to decline; the journal's publishing history was chequered over the next few years. Despite many problems, the Alumni Association of the University of Manitoba was subsequently incorporated and celebrated a successful "alumni week" on the Fort Garry campus. The association also began organizing alumni activities throughout the year, especially a very popular annual curling bonspiel. In 1935 the Manitoba Agricultural and Home Economic Alumni Association merged with the Alumni Association; a $6 membership fee was instituted. The university was not alone in concern for keeping in touch with its graduates. In 1937 the St. John's College Graduate Society formed, with Canon Walter Barfoot as president and W. L. Morton as secretary. The society began

Fort Garry site looking west from the campus, c. 1941 (UMA).

with fifty paid members, and planned affiliation with the university Alumni Association. Not until 1946, when the university agreed to provide the Alumni Association with sufficient funds to hire a full-time secretary and set up an office on the Broadway campus, was the association really put on its feet.

In the later 1930s, both the university and some of its colleges celebrated anniversaries. The sixtieth anniversary of the founding of the University of Manitoba was marked modestly in 1937 by the publication of a volume of essays, entitled *Manitoba Essays*, mainly written on academic topics by faculty members. The volume was edited by Philosophy's Rupert C. Lodge, generally regarded within the university community as its leading ornament on the arts

side. Lodge's introduction was a model of restraint of enthusiasm for the institution being honoured. A year later, Wesley College celebrated its fiftieth anniversary with the publication of a Golden Jubilee volume. In it Watson Kirkconnell wrote that Wesley "had won for herself in the hearts of students and graduates a loyalty comparable, in Canada, to nothing so much as to the clanlike devotion of Queen's alumni to the Alma Mater." The difference in the tone of the two commemorations was instructive.

As the end of the 1930s approached, Canada finally began to come out of the Depression, only to have to face the prospect of renewed international war. In December 1938, the university's BoG had made a submission to the

Dance advertisement from
The Manitoban, 1936.

Don't leave her home
on
Hallowe'en

Take her to the
ANNUAL PUMPKIN BALL
- Two brand new orchestras -
- Two Super Ballrooms -
ROYAL ALEXANDRA
Saturday, October 31st.

9 p.m.   1.50 per Couple

Rowell-Sirois Commission, which was
investigating the constitutional arrangements
for Canada that had proved so inadequate to
cope with the economic emergency. The
submission pointed out that the legislative grant
to the university had been cut from $501,000
in 1929–30 to $257,000 in 1937–38, during a
period when the entire endowment of the
university had been lost through defalcation.
Salaries of staff had been reduced by 20 percent
during the 1930s, and had not yet been
restored. The BoG hoped that financial relief
might be provided by the federal government,
but such wishful thinking was still a generation
away. One of the few signs of economic upswing
visible around the Fort Garry campus in 1939

was the decision by the municipality to pave the
west side of Pembina Highway.

In 1939 the University of Manitoba reported
an enrolment of 3067 males and 1694 females,
up from 1776 males and 831 females in 1932.
The out-of-province enrolment in 1939 was
332, or 11.8 percent of the student body, and was
heaviest in medicine and home economics. The
percentage of students from Manitoba outside
Winnipeg—26.9 percent—was exactly the same in
1939 as ten years earlier. The ethnic composition
of the student body was still predominately
British, at about two-thirds, but twenty-seven
national origins were now represented.
According to the University of Winnipeg's
historian, Gerald Bedford, organized student life
at the U of M at the end of the Depression
decade was dominated by United College. United
students controlled the *Manitoban* and held most
of the top elected offices in UMSU, for example,
and United teams were frequent winners in
inter-collegiate athletics.

United students were responsible for the
institution of Sadie Hawkins Week in January of
1939, which spread quickly across the university.
Sadie Hawkins was a comic-strip character
created by American cartoonist Al Capp in his
popular "L'il Abner." Sadie was a singularly
unattractive-looking young lady with buck teeth,
whose father declared that for one day each
year, she would be allowed to take the lead in
the courtship ritual. Daddy waited with a
shotgun to marry her to any male she could
capture. Naturally the males ran and hid.
Translated to the Canadian campus, Sadie
Hawkins meant a variety of social activities in
which girls supposedly invited boys and paid for

COTC at the Minto Armories, Winnipeg, 1939 (UMA).

tickets. Sadie Hawkins week symbolized in many ways the position of women at the university. They constituted just over one-third of the total enrolment and nearly half the arts enrolment, and filled every available room in Taché Hall, but first-year female students were still referred to as "freshettes" and female sports teams as "Bisonettes." For most of the year, university women were expected to remain subordinate to males. One totally female world was the world of the sorority, still going strong on the campus. The Dean of Women Students had failed to convince the sororities to wait until second year to recruit members, but did convince them to cut the rush period from one month to two weeks, ending at the close of September.

Then came the war. For the University of Manitoba, as for most of Canada, war meant more deferral and more disruption, an extension of an already prolonged period of abnormality. The war also had a tremendous impact upon the university. On the academic side, it provided a great impetus to science, engineering, and medicine, as well as a disastrous disincentive to the arts and humanities, from which it could be argued those disciplines have never quite recovered. On the social and extracurricular side, the war postponed the reappearance of much that had been cut during the Depression years, particularly in the area of athletics. Military or war-related training absorbed much of the spare time of both male and female students. Early in the fall term of 1939, the official size of the Canadian Officers Training Corps (COTC) was raised from 150 to 800, and the number of actual participants exceeded 700, the largest

Poster and program for *You Can't Beat Fun.* Opposite: The show's creators (l to r): U of M students Earle Beattie, Samuel Seetner, and Edward Parker (UMA).

corps in western Canada and perhaps the largest in the nation. A year later, compulsory military training began for all male students over the age of nineteen, unless they were excused on military grounds. Those over twenty-one were responsible for six hours' training weekly, as well as for a two-week stint at camp in May.

Student thespians managed one last hurrah before the grim realities of war bit deeply into campus life. In the fall of 1939, the UMDS managed to persuade the UMSU council to permit it to stage the world premiere of an original musical revue written, produced, and performed by U of M students. *You Can't Beat Fun* had music by Samuel Seetner, a book by Earle Beattie, stage conception by Edward Parker, and lyrics by Beattie and Seetner. Appropriately, the collaborators represented different constituencies of the university. Seetner was a student in Science, Beattie was in his third year at United College, and Parker was enrolled in the Faculty of Law. Using a large cast headed by Monte Halparin, the revue was presented to sold-out houses at the Civic Auditorium Concert Hall on 11–13 January 1940. An extra night was added at the last minute because of the heavy demand for tickets. Set at Swingmore College, the show was billed as "The Gayest and Slaphappiest Satire on Campus Life," featuring "Comic Professors of Love, Rhythm, and Hotcha." Less than a month later, the Glee Club presented its annual Gilbert and Sullivan extravaganza, *H.M.S Pinafore. The Manitoban* quite rightly commented of both shows that "Canada today needs a good laugh to come out of its war jitters." Unfortunately, wartime restraints soon meant the end of such

elaborate productions for several years. The same issue of *The Manitoban* carried a long story on a student "ghost-writing" service operating out of New York City, which had a staff of seven writers and six typists. The *'Toban* did not comment on whether U of M students had employed such services, but thought that most Manitoba undergraduates "would give their eye-teeth to be spared the effort of writing essays."

In 1941 a university report noted a discipline committee was considering expulsion for two students refusing military duty. A Senate recommendation for compulsory first-year physical education for students in arts, science, agriculture, and home economics was

UNIVERSITY OF MANITOBA
DRAMATIC SOCIETY
PRESENTS

for the first time on any stage
A MUSICAL PLAY

"You Can't Beat Fun"

Music by SAMUEL SEETNER : Book by EARLE BEATTIE
Stage Conception by EDWARD PARKER
Lyrics by Beattie and Seetner

Directed by David H. Yeddeau

THE PLAYERS

NINE PATRIARCHAL PROFESSORS—
Ralph Colpitts, Jerome Cohen, Colin Hay, Abe Simkin, Howard Steppler, Monte
Syme, Ken Wares, Harold Bookbinder, Saul Weinstein.
DICK BILLINGS
HIS PA
JOHNNY ARMSTRONG .... BERNARD MOSS
HIS FATHER .... MORTEN PARKER
JOAN WILLIAMSON .... MONTE HALPARIN
BETTY WILLIAMSON .... LOUIS KALESKY
THEIR DAD .... JUNE EDMISON
THE FACULTY— .... JESSIE FISHER
Dr. Diddlefritz, President of Swingmore College .... GEORGE MUIRHEAD
Dean Hiccoughs, Professor of Love
Dean Dingbat, Professor of Rhythm
Flora Ironsides, Dean of Home Economics
Dr. Seabright, Substitute Professor .... MONTE SYME
JOEY JIVE .... MORLEY MARGOLIS
MISS SNODGRASS .... MAX CHAM
MISS STRYCHNINE .... VICKI STEACY
THE STUDENT COUNCIL .... MORTEN PARKER
Chairman .... JOE JAMPOL
Secretary .... LILY NITIKMAN
New Chairman .... PAT HALTER
New Secretary
Montmorency (Canary Club) .... HOWARD STEPPLER
Sorority Sister .... OLIVE McLAY
Editor of the Yearbook .... MONTE HALPARIN
Jimmy Juggle (Social Committee) .... IRIS GREENFIELD
Co-ed Chieftain .... HART FAINTUCH
Other Members: Audrey Putnam, June Greenfield, Lily Nitikman, Doris .... VICKI STEACY
Marter, Jessie Fisher, Jerome Cohen, Bernard Moss. .... HAROLD BOOKBINDER
SOLOIST, CO-ED BALL .... NEVILLE WINOGRAD
COAT CHECK GIRL .... JUNE EDMISON
THE TWO SEE-MEN .... GWEN RAMSAY
.... MARIE McGUINNESS
{ DON KENNEDY
{ JOE KENNEDY

CHORUS
THE CO-EDS
SOPRANOS—
June Greenfield, Iris Greenfield, Audrey Putnam, Olive McLay, Doris Marter,
Minnie Isenberg, Lucy Black, Enid Nemy, Marjorie Patrick.
CONTRALTOS—
Donalda Long, Lily Nitikman, Grace Maza, Dorothy Stoffman, Rose Rabinovitch,
Betty Pickup, Ruth Simon, Jocelyn Saul, Pat Halter.
THE MEN
TENORS—
Harold Bookbinder, Earl Pashkovsky, Irvin Kleiman, Jerome Cohen, Abe Simkin,
Colin Hay, Ralph Colpitts, Hart Faintuch.
BASS—
Neville Winograd, Roy Bader, Ken Wares, Paul Ringer, Lazer Diamond, Ralph
Palmer, Ted Croasdell, Howard Steppler.

postponed "for the duration" because of the demands of compulsory military training on all male students. In a 1940 Canadian Students Association poll, U of M students voted 273 to 773 against conscription. In the same poll, the student body voted 663 to 25 in favour of complete freedom of speech, press, pulpit, and assembly, except in matters of military information. War work was also instituted for all female students, who were "voluntarily" to spend three hours per week receiving instruction in skills "designed to prepare them for service in a national emergency." This instruction, in which the university led the nation, was made compulsory in September of 1942. Enrolment in university-level work at United College fell from 357 in 1939 to 267 in 1941, and in the affiliated colleges enrolment dropped from 602 to 429. The bottom also fell out of arts

Monty Hall on the Wartime Years

When I walk down Portage Avenue--even today--I recognize half the people.
I know them--or I think I do. Sure, they've changed the store fronts, and
Childs Restaurant no longer exists, but the wind at Portage and Main still
howls as it whips around the corner, reminding you that this burgeoning
metropolis still sits in the middle of a prairie. So Moore's Restaurant is
gone, too. Chicken à la King for 35 cents after a college dance! You poor
children of today with your $10 steaks; what do you know of long walks
home from the South End to the North End after seeing your date home--all
to save the 8 cents streetcar fare. Of course, you don't even know about
streetcars! And working your way through college five nights and two days
every week just to pay the tuition, which was $150 a year for Junior
Division; and then the incredible jump to $250 a year for the Senior
years. What is Junior Division, you ask? You know that long, low, flat
building at Osborne and Broadway? Ah, that's gone, too, has it?

You'll never know what college life is like until you get on the old Park
Line streetcar #97 and take that Toonerville Trolley ride all the way to
"Aggie," the site of your beautiful campus of today. Tell me, do the kids
of today drive out to class, or do they take buses? Do the boys stand up
and give their seats to the girls? Do they harmonize to "Shenandoah" and
"Kentucky Babe"? Do they still pack their lunches when they go to classes
and trade sandwiches in the common room? Does anyone bring red salmon
sandwiches? Yes! red salmon! During the war years, salmon was rationed,
and a poor ersatz white salmon was canned. Anyone who had red salmon was
immediately discovered at lunch. That culprit shared his illegal fortune
with his neighbour or risked having the entire lunchroom made aware of his
mother's unpatriotic hoarding.

Junior Division with the famous catchphrase: "I'll meet you under the
clock." That's where the famous Arts-Science free-for-all took place, lab
coats flying in the fray. Roy Matas and I teamed up. I picked an Arts
student out of the throng, turned him to face Matas and--ZONKO!--another
Science knockout. Junior Division--Pre-Med--and waiting for the inevitable
letter, the reply to your medical school application. Sorry, it said, an
impersonal Gestetner blue, maybe next year, or next lifetime.

The war comes and we all join the COTC. Fort Osborne Barracks, Camp Shilo,
the same drill every week, nothing new. Schoolboys playing at soldier,
laughing, giggling at the klutz in front of you who keeps starting off on
the wrong foot, while your lieutenant or captain is some professor who
remembers those great glamorous days of Verdun and Marne when men were men
and both sides took a million casualties in one week. . . . Freshie Day--
track and field--box lunches and everyone so orderly. Pass your lunches
down to the aisle--neatly please--and then down each row to the waste
bins. And migod they did!!! Try that today in your stadium. Maybe we cared
because we had so little that even the right to go to college was
something we protected.

Monty Hall (Monte Halparin) graduated from the university in 1943.

enrolment at the university itself. Contrary to earlier expectations, wartime registrations did not so much fall as redistribute themselves, out of arts and into more approved (i.e., "practical") subjects. Only women were left in most of the humanities courses. This was not necessarily a bad thing. One English department course in Milton at the end of the war included as students Peggy Wemyss (later the novelist Margaret Laurence), Patricia Jenkins (later the novelist Patricia Blondal), and Adele Wiseman. Few Canadian instructors in literature ever had a greater opportunity to teach such a high-powered class.

A combination of government directives and the general climate of opinion led students to shift from arts to "approved" training in fields such as science, medicine, and engineering. The federal government classified the universities as essential war industries, and provided loan funds for students to enrol in science and engineering. The government also assisted the university to accelerate the medical course. Students in science, engineering, agriculture, and architecture were subsequently prohibited from joining the armed forces without permission. By 1943 only eighteen full-time students eligible for military service were left at United College. Officially, all students pursuing degree courses successfully were contributing to the war effort, but there was the matter of one's conscience, as well as the unspoken question of whether arts students would be exempted in case of a general mobilization.

Both the president of the University of Manitoba and the principal of United College

Margaret Laurence

(1926–1987), regarded by many as Canada's greatest novelist, has had her work translated and published throughout the world. Laurence (then Peggy Wemyss) graduated from the university in 1947; her classmates included Adele Wiseman and Patricia Blondal, both of whom also became important writers. Laurence is best known for her novels set in the fictional Manitoba town of Manawaka. Two of these, *A Jest of God* (1966) and *The Diviners* (1974), won the Governor General's Award.

were critical of government policy. In November of 1941, Principal Graham told his board that the decline in arts enrolment had "very definitely been accelerated by propaganda emanating from Dominion government agencies encouraging students to take technical studies in preference to arts courses." He was particularly upset by suggestions from one Dominion bureau to the Senate of the university that the shift of study take place before students had even matriculated. Graham saw this as "constituting an encroachment upon intellectual freedom" that was "very close to being fascistic." A year later, in October 1942, rumours began circulating that universities would soon drop arts teaching altogether in order to concentrate on technical training. *The*

Manitoban reported President Smith as writing to government, insisting that "students graduating in Arts are just as valuable to the war effort as those taking Engineering, Science, Medicine, Dentistry, or any other technical course." So much national unrest developed over this aspect of government policy that Prime Minister King issued a statement early in 1943 that universities should continue to teach arts, and that a few students should even be carried through the postgraduate stage in social science.

The university and United College attempted to show at least symbolic support for the arts disciplines by proposing dramatic restructurings of the curriculum. At the U of M, President Smith himself shepherded through the necessary academic channels an integrated series of interdisciplinary courses in humanities, social science, and science—a sort of core curriculum—which would be required of all students. One of the keys to the scheme was the introduction of small tutorial groups in each course. Senate approved the package, but deferred implementation until the necessary financial resources were available. The money was never to be found. Late in 1943, the United College faculty approved a resolution supporting "an attempt to reorganize the curriculum in Arts with a view to presenting the student with a clear picture of the culture of which he is a product and of his duty as an educated man to defend the best in his tradition and inheritance, and to launch a fresh attack upon the intellectual problems of his generation." Not much ever came of this resolution, however.

Opposite: Scenes from the
science graduation dinner,
1943, including (middle and
bottom) Monte Halparin,
UMSU president, and Hugh
Saunderson, then Dean of
Arts and Science (UMA).
Left: COTC troops at the
university (UMA).

One of the concerns of the government was that the wartime policy of deferral from military service of young men attending university would lead to draft dodging. The university attempted to answer this concern in 1942 by announcing publicly its resolution "to prevent the institution from becoming a refuge for an young man poor enough in spirit to desire to evade his military obligation by merely remaining on as a student." Any student doing poorly academically was to be reported to the military authorities at the place of his residence.

Later in 1942, the government announced that all physically fit male students must enrol for the Canadian Officers Training Corps, must perform military training, and must pass examinations in order to remain registered at the university. Early in 1943, the university publicly reported that ninety-seven students, including eighty-nine men, would have to drop their courses because of low grades. President Smith repeated at this time that students must not enrol at university solely to gain exemption from military service, but must work hard at their studies. Later that year, Smith was able to counter implicitly the worry about student slackers by pointing out in his annual report that over 2500 U of M alumni were serving in the Canadian Armed Forces, with sixty-nine known dead, twelve in prison camps, and fourteen being awarded military distinctions. He also noted that fifty-three members of staff were on wartime loan to the government. By 1944 more than 3000 graduates and former students had joined His Majesty's armed forces

Science students, early 1940s (UMA).

since the start of war. United College's participation in the war effort, as of summer 1945, consisted of 890 former students in active service, with 458 commissioned, 35 decorated, and 141 casualties (101 killed, 7 missing, 24 wounded, and 9 imprisoned, all subsequently released).

The war had considerable impact upon both the physical plant at the university and on

student use of that plant. In 1940 the Canadian Army leased the student residences at Fort Garry as a barracks for men in training and, beginning with the end of classes in 1940, began using the campus for drilling the recruits. A roller-skating rink from River Park was moved to Fort Garry as an indoor drill hall. As a result of the loss of the residence, university students were forced to seek alternate housing accommodation. Moreover, students lost access to the Student Union facilities of Taché Hall. The result was a considerable decline in organized social life, with most activities that remained using off-campus venues. The downtown auditorium roller-skating rink was popular, and an annual ice-skating night (which would turn into a Winter Carnival) was instituted at the amphitheatre rink. Bowling became very popular and downtown movie-going reached new heights. Co-eds brought a ball of wool as an entrance ticket to a 1942 co-ed ball, held off-campus, and more than 500 balls were collected for the war effort. Most observers agreed that soldiers and students managed to share the campus with minimum friction. The colleges continued to operate their residences throughout the war, and there is some evidence of a greater amount of normal student life in the colleges than at Fort Garry.

The demands of military training and the pressure to pass examinations combined to deter male participation in many extracurricular programmes. Because of extensive drilling and training on Saturday, for example, it became impossible to organize social activities on a Friday night. Organized athletics were reduced to the barest of minimums.

ICE CARNIVAL

The Athletic Board of Control presented its Annual Ice Carnival on February 20th, 1945. Close to 1200 were in attendance.

The program opened with a figure skating review by members of the Winnipeg Winter Club. Miss Sheila Smith opened with a brilliant solo. She was followed by a comedy with Robert Purvis and Ross Smith called "A Skating Lesson." Misses Lois Parkhill and Margaret Chown paired in a number followed by Miss Joyce Lamont in an excellent solo. Ross and Sheila Smith in a duet displayed the beautiful skating form that won for them the Canadian Junior Pairs Championship last year. The skating program concluded with a chorus of talented University girls, the Misses Joyce Lamont, Isobelle Hamon, Louise Parkhill, Kathleen Stewart, Frances MacCharles, Catherine Stewart, Evelyn Hipperson, and Margaret Chown. Margaret Chown handled arrangements for this very successful program.

The Engineers under the direction of Eric Bergenstein presented an adapation for ice of the well known drama "Snow White and the Seven Dwarfs." As always, the Engineers' skit was very amusing and greatly appreciated.

This year, as an experiment, the hockey game was a play-off game between the finalists of the Senior Inter-Faculty Hockey League. The game was one of the best ever played at any ABC Ice Carnival and was particularly well received by the audience. The Engineers enjoyed it even more than the rest of the crowd, as their team wound up victors 7 to 4 over Science in a fast, wide-open game.

The grand climax of the evening was the selection and the crowning of the Carnival Queen. The judges chose Miss Margaret McInnes of Home Economics who was truly a Queen among Queens. She was crowned by Dr. Hugh Saunderson, Dean of Arts and Science, and reigned supreme for the rest of the evening. The other candidates, who during the evening constituted the Queen's entourage, were Joyce Lamont of Interior Decoration, Sybil Williams of Medicine, Jeanne MacDonald of Science, Jean Malcom of Arts, Margaret Hall of United, Susan MacQuarrie of St. John's, and Geraldine Smith of St. Mary's.

The judges were Dr. Hugh Saunderson, Dr. R.A. Warle, Prof. J.R. Cavers, Mr. Ted Schrader, and Mr. Roy Kerr. Bob Shannon, one of the University's returned men, acted as Master of Ceremonies for the evening. The entertainment was followed by skating till 12 p.m. and dancing till 1 a.m.

From *Brown and Gold* (1945)

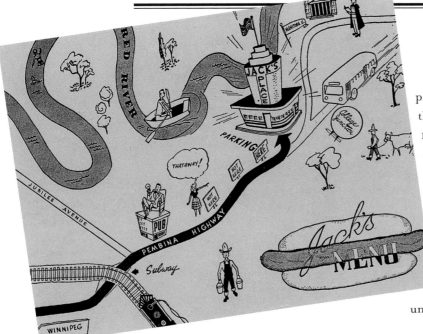

The ad for Jack's Place, a popular student hang-out, from the 1945 UMSU phone directory (UMA).

Sorority rushing was cut to a single week. A few frivolous (and not so frivolous) activities still persisted. In September of 1944, Peggy Wemyss enrolled at United College and moved into Sparling Hall, where she engaged in water-bombing—an exercise in which paper bags full of water were dropped from third-floor windows onto passers-by below. Her wardrobe consisted of two sweaters, two skirts, two blouses, one good dress, one pair of sensible shoes, and one pair of high-heeled shoes. Wemyss decided against joining a sorority, and became part of what her biographer calls the college's lunchroom and coffee-shop crowd instead. There was still a Freshie Week, and in 1943 United College's Patricia Ann Jenkins was selected as Freshie Queen. On 29 January 1945, the Athletic Board of Control held an unauthorized dance in the Rez auditorium, which resulted in an undisciplined crowd invading the residence. The crowd caused a disturbance until midnight and did $125 in damages, a considerable amount at the time.

In February of 1945, the annual ice carnival presented by the Athletic Board of Control at the amphitheatre attracted an audience of 1200. The programme included skating exhibitions, an on-ice skit by the engineers, and a hockey game (the senior inter-faculty playoff, won by the Engineers over Science, 7 to 4). No one had to ask why no arts team had made the final. The climax of the evening was the selection and crowning of the Carnival Queen, and the entertainment was followed by skating until 12:00 and dancing until 1:00 a.m.

But this event occurred late in the war. Most student life had been very serious from 1939 to 1945. Debating important social issues was an extremely popular activity, and in November of 1943, a group of students organized a campus society of the CCF. A club called the Practical Democracy Club emerged about the same time, committed to free enterprise. Other serious clubs, such as the International Affairs Club, flourished during the war years. So did Hillel (founded by Jewish students in 1944 to replace the old Menorah Society), the Inter-Race Fellowship (also established 1944 to create understanding between racial groups on the campus), and a chess club.

The wartime period was not free from controversy. From its institution, the programme of compulsory extra war-work classes for women was unpopular among many students, who complained about a system that seemed totally divorced from active participation in community enterprises. The students also grumbled that academic courses required extra study, and voted with their feet for the practical

A view of the Administration Building, looking down what was known as the Avenue of the Elms, c. 1940s (UMA).

ones—238 students signed up for typing, for example. The Committee on Women's War Work recommended in the spring of 1943 that the compulsory aspect of the programme be discontinued, but the almost all-male university Senate reaffirmed the requirement by majority vote. After continued agitation, the Senate finally agreed on 3 February 1944 to make the programme a voluntary one.

A few weeks later, on 10 March 1944, a *Tribune* editorial applauded the decision of the university's Discipline Committee to discipline a student who had written a poem entitled "Atrocities," published anonymously in a recent issue of the literary supplement of the *Manitoban*. The student was Albert Hamilton, the president of UMSU and a COTC cadet, who had already declared that he would volunteer for active service. Nevertheless, his poem was highly critical of Canada's war leaders, who were, it suggested, little better than those of the enemy. The Discipline Committee had labelled him "an

Wemyss, Jean Margaret
Neepawa, Man.

When Peggy was a little girl, her mother inadvertently dropped her onto a volume of Robinson Jeffers on the floor. She has been writing poetry ever since. Seriously, she plans a career in journalism; after which, successful or otherwise, she will settle down, marry a man with at least one million dollars and raise an average Canadian family.

The entry for Margaret Laurence (then Peggy Wemyss) in the 1947 *Brown and Gold*. Two of her classmates, Adele Wiseman and Patricia Blondal (right), also became important Canadian writers.

arrant" fool, rather than a criminal, said the *Tribune*, but he could not be let off the hook. The committee's decision was to withhold the awarding of the offending student's degree until he received an honourable discharge from the armed force of his choice. The editor of the supplement, Jack Ludwig (later a prominent novelist teaching in the United States), was summarily expelled and only later received his degree. Whatever the *Tribune* might opine, this disregard of the fundamental right of free speech was particularly unfortunate coming from an institution that should have been committed to its preservation and whose students had in 1940 indicated their full support of free speech.

Only a few days after the administrative decision on "Atrocities," Hyman Solokov, a lawyer speaking on behalf of the Abukah Society, charged publicly that the university's medical school practised racial discrimination by

operating an unofficial quota system against Jews. This question remained in abeyance for the moment.

Probably the outstanding controversy of the wartime period broke out early in 1945. It was really a replay of earlier debates over the location of the university, provoked by a university announcement that it would give priority to the consolidation of its campus at Fort Garry in the postwar period. The *Tribune* editorialized on 21 February 1945 against moving the Junior Division to Fort Garry. "We want a popular, democratic University to which students have ready access," thundered the newspaper, and removal to Fort Garry "means that the University of Manitoba would have far less impact on this community than it should have." *The Manitoban* contributed to the debate by sponsoring a poll that indicated that a majority of students favoured the Broadway site—201 students in the Junior Division wanted Broadway, while only 88 wished to remove to Fort Garry. The *'Toban* called for the creation of a unified university in the heart of the city, noting that all the colleges were on record as desiring to remain downtown. The University of Manitoba Student Council, which included a number of college representatives, went on record by a vote of 12:4 in favour of reuniting the university—on the Broadway site. In March of 1945, the *Tribune* published a map showing a fourteen-acre site in the middle of

Chemistry lab, c. 1943 (UMA).

downtown that could be purchased cheaply for the university. The debate continued sporadically for many months.

St. John's College, which had gradually wasted away during the Depression, showed its preferences in 1945 in two ways. First, it moved from its isolated location in the North End to the corner of Hargrave Street and Broadway Avenue, buying the Music and Arts Building (formerly the Ashdown home) for $70,000 and positioning itself within walking distance of the Junior Division of the university, United College, and St. Paul's College. That same year, the college rejected an offer from United College to combine arts instruction and move physically to the United campus, on the grounds that this was the first step to absorption. Despite its move, St. John's still hoped eventually to relocate to the Fort Garry campus. The move to Broadway, combined with the post-war influx of veterans, temporarily raised enrolment from 28 in

1944–45 to 107 in 1946–47, although the college's reputation for producing "gentlemen scholars" was no longer necessarily a positive one.

The Manitoban had opined in 1944 that most U of M students leaned toward socialism—as did increasing numbers of Canadians in general, most of them attracted by the CCF's emphasis on the need for post-war reconstruction. As early as 1943, it was clear that the universities would play a leading role in that reconstruction. President Smith, in his 1943 annual report, addressed the challenge of "Planning for the post-War period," particularly the ability of the university to respond to large numbers of "rehabilitation men and women." This challenge came concretely to the university late in 1944, when the Department of Veterans Affairs (DVA) requested from the university a programme of courses in first- and second-year arts for 110 RAF people trained under the Air Training plan but not needed. The DVA wanted the courses to start in April 1945, so that those taking them could enter a regular university programme in September 1945. The veteran flood had begun, and the university would never be the same again.

Chapter 5 ❧ 1945–1958

At the 1949 convocation of the University of Manitoba, one of the graduates in honours languages listed in the programme was John Wolpe. Few of those attending the ceremony knew of his unique history. Wolpe was a Jew who had escaped from a concentration camp and had attached himself to the Royal Winnipeg Rifles at Calais in 1944. He somehow acquired a uniform and became known as the "Unenlisted Rifleman." Wounded during the Rhineland campaign, he was evacuated to a Canadian military hospital. There he was discovered to have no documents whatever. This story has a happy ending, however. Johnny Wolpe was enlisted and given a unique regiment number, U2343. With the aid of the Canadian Legion, he was brought to

Manitoba after the war, where he resumed his studies. After graduation he moved to the United States to teach languages. Wolpe's graduation can be seen to have ended symbolically the veterans' era at the university. He was only one of the most unusual of thousands of returning veterans who attended the university after World War Two, finding in the experience a new opportunity in life.

The post-war period was one of unparalleled growth, new challenges, and change everywhere in Canada. Institutions of higher education like the University of Manitoba were at the leading edge of many of the new developments. The universities educated the returning veterans on an emergency basis, and then turned to face a new challenge of expansion. By itself the

Opposite: The U of M cheerleaders, 1950 (UMA).

Veteran student and family, c. 1946 (UMA), probably filmed by the National Film Board in the Veterans Village.

post-war Baby Boom meant a great potential increase in the number of young people seeking admission to higher education. But when the Baby Boom was combined with profound changes in Canadian education in the 1940s and 1950s that democratized access to education for all students, the result was an enormous new pressure on the universities. Politicians,

educators, and parents alike could agree that improved education was essential if the younger generation were to cope with an ever-more complex economy and society. The Russian launch of Sputnik in 1957 merely provided additional ammunition for the advocates of fast-track science. There was less agreement over the extent to which education should be driven solely by vocational considerations. In any event, a significant shift occurred in the financing of Canadian higher education, with the federal government providing funding for the first time to meet the new situation.

The U of M struggled with the larger national issues that faced all higher education in the post-war years at the same time that it had to deal with some concerns that were quite local. In 1950, for example, the university shared with the Red River Valley the impact of the greatest flood seen in Manitoba since its settlement. On another level, older questions, such as the relationship of the colleges to the university and the extent to which the university would centralize its facilities at the Fort Garry campus, continued to be agitated.

In September 1944, Sidney Smith resigned as president to become Principal of University College at the University of Toronto. A year later, he became president of the University of Toronto itself, and later served as Minister of External Affairs in the first Diefenbaker government. Smith was succeeded, for a period of six months, by H.P. Armes, the U of M's Dean of Arts and Science. In June of 1945, A.W. Trueman of New Brunswick was appointed president. Trueman, a graduate of Mount Allison and Oxford, had been head of Mount Allison's English Department and Superintendent of Schools in Saint John, New Brunswick. By his own admission, he was "something of an innocent" when he took office, knowing "little or nothing of its reputation, or of the local ground rules under which it operated." During his brief three-year tenure, he apparently never did learn the rules.

Veteran student and family, c. 1946 (UMA), again filmed by the NFB in the Veterans Village.

In his first meeting with the provincial premier, Stuart Garson, for instance, he was subjected to an angry eighteen-minute lecture by Garson because of a misunderstanding over a group of U of M students who had visited Garson a few days earlier.

In his first annual report in 1946, Trueman returned to a constant theme of his predecessor, saying, "With all due respect to the claims of science and technology as great forces in the shaping of modern life, it is difficult to see how the present difficult problems of provincial, national and international scope can be discussed intelligently and solved unless we develop more and more in our people the kind

A.W. Trueman on University-Government Relations

Sid Smith had told me, on the eve of my departure for Manitoba, that he was sure I would like the young Westerners--informal, outspoken, and full of "git-up-and-go." He was right, although they got me, on one occasion, into deep trouble--though only briefly. A great deal of University instruction was carried on in the city itself in a large temporary building situated on Broadway just across the street from the Legislative Building. Admittedly, conditions in the temporary buildings were not good. Everyone with whom I had talked told me that our location in the downtown building was temporary, and that the Board was anxious to consolidate instructional facilities on the Fort Garry campus as soon as possible.

During my early days in Winnipeg, I secured an appointment with the Premier, Stuart Garson, to make myself known to him and to have a general talk about University affairs. Just before I went to keep the appointment I learned, to my surprise, that a delegation of students had gone to the Premier to report on conditions in the temporary buildings and to ask for improvements. Amused by this gutsy, young, Western performance, I rather easily assumed that Garson, too, would be amused by its brashness, naiveté, and impropriety. When I walked into his office I said, by way of starting the conversation, "Well, Mr. Premier, I hear that you have had a visit from some of our students," and I'm sure I grinned as I said it. He replied, "Yes, I have. Sit down!" And then he rode me with spurs for eighteen minutes by my watch, obviously in a rage over the whole affair, and resentful of me for the part he assumed I played in it.

The first time he stopped for breath I broke in to protest that the students had acted on their own volition and quite without my knowledge and consent. He refused to believe me. Thrusting across the desk the latest issue of The Manitoban, he said, "Look at this!" There on the front page were two feature articles, one on the students' protest to the Premier about conditions in the temporary building, and one reporting an interview with me in which I was correctly quoted as having said that I hoped we would soon be able to abandon the downtown temporary building and move to more satisfactory quarters on the Fort Garry campus. Because of the juxtaposition of the two articles, the Premier assumed that I and the students were in cahoots, and that I had inspired the delegation. He saw the arrival of this delegation, followed so promptly by my visit to his office, as a calculated criticism of the Government and as an attempt to whip up publicity and exert pressure on the Government to provide funds for more building on the Fort Garry site. When finally he stopped, I said: "Mr. Premier, I completely agree that it was quite improper of the students to come to you in this way and for this purpose. Obviously they should have come to me. I reiterate that I knew nothing about their visit to you. I learned of it only shortly before I came here. Mr. Premier, you must believe what I say." He looked at me for a moment, his anger having cooled, and said, "Of course I believe you, Mr. President." And after that I was on excellent terms with him. But what a hell of a way to begin my relations with the Government!

From A.W. Trueman, A Slice of Time: Memoirs (1982).

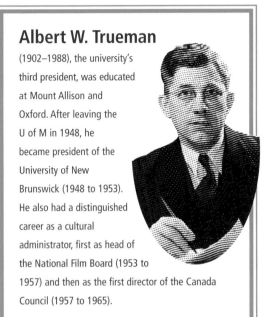

Albert W. Trueman

(1902–1988), the university's third president, was educated at Mount Allison and Oxford. After leaving the U of M in 1948, he became president of the University of New Brunswick (1948 to 1953). He also had a distinguished career as a cultural administrator, first as head of the National Film Board (1953 to 1957) and then as the first director of the Canada Council (1957 to 1965).

of knowledge, the kind of intellect, and the kind of judgment which have their sources in the investigation of History, Language, Literature, Philosophy, and the Arts generally." The new president also announced in his report that the Junior Division would be moved to Fort Garry and that the Western Civilization course programme developed under Sidney Smith would begin. He did not specify a date for either of these developments, however.

In fairness, Trueman and his administration had little time to devote to long-term policy immediately after the war. Accommodating the returning veterans was by itself a full-time job. Physical space was also a problem. The university's main residence, occupied by the Canadian army as a barracks from 1940 to 26 August 1945, was put back to student use within a few weeks of its return to the university "amid

scenes of almost indescribable confusion and disorder." The building was in need of extensive repair, but there was such a shortage of housing accommodation in Winnipeg that it had to be pressed into service immediately. Food service was a constant problem because of

Science classroom, c. 1948 (UMA).

the inadequacy of kitchen facilities and the shortage of foodstuffs in the city. Many of the 320 male residents were ex-servicemen who chafed at any rules and regulations.

Given shortages of construction material and the high cost of labour, it was virtually impossible to conceive of permanent buildings. Instead, twelve army huts erected on the campus during the war were put to use, as well as two small army houses, and a frame building ten metres by thirty metres. A temporary cafeteria, used by the university while the army had been in residence, and the large drill hall erected by the army, were also adapted to service. United College opened classrooms in a skating shack, in the basement of Elim Chapel, and on the second floor of the Veterans' Army and Navy Hall. The influx of returning students put considerable pressure on the existing teaching staff, which was further exacerbated by a national bidding war for faculty that had occurred over the summer of 1945. Manitoba faculty salaries had long lagged behind the national average, and United College was particularly hard hit, experiencing a considerable exodus of high-profile faculty, including Arthur Phelps in English and Arthur Lower in History, to other universities.

The great student issue of 1945–46 was the location of the campus. In the autumn of 1945, a general debate on the site question was resurrected in the student newspapers and public press. Professor Russell of Architecture supported the Fort Garry site in a *Manitoban* article, and the *Winnipeg*

University of Manitoba
vs.
North Dakota State College

Saturday, October 23rd, 1948
OSBORNE STADIUM
2.30 p.m.

Drill Team

Opposite: Registration for U of M adult education classes, c. 1950 (UMA).

Tribune printed an editorial that claimed that since affiliated colleges would remain downtown, the permanent site should be Broadway. It was clear to many, however, that the existing Broadway facilities were far from adequate. Author Barry Broadfoot, who was one of the returning veterans who became a student, has described the downtown campus as "an arsonist's delight," with "a canteen, a hike along a long, dark corridor lined with lockers, down a flight of steps and into a dungeon filled with rickety tables and chairs and a counter serving sandwiches, hotdogs, pie, coffee, tea, and soft drinks at prices that should have paid off any operating deficit the university might incur."

The immediate post-war generation of students was a particularly serious and studious one, but there was an undisputed need for a student union building and other recreational facilities. A special meeting of the university's BoG in August of 1946 set up a committee to appeal publicly for funds. The committee was composed of representatives of UMSU, the BoG, the Alumni Association, and Friends of the University. A fund of $131,000 was raised and was matched by a grant of $130,000 from the Manitoba government. As a result, a double hangar at Neepawa that had been used by the RCAF was purchased for $9400 and reassembled on the Fort Garry campus, west of the old Chemistry and Physics Building. It was to contain a basketball floor and a one-storey lean-to, housing athletic offices and student offices. By

NOVICE SINGLES
1947

The Returning Veterans

Then it was all over, first in Europe and then in the Pacific, and there we were, milling about, passing in and out of the tiny, cramped registrar's office at the Osborne Street campus of the University of Manitoba, dozens of us that day early in October, just as there had been dozens on each of the previous thirty days. In a way I, like the rest, moved about hesitantly, all of us perhaps fearful of what we would find. . . . There were so many of us.

So, on this happy morning as we milled about, looking for faces we had seen or known in some camp in Canada or some far-off place, we were essentially children again, as bewildered as we had been when we enlisted. In the services we knew only too well what it was like to be screwed, blued, and tattooed, blancoed and snafued, rushed somewhere in half a day to wait nine days for something to happen; the unnecessary required paperwork for which the forms were missing or which would be thrown away anyway, and the unending blather and gossip and I'm-in-a-lifeboat-Jack mentality. Each of us, in our own way, had learned to cope with the stupidities of service life. Now, seeing the disarray and confusion, we wondered if we were running into it again.

I had filled out forms, signed them, and been given three cards; I had been handed a large sheet that showed what subjects I was required to take and where and when they were, and another sheet with a list of books I would need, and a booklet stating the rules and regs of the university, all emphasizing what a lucky guy I was. I threw the booklet away and whenever I needed to know something I asked someone who knew. Army style.

I had to assume that the university had been told and warned and also cautioned that this tight little island was about to be invaded and would never be the same again. I imagine the deans and professors and lecturers and administrators had all nodded, smiled, and said yes, we understand. We were to be treated no differently from the boys and girls coming in from the high schools. But again, yes, we were to be treated differently. They were told to treat us gently, carefully. Some of us, they were told, had been away from the real life for two, four, six years. Our learning habits would probably be somewhat different. We might want to know something that came up at a lecture and we'd want to know it now! That must have terrified them! Our social graces might not be all they might have desired because after all, so many of us had been deprived of the cultural advantages of the high-school monthly dances. We might try to take control. After all, hadn't many of these chaps, good fellows all, but hadn't many taken part in controlling the world? They might have been told that many of us had learned that the way to make something work was by bloody well making it work. That is different from controlling. You can make something work and then turn the machinery back to the one who had controlled it but couldn't make it work.

Barry Broadfoot graduated from the university in 1949. He is the author of many well-known popular histories, including Next Year Country and Ten Lost Years. Excerpt from his memoir, My Own Years (1983).

1946 the inter-collegiate athletic programme had pretty well returned to normal. In that same year, St. Andrew's College opened its doors on Church Avenue in the North End, in the building recently vacated by St. John's College. It initially offered grades eleven and twelve and a four-year course in theology, and was not affiliated with the university.

Registration in 1946–47 was 6488 (5025 men and 1463 women) in regular courses, with a total registration of 9514. The percentage of those enrolled in regular courses who normally resided in Winnipeg was 58.4 percent, with 28.3 percent from rural Manitoba and 13.3 percent from outside the province. There were 3215 veterans registered. To cope with the increased numbers, the registrar had begun using IBM equipment to prepare examinations registers and to record examination results. The total enrolment at United College was 1175.

The increased enrolment produced a great shortage of outside accommodation for students, especially women. The number of downtown students using the YMCA in 1946 was 498, and 193 women, most from Home Economics, lived in residence at Fort Garry. The residences for both men and women were social centres, and the university attempted to maintain some parietal supervision. A night porter checked students in from 10:30 p.m. to 2:00 a.m., when the front door was bolted; late leaves commenced at 11:00 p.m. A full men's residence held nine Sunday evening programmes with short plays and skits; average attendance was 350. In the year 1947–48, fifteen residence dances were held during the year, with an average attendance of 300.

Many of the veterans were married with family responsibilities; they had little time for traditional student activities. The married veterans also provided a challenge for living accommodations, which was met to some extent in the summer of 1946 by beginning the

Faculty in front of the Broadway site prior to convocation, c. 1948 (UMA).

construction of "Veteran's Village" (or "Veterans' Village"; the spelling was never agreed upon). This village was located at the Fort Garry campus near the river, with seventy-two huts arranged in three circles of twenty-four huts each; another thirty huts were built a year later on the opposite side of the campus. Within every circle was a central washroom and laundry facility. Each hut was four metres by eight metres in size, comparable to the accommodation of many families in the city, and was build on skids with lumber salvaged from the Transcona Concrete Plant. The roofs were of asbestos shingles and the walls of buckboard, partitioned into two rooms. The huts were heated by Quebec stoves. Hastily

constructed on an emergency basis, the huts had no insulation, paint, cupboards, floor coverings, or running water. But they were quickly the homes of over 100 children and their parents. One young child, her father has written, slept for three years in a porch added to the hut. "Swaddled in ten blankets, she survived winter temperatures of minus 30 degrees Fahrenheit without catching a single sniffle, although she often awoke with lips blue from the cold." Other children, who slept nearer to stoves, constantly risked carbon monoxide poisoning. The university established a special medical clinic for dealing with the young children residing in the village. In 1947, with veteran enrolment at 2432 (of whom ninety-one were women and twenty-one were Americans) another Veteran's Village was constructed to house another 102 married veterans' families.

The veterans' villages were intended to be very much temporary, like the era of the veterans itself. The post-war emergency was over by 1949 in almost all senses of the word. Much of the demand for housing accommodation ended, and there were empty rooms in both the men's and women's residences. Nevertheless, the villages continued until the early 1950s, and were lived in over the years by over 400 adults and more than 600 children. Few veterans availed themselves of the federal government's Veteran's University Loan Fund, and the veterans did not appreciably improve the financial situation of the university.

As the veteran registrations began to decline, the university's revenues decreased faster than the expenses. The Manitoba government increased its contribution to the university after the war, from $390,000 in 1945 to $750,000 in 1948, but the financial needs of the university rapidly outran the revenue. The province's premier was Douglas Campbell, who prided himself on balancing budgets and not spending an unnecessary penny. His government was not particularly sympathetic to the cries of the university for still more money. Improved salaries and working conditions for academic

staff were essential to keep the university nationally competitive, claimed its spokesmen. A number of new buildings were urgently needed if the university were to honour its commitment to close the downtown campus. Construction of a new engineering building was begun in the spring of 1948, but a new library building was also desperately required. The university was still responding to demands for expanded services,

Opposite: Returned veterans in the classroom, c. 1946 (UMA). Above: Chemistry lab, c. 1946 (UMA).

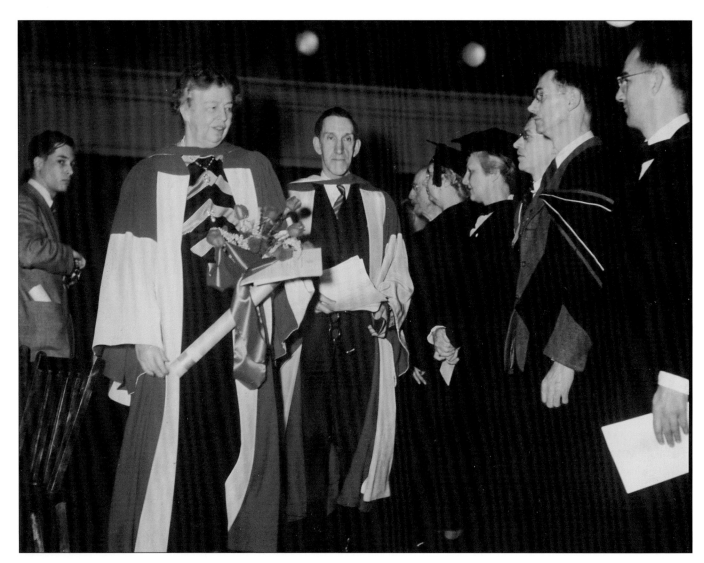

Eleanor Roosevelt (seen here with President Gillson) visited Winnipeg to speak at a special convocation, March 1949 (UMA).

which were usually met without provisions of additional funding. In 1949, for example, the Department of University Extension and Adult Education was organized. It had no clerical staff, and, according to government instructions, was not to create a complex provincial system of adult education, but rather to organize and coordinate a conventional system of university education.

In 1948, as the veterans began to complete their studies, President Trueman suddenly announced his resignation in order to become president of the University of New Brunswick. At the time, there was speculation that he left the U of M because of continual disputes with F.W. Crawford, the university's powerful comptroller, who shared with Premier Campbell a belief in pinching every penny.

Crawford also insisted that the comptroller had the final word in fiscal matters, thus maintaining the university tradition that the president was not really the institution's chief executive officer. Trueman was succeeded by A.H.S. Gillson, a Cambridge-trained

In April 1950, however, it became apparent that the flood that year was of a far greater dimension than any in living memory. Eventually, the 1950 Flood became the focus of international attention, as all of southern Manitoba and Winnipeg battled the flood

mathematician and former Dean of Arts and Sciences at McGill.

Under Gillson, the university planned in 1950 to move from its Broadway buildings and unite the entire graduate programme at Fort Garry. However, a different sort of move occurred in the spring of that year. The Red River, which flows north past the university's Fort Garry campus and through the centre of Winnipeg, was well known for spring flooding.

waters. At its peak, over 80,000 Winnipeggers had to be evacuated—the largest evacuation in Canadian history—and large portions of the city and Red River Valley were under water. Just before the flood occurred, the east wing of the student union building was opened with a basketball game between Bemidji State and the University of Manitoba, played on a new $50,000 basketball floor. The Bisons had only just returned from the Dominion Senior finals.

Canoeist in front of Tier Building during 1950 flood (UMA). Following page: Aerial shot of the Fort Garry campus during the height of the 1950 Flood. The Veterans Village is at the lower left of the photo (UMA).

Two views of the newly opened library, 1953, one by *Manitoban* cartoonist Dave Williamson and the other an official photograph (UMA).

Six weeks later, that basketball floor was under water as the Red River overflowed its banks; virtually the entire Fort Garry campus would be inundated. With a number of campuses scattered around the city and a large staff, the U of M was bound to be intimately involved in the flood crisis.

Thanks to timing beyond anyone's control, the great flood did not much disrupt the teaching life of the university. Classes were finished, most examinations had been taken, and both students and faculty were beginning their summer break. A few examinations were scrapped at the medical school, and the convocation set for 23 May was cancelled. Students, faculty, and staff alike joined the thousands of volunteers working to sandbag the dikes of Winnipeg. The university had offered residence space to refugees from the rampaging river; at the end of April, students hastily moved out of the residence building, and 135 Morris refugees moved in. But the rising waters soon drove virtually everyone from Fort Garry.

The river near the Fort Garry campus had been controlled until noon on 5 May. Water rose rapidly that afternoon, however, and as it

removed to upper floors. Unfortunately, the local pumping station failed on 9 May, and all electrical services were discontinued the next day. A university report dated 14 May indicates that normal business was suspended on the campus. Heat was being provided in the student residence with an oil heater and cooking was done on four propane gas stoves. The water had virtually cut off the campus from the city, but the university operated a small motor boat on a

reached the steam pipes in the tunnels, the heat was cut off. Power was cut off at 9:00 p.m. on the same date. By Sunday 7 May, the Fort Garry campus was without heat, light, or telephone service, although an emergency overhead power line was being put in place to provide temporary service to the student residence. At the president's house, President A.H.F. Gillson and his wife were still in residence, cooking their meals over an open fireplace. An administration memorandum of 8 May reported that the university could carry on under the present levels of water, although all property should be

scheduled basis from the Fort Garry Municipal Hall to a site south of the campus, where passengers could be carried to the campus by university truck. All university offices had been moved to the Broadway buildings. Ironically enough, this move occurred on the eve of the projected vacating of the Broadway campus. On 18 May, the water stood level with the top of the metal newel post at the bottom of the stairs in the Engineering Building leading up from the basement to the main entrance of the new addition. Fortunately, by this time the crest had been reached and the waters began to recede.

The Broadway Campus in the 1940s

My first two years in Arts at the University of Manitoba were spent at
Broadway Division. The low rambling building that became known as Broadway
Division had been jerry-built as a temporary structure during World War II
--or was it World War I?--and continued to serve as a long-term temporary
home for first and second-year Arts and Science students while the powers
that be wrangled over the site of the University of Manitoba. In my time
the building was held together with an annual fresh coat of paint and the
dance and election posters plastered all over its walls. It was extremely
draughty and the heating was, to put it kindly, uneven. There were a few
hot spots so one drifted in and out of extremes of temperature as one
flitted like a bee from class to class, seeking the nectar of knowledge.

These were the days before pantyhose and no young lady wore slacks--they
called them slacks then--to school. Unthinkable! As for jeans, they
existed, but only for western ranch hands, not for pearl and cashmere
sweater girls like me. I wore skirts and sweaters and saddle shoes and
bobby sox and in cold weather seamless nylon stockings. I wouldn't have
been caught dead with overpants--woolly things mothers like mine bought
for girls like me so we shouldn't end up with bad kidneys or freeze our
private parts and be unable to have babies. One of my classmates hated
stockings, so she kept wearing leg paint, an invention carried over from
the war when it was patriotic not to wear nylon stockings because they
were all being used for parachutes and the black market in Europe.

Remember Pep Rallies? I don't know if there still are such things--and
whatever happened to Tea Dances? In those days Pep Rallies were held over
the lunch hour in order to incite school spirit and push the next event
the Big Wheels of our student administration were planning: a dance, a
football game, a drive for something--though seldom political. The HOH
Club, another form of H2O, was a pep rally without the pep. Students,
mainly science men, gathered in a lecture theatre to eat their lunches in
communal silence. Occasionally someone, if the spirit moved him, would get
up and say, "Hoh!" Even more occasionally, someone might tell a joke.

The centre core of Broadway Division had the equivalent of a town square:
corridors entering it from three directions, with a door to a large
lecture hall on the fourth side, with a wall of bulletin board facing
stage left and stage right, respectively, the entrances to the Women's and
Men's Locker Rooms. Coming in from the north side, a girl had to do a
diagonal cross to her locker room door. All the boys in Broadway Division
held up the wall on her right, lounging and leaning outside their locker
room door, watching all the girls go by. Males had Power in those days--
unquestioned. Was Heather Robertson in 1962 the first female editor of the
Manitoban? It sure didn't happen in my time. Even though I was a serious
student, it was still expected and assumed without question that I would
marry young and have a family. The assumption was in the air I breathed.

Betty Jane Wylie graduated from the university in 1952. She is the
author of many books, including Family, An Exploration, and Beginnings.

Seventy-fifth anniversary convocation at the Winnipeg Auditorium, 1952 (UMA).

Like most institutions in southern Manitoba, the U of M had to face the cleanup and rehabilitation, the preliminary costs of which were initially estimated at $250,000. The university initially anticipated that it would have to bear some of the costs of rehabilitation itself. When the university reopened in September 1950, the first issue of the *Manitoban* reported that damage to the new UMSU building under construction had been considerable. The basketball floor had been so warped that it rose a metre in the centre. Workmen were waiting for the moisture to dry out before laying the floor again. After the flood, the university calculated its total flood damage at $227,835. Later, a nine-metre-wide dike was built through the university grounds as part of a provincial flood prevention programme; it remains today as the principal reminder of the 1950 flood.

The student president of UMSU, Arthur V. Mauro, welcomed fewer students back to the campus. Regular enrolment dropped from 4489 in 1948–49, to 4019 in 1949–50, to 3641 in 1950–51. The decline was caused

Above and right: Science students in freshie parade, c. 1949 (UMA).

mainly by the phasing out of the veterans. Over the summer of 1950, while the university was still cleaning up from the flood, the Junior Division of Arts and Science moved to Fort Garry, leaving only the Faculty of Medicine and the School of Art (which had become affiliated with the university in July 1950) physically removed from Fort Garry. The addition of the School of Art as a new and separate faculty was almost lost in the ballyhoo over the closure of the Broadway buildings. The Fort Garry campus was revamped by moving Home Economics into a renovated Horticulture Building and vacated departments from the Horticulture Building into a renovated barn.

The enrolment decline of the early 1950s was deceptive, only the lull before the storm. Population statistics and school enrolments pointed to enormous enrolment pressures at every university in Canada for the next fifteen years. Several actions in 1951 on both the local and national levels anticipated the new developments. Locally, on 23 May 1951, the first sod for a new university library was turned by Premier Douglas Campbell and Chancellor Dysart. On the same day, the first convocation was held on the Fort Garry campus in the east wing of the new gymnasium, followed by a garden party on the great square west of the arts building.

On the Dominion level, on 19 June 1951, the Canadian Parliament decided to appropriate $7 million for higher education in Canada. For the first time, the Dominion would become involved in university funding. Grants could not be more than 50 cents per head of population, and the grant was to be divided in

Left and below: The Home Management House (left top), better known as the "Practice House," was built in 1939 for the Department of Home Economics' home-management programme. A stately Georgian residence, it contained all the features of an upper-middle-class home of the period, including an elegant living room and dining room, as well as an office and living quarters for a live-in staff person.

Each month, ten to twelve students moved into the house and operated it as a household, cooking, cleaning, and planning menu (photos c. 1952: C. Jewers). Its most unique feature, which now seems either quaint or mildly disquieting, was the "practice baby." Each year, an infant was "borrowed" from the city's Child Welfare Association, and, under the supervision of Home Ec staff, students learned how to care for a young child in a home setting. In 1957, the programme left the Practice House and moved to a small apartment block. The House was then used as a residence for university administrators and later became the home of the Alumni Association.

The Practice House and "practice baby" have been immortalized in Carol Shields's novel *The Republic of Love*. Its hero is a former "practice baby," and he is introduced to readers this way: "As a baby, Tom Avery had 27 mothers."

Dr. Bruce Chown, whose work led to the cure for Rh disease among the newborn (UMA/T).

each province among eligible institutions, according to the ratio of their enrolment of eligible students to the total number of students enrolled. The appropriations were a direct result of recommendations by the Commission on Arts, Letters and Science chaired by Vincent Massey, which had examined culture in Canada during 1949 and 1950. (Massey, as Governor-General, laid the cornerstone for the new U of M library on 28 October 1952; it opened on 26 September 1953.) Under the federal formula, the province of Manitoba got $388,250, based on a population of 776,500. The U of M, with its 2828 students, got $279,151.75, and its affiliated colleges, with 1104 students, got $109,098.25. While these grants were important sources of funding for every institution of higher education, in Manitoba they were particularly welcomed by the denominational colleges, all of which had been experiencing considerable financial difficulties, and marked a renewed interest in the colleges throughout the decade of the 1950s.

Also in 1951, the university was able to take advantage of an unexpected windfall on its endowment lands. Oil and natural gas had been discovered on the lands in the southwestern part of the province, and 19,000 acres were leased to Imperial Oil for a down payment of nearly $100,000 and unknown annual royalties. Unfortunately, the natural gas and petroleum fields in Manitoba proved of only limited importance, and would not provide the same sorts of long-term income as occurred in the province of Alberta.

The year 1952 marked the seventy-fifth anniversary of the founding of the university.

The occasion was remembered with a week of celebrations in October, including a commemoration service in St. John's (Anglican) Cathedral. A history of the university, which would cover its first seventy-five years, was commissioned. Written by the university's most distinguished historian, W.L. Morton, it was eventually published in 1957 as *One University*.

The university was at a critical juncture in its life. Many of its students were now commuters to the Fort Garry campus, but the main

Varsity Variety show, c. 1950s. This annual musical comedy revue was an important part of campus life in the 1950s (UMA).

BARNEY CHARACH

university was still relatively small, little altered in faculty size or student numbers since the 1920s. Its administrative structure was still traditional, even patriarchal, in nature. The affiliated colleges, all of which were still located downtown, operated quite independently of the main campus. Many of the colleges—such as St. John's, St. Paul's, St. Mary's—were quite small. United College, Brandon College, and St. Boniface College were much larger and had very different pretensions.

While the university had a number of professional faculties, none was very large and— with the possible exception of the medical school—all had limited research aspirations. Much of the ground-breaking research at the medical school happened in the Department of Pediatrics, founded in 1946. Pediatrics was headed until 1954 by Dr. Bruce Chown—who was responsible for major breakthroughs in the diagnosis and treatment of Rh haemolytic disease among newborns—and then by Dr.

BARNEY CHARACH

Naming of the Freshie Queen, 1959 (P. LeBoldus).

Harry Medovy. Rh haemolytic disease caused roughly 10 percent of the foetal and newborn deaths in North America, and the work by Chown, his research team, and his successors at Pediatrics saved the lives of thousands of children. Chown and Medovy also took the lead in pressing for a new children's hospital, which was opened adjacent to the Winnipeg General, in 1956; the hospital created its own foundation in 1959, one of the first in the province.

In addition to the consolidation of most teaching at Fort Garry, other changes began in the early 1950s, many of them the consequence of closing the downtown buildings. A new building boom at Fort Garry was inaugurated by the opening of the campus's first stand-alone bookstore in the spring of 1952. The new facility was designed by Professor H.A. Elarth of the Department of Architecture, and also served as the university bus depot. The bookstore was furnished in white rubbed birch and

illuminated with some of the first fluorescent
lights installed on the campus.

The year 1952 was also the beginning of a
campus tradition that dominated much of the
university's extracurricular life over the next two
decades. That year, the Glee Club, which had
been staging an annual operetta (usually by
Gilbert and Sullivan) since the 1920s, turned to
a more modern production. Under James
Duncan's direction, the Glee Club presented
Brigadoon by Alan Jay Lerner and Frederick
Loewe, thus beginning a nearly twenty-year run
of the production of Broadway musicals on the
campus. The heyday for the musicals was the
1950s. Producing Broadway musicals required
enormous student participation, not only in the
main roles, but in the chorus, the dancing
troupes, the orchestra, set design, costumes,
and technical work. No student ever got a single
academic credit for participation, which, for
many stage-struck undergraduates, was a year-
round business. The Glee Club chose the show
itself, and auditions began in late September.
The show opened downtown at the Playhouse
Theatre in early February after weeks of
rehearsal. Each performance closed with a
rendition of "On Manitoba," with its
stirring "Iji ittiki kiyi yip."

Several other developments in 1952
foreshadowed a changing relationship
between the university's Board of Governors
and both its faculty and staff. For many years
the BoG had operated without paying much
formal attention to other constituent parts
of the university community, none of which
were represented upon it. On 25 March
1952, UMSU unanimously passed a

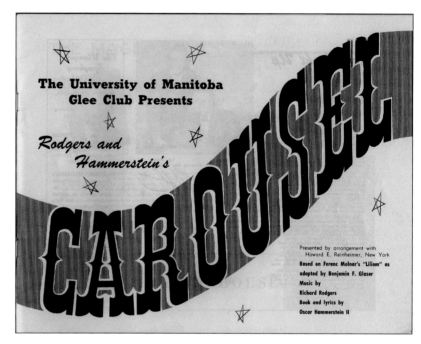

The University of Manitoba
Glee Club Presents

*Rodgers and
Hammerstein's*

CAROUSEL

Presented by arrangement with
Howard E. Reinheimer, New York
Based on Ferenc Molnar's "Liliom" as
adapted by Benjamin F. Glaser
Music by
Richard Rodgers
Book and lyrics by
Oscar Hammerstein II

resolution to re-establish the School of Social
Work, which had been abolished by the BoG at
the end of the term because of alleged lack of
funding. This was one of the first occasions in
many years where the student organization had
expressed an opinion on university academic
policy. In August of 1952, the Association of
Academic Staff—which had been formed in
1950 under the chairmanship of W.L.
Morton and was open to all
members of the teaching staff in
all faculties—announced that it
represented 95 percent of the teaching
staff, in a press release that broke
tradition by being distributed without
prior notification to the BoG. The
association would soon join the
Canadian Association of University
Teachers (CAUT) and begin agitation for
faculty representation on the BoG. United

The cover of *The Medicoban,* the notorious 1953 medical students' parody of *The Manitoban* (UMA).

College formed a local branch of CAUT, named the United College Association, in the spring of 1953.

The UMSU criticism of the administration and the BoG in early 1953 erupted into a major row over the planning of a new UMSU building, with the students charging that student opinion was being disregarded. On 23 January 1953, the BoG suspended the student newspaper, *The Manitoban,* allegedly over an indecent issue produced by medical students, who advocated a "straight-forward approach" to "student writing and thinking." Headlined articles had included "Keeping Plastered" and "Things to Do till the Pub Opens," and the front-page story featured the three major world leaders gesturing at the navel of a coed garbed in a bikini under the banner "Big 3 Split on Navel Site." *'Toban* editors insisted that the paper was really being punished for its criticisms over the building controversy. The issue blew over, and the newspaper was allowed to resume publication on 1 February, although not before the *'Toban,* UMSU, and the campus radio station all promised never to permit the moral standard of the university to be similarly sullied again. Like the UMSU resolution on social work of the previous year and the formation of a faculty association, this little tempest suggested that the university was

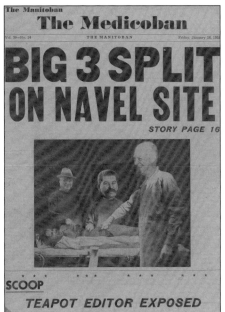

entering into a new era, one in which the students and faculty would insist on more involvement in administrative decisions.

While campus entertainment was changing from Gilbert and Sullivan to Broadway, to reflect a more modern society, the winds of change had not yet had an impact on the composition of the student body. If anything, student ethnic origins lagged behind the composition of the Canadian population after post-war immigration. A survey published by the *Free Press* early in 1953 demonstrated that very nearly half the student body still regarded itself as British or Irish, and, assuming that most of the 269 "Canadians" were also of British origin, it was more than half. Most of the remainder of the students came from European backgrounds, with only a smattering of students from racial minorities or underdeveloped nations. The survey also demonstrated that many students, like many Canadians of the time, were uncertain as to whether to identify themselves by national, ethnic, or racial origins.

On 1 September 1954, President Gillson resigned from the position he had held for five years and, nine days later, died at his home. His successor, Hugh Hamilton Saunderson, had attended the U of M from 1920 to 1924 (and won the University Gold Medal). He was the first U of M graduate to become its president. After graduate work in chemistry in eastern Canada, including a PhD from McGill, he had returned to the university, teaching chemistry and serving as Dean of Residence in the 1930s, and Dean of Arts and Sciences from 1945 to

after his address with stockings over their faces, one leading a chicken. The leader of the intruding party welcomed Saunderson with student "demands," including one that the water fountains would run with beer and another that students be paid. The chicken

President Saunderson and family in 1954 freshie parade (UMA).

1947. He then worked for the federal government in Ottawa until becoming the university's sixth president. Saunderson remained president for sixteen years, and shepherded the university through its expansions of the 1950s and 1960s.

At Saunderson's formal installation as president, four young men entered the hall

broke loose and fluttered onto the laps of some of the platform party. Saunderson wisely viewed the incident as an example of student hijinks and, to the dismay of some of his colleagues, did not punish the students.

Saunderson displayed a similar easygoing manner in his message to new students that first year of his presidency. Writing in the *Freshie's*

Handbook, he entitled his remarks "Welcome from One Freshman to Another" and went on:

> Let me welcome you most heartily to the University of Manitoba. Because I arrived a few days before you came, I can welcome you, but we are really starting off together on a new adventure.

> Like most adventures, we are starting out with some doubts. At least I am, and I suspect that many of you share my feelings.

Nevertheless, the new president concluded, that with resolve and purpose, together he and the students "should have a stirring and useful trip. Welcome, fellow adventurers!"

As one of his first major academic actions, after clearing the installation platform of chickens, Saunderson invited the affiliated colleges—particularly St. John's and St. Paul's—to relocate on the Fort Garry campus. In his autobiography, he justified this decision, which he had taken on his own initiative, as one concerned with "the development of character and the encouragement of things of the spirit." In another passage, he emphasized the need for the university to produce "clear minds, healthy bodies, and a high regard for things of the spirit." Saunderson argued that having St. Paul's and St. John's on the campus "would emphasize not only our history, originating as we did from the colleges, but also would provide a religious emphasis not available in a lay university." This move by Saunderson opened a protracted period in the history of the university (it lasted until 1970) in which an attempt was made to find a

place for the existing colleges, and even, ultimately, to create a new one. This effort was chiefly motivated by two related realizations, not necessarily shared, however, by all members of the university. One was an appreciation that as the institution became larger, it would lose much of the personal intimacy among students and between students and faculty that had characterized its earlier history. The other was an understanding that the colleges were most likely to serve as the bastions of the liberal arts in what was probably to become a university dominated by professional faculties. By 1956 St. Paul's College and St. John's College had both announced decisions to relocate to the Fort Garry campus.

In March of 1955, the academic standards of the university came under scrutiny when a story in the *Winnipeg Tribune* reported that only 27

BARNEY CHARACH

percent of first-year arts and science students had passed all their Christmas examinations. A junior dean was subsequently quoted as blaming the problem of Christmas failures on an extended freshie week, which continued throughout the entire month of September and included both sorority/fraternity rushing and a constant succession of parties and dances. First-year students did not settle down to their studies until many weeks into the term, said this informant. He did not mention the production schedule of the annual musical. Probably as a result of this publicity, the university administration and UMSU decided to return to a single week of freshie activities, culminating with a freshie parade running along Main Street to Portage and then south to Memorial Boulevard and the Legislative Building, and a gala dance at the Winnipeg Auditorium. This first official freshie

parade, involving a motorcade of thirty floats and half a dozen local bands, took place in September of 1955. It was followed by the Royal Premier Dance and the crowning of the Freshie Queen, chosen from candidates from a number of colleges and faculties.

The administration and UMSU reached another joint decision on a more serious note when President Saunderson persuaded UMSU to inaugurate in November of 1955 the first Festival of the Arts. This celebration included lectures, musical programmes, an elaborately staged UMSU production of *Hamlet*, artistic discussions, and exhibitions. Over the next few years, the festival featured such well-known speakers as Laurens van der Post in 1956 and Sir Herbert Read in 1957. It has continued in various guises (including a period as the Festival of Life and Learning) until the present day.

In 1956 a number of embarrassing situations at the university were publicized in the Winnipeg newspapers. The first embarrassment was a leaked pharmacy examination, or at least the rumour of a leaked exam. Several students admitted they had been told on the telephone by an anonymous voice the night before the examination that someone had a copy of the paper, and a few even said they had been given one or two questions. A subsequent faculty committee was unable to find anyone whose marks had improved, however. The second embarrassment involved the Faculty of Education. Canadian universities were beginning to expand and were head-hunting new faculty. The U of M, where faculty salaries were relatively low and teaching commitments relatively high, was prime recruiting territory.

BARNEY CHARACH

Campaign poster (1952) for Women's Association (C. Jewers); freshie parade, c. 1958 (R. Malaher).

In the early summer of 1956, all five full-time staff in the faculty resigned to join former Dean Scarfe at the University of British Columbia. A disruption to the faculty could have been a disaster. Dean Scarfe rejected vehemently a suggestion from a member of the U of M administration that UBC had behaved reprehensibly in raiding faculty. Fortunately, a new dean was appointed and the faculty opened in the autumn "as if practically nothing had happened." Well, almost nothing. In the course of the transition it was discovered that for many years staff had allowed students to take examinations in evening and summer school without submitting the necessary essays to complete the courses. Thousands of students still had incompletes. The departing staff offered to mark the delinquent essays, but many students were unable to submit them. Eventually, partial credit had to be given for half-completed courses.

The final embarrassment involved newspaper reports in August of 1956 that far more U of M students failed three or more subjects than at other Canadian universities. Only 40.4 percent of students had clear passes at the U of M, reported the *Tribune*, while percentages were 55.4 percent clear passes at Saskatchewan, and

75.08 percent at Queen's. President Saunderson blamed the failure rate on students' lack of hard work. The question of exam results would not go away, however, and the issue re-emerged regularly in the press over the next few years. A Winnipeg school trustee called for a probe of the examination results.

Despite these problems, attendance at the university continued to be an invigorating experience for many U of M students. One of these was Eric Wright, a young immigrant from Britain. Wright came to Canada in 1951, and first worked in Churchill, Manitoba. After the experiences of war-time Britain and the isolation of Churchill, Wright found the university to be "paradise.... I expected the University of Manitoba to be every bit the experience I imagined Oxford to be, and it was. In 1952, most youths who grew up in Canada in circumstances parallel to mine—one of a family of ten, say, on a farm in the Saskatchewan dust bowl—would have been just as unlikely to regard university as a possibility as I did in England. I was privileged now, and I knew it."

Wright was especially impressed by one of his English professors, the young poet James Reaney. Reaney, a native of southern Ontario, taught at the university from 1949 to 1957. In that period he won two Governor General's awards for poetry, and later became even better

St. John's College, c. 1955. St. John's students still wore black gowns in the 1950s (UMA).

Insert: Israel Asper as a
pressman at the *Manitoban*,
1950.

Israel Asper

Asper graduated with a law degree from the university in 1957. He was an extremely active student. A debating champion, he worked on the *Manitoban*, was UMSU publicity chair, and organized the Varsity Variety musical revues. Since then, he has built one of Canada's largest media groups, which includes the CanWest Global TV network and *The National Post* newspaper. He is also active in many philanthropic enterprises, such as Winnipeg's Asper Jewish Community Campus.

known as the author of one of the seminal works of Canadian theatre, *The Donnellys* trilogy.

During this period of change, the university was also able to celebrate its roots in the original Manitoba Agricultural College. In June of 1956, the Faculty of Agriculture celebrated its fiftieth anniversary. More than 1000 graduates returned to the campus for the festivities. They were able to tour a modern farm of 1284 acres, with 96 dairy cattle, 111 beef cattle, 196 sheep, and 362 pigs, as well as to revel in the research achievements of a faculty that was on the cutting edge of many developments in agriculture.

In the *Annual Report* of the university for 1956–57, President Saunderson discussed at length his visions for the university. There was a need, he wrote, to keep collegiality in a large institutional setting, which simultaneously had to balance liberal arts and professional training, was

Architecture students'
lounge, c. 1958 (UMA).

The new building of St. Paul's College, 1958 (UMA). Note the presence of wheat stooks just outside the building.

limited in resources, and had two-thirds of its students from greater Winnipeg, mainly living at home. Lacking the integrative force of residences, the president insisted, some other device had to be found. Saunderson suggested that the answer lay in the combination of the liberal arts college and professional faculties. "Our university of the future will probably have in it a number of professional and technical faculties, each of which will provide the special facilities needed in its branch of knowledge. Joined to them in the University will be a number of colleges, each of which will provide facilities and opportunities for students with different interests to live and think and and discuss together. Each college would teach a number of subjects but it wouldn't be expected to, nor could it reasonably find money to, provide classes in all the many fields of learning. Other colleges would provide some of the same classes and some different ones. The colleges jointly could provide a far broader educational opportunity than any one could afford. Students at one college could readily and regularly attend classes at another which offered a course they desired." This view of the future led him both to welcome St. John's and St. Paul's— which had both announced their decisions to move to the campus—as well as to contemplate publicly the need to establish a new college in arts and science.

While the colleges began their new buildings, both the university and the *Tribune* continued their investigations of the university failure rate. In June of 1957, the university announced that a blue-ribbon committee would examine the failure rate. President Saunderson suggested four factors: (1) inexperience in writing examinations; (2) differences between high school and university expectations; (3) bad motivation; (4) the involvement of students in too many extracurricular activities too soon. In one story in late August 1957, students interviewed by the *Winnipeg Tribune* offered their own reasons for failure. One insisted he only went to university because "you're a social outcast if you don't go to university." Another said he found opening social activities a problem. "There was a dance practically every night," he said. "It was fun—but it set a pattern a lot of us never did break." A third found entering university from grade twelve a problem, particularly since he had no knowledge about how to write an examination. A subsequent poll in the *Manitoban* on how to combat the failure rate got only three replies. "Apparently the students are neither interested nor concerned," reported the paper's editor. The university administration was concerned, however, and responded in the short run by further restricting the activities of freshie week,

Taché Hall residence lounge, Christmas, in the early '50s, as the furniture indicates (UMA).

The "strip" on Pembina Highway on the way to the Fort Garry campus, c. 1955 (UMA/T).

which was reduced to three dances, the freshie parade, pep rallies, a theatre night and fashion show, and the crowning of the freshman queen at the gala dance on Saturday night. Limitations on freshie week did little good in the short run. *The Tribune* reported in February of 1958 that almost half of the students writing first-year French, physics, and zoology at the university had failed their December examinations.

Other changes in the traditional rites of students occurred about the same time. The annual Sadie Hawkins dance, a fixture for many years, was abandoned in 1957 in favour of a Winter Carnival. The snow sculpture contest for the carnival produced a number of entries, including a Purple-People-Eater with Flying Saucer and an Abominable Snow Man. There

was also a Snow Queen. One columnist for the *Free Press* noted that at the university, "every time a dance is held a queen must be chosen. Every campus activity from bobsledding to advanced basket weaving has its queen.... The strange thing about the whole queen bit is that they never seem to crown the same one twice." The writer concluded by waxing nostalgically about "the sweet heart of Sigma Chi." But, in truth, the popularity of the "Greek World" was on the decline. Three sororities had withdrawn from campus in 1956, and membership in the eight remaining active chapters was only 131, down from 160 in 1955, and 181 in 1954. Rushing for sororities in 1957 was moved to October, with students not eligible until their second year. The Dean of Women Students announced that

Students at campus bus stop, c. 1955 (UMA).

the U of M was the last Canadian university to take this step. That same year, intramural athletics greatly increased in popularity, with a participation rate of 35.2 percent for women and 47.4 percent for men at the Fort Garry campus. The most popular sport was six-man football, which drew large crowds for big games between the various faculties and colleges.

A real sense of expansion invaded the Fort Garry campus by 1958. The number of students enrolled in regular courses had grown more rapidly than anticipated, and stood at 5259 after the 1958 registration. There was much construction and projected construction at Fort

Garry and downtown. The new home-management apartments—made necessary by the move of the home-management programme from the old Practice House—were completed, work was advanced on new buildings for dentistry and architecture (the Russell Building), and the engineering building had been expanded. Moreover, planning had started for new buildings for chemistry (the Parker Building) and physics (the Allen Building), and planning was underway for a new building to house the School of Commerce and the psychology department. And in February of 1958, the university got its very own Bendix

Henry Friesen

Born in Morden, Manitoba, Friesen graduated from the Faculty of Medicine in 1958. During postgraduate work at McGill and Boston, he discovered the human hormone prolactin. He returned to the U of M in 1972 as head of the department of physiology, where he did important research in human growth hormones. Later, as president of the Medical Research Council of Canada, Friesen has led the transformation of the structure and funding of medical research in Canada.

computer, the fifth university in Canada to obtain such a powerful resource. It was immediately nicknamed "Jasper."

The colleges continued to be in the spotlight in 1958. An Academic Policy Committee, chaired by Acting Dean W.L. Morton, recommended to the BoG the establishment within the Faculty of Arts and Science of a college-type unit "in which there would be both instructional and residential accommodation." In February that year, an Arts Building Committee was created to study the space needs of the faculty and "to investigate the feasibility of an Arts College."

In September of 1958, St. Paul's College opened on the Fort Garry campus in a new building containing classrooms, library, cafeteria, faculty offices, and chapel. Female students were admitted in large numbers to St. Paul's for the first time. Almost from the beginning, the dean of the college was projecting great enrolment increases over the next ten years. At the same time, St. John's College opened for business at its new building on the Fort Garry campus, although the facility was not completed until the following year, when the chapel and women's residence were added.

The moves were traumatic for many collegians, particularly in terms of the tranquility of the new location, far removed from the traffic and bustle of Portage Avenue. Students and faculty accustomed to downtown complained about the want of amenities in the outer reaches of the suburbs. There were few restaurants, Pembina Highway and University Crescent were narrow two-lane roads, and only Pembina was paved. The Southwood Golf Course was virtually the only break in the wilderness between the campus and the centre of Fort Garry, north of McGillivray Boulevard. The difficulties of life in the outer suburbs of Winnipeg were brought home to all at the university on 18 November 1958, the day of one of Manitoba's occasional great snowfalls. University classes were not cancelled, and bus drivers struggled valiantly to get professors, staff, and students to the campus. A young pianist performed the last concert of the Festival of the Arts in the Agriculture Auditorium that noontime before a very sparse audience, and the Dramatic Society's production of *A Midsummer Night's Dream* that evening was snowed out completely.

Chapter 6 ❧ 1958–1970

On 11 August 1958, the University of Manitoba tore down its stone and metal gates at its Pembina Highway entrance at Matheson Road. These gates had been constructed in the early days of the Agricultural College's development at Fort Garry. They were taken down because they were too narrow to admit more than one car at a time. Occurring at around the same time was a commercial expansion of Pembina Highway near the university entrance, as motels and service stations made their way out from the "subway" at Jubilee. On 23 February 1961, the last of the presence at Broadway—the Extension Department—made its move to the campus one step ahead of the wrecking balls.

These actions were symbolic of the sense of expansion and development being experienced everywhere in the province as well as at the university. In 1958 the Manitoba government, headed since 1948 by the fiscally conservative Douglas Campbell, was taken over by the Progressive Conservatives of Duff Roblin. Campbell and his predecessors, responsive chiefly to the rural voters of the province, had practised "pay as you go" policies since the 1920s. Roblin's government put the emphasis on the "progressive" part of their party's name, and were supported by an increasingly urban electorate in a series of elections. The Tories (many thought of them as "Red Tories") built a floodway, developed a provincial health-care system, and provided greatly increased funding

Freshie parade, 1962, with Vonnie Von Helmolt, Bob Ackman, and Gerald Schwartz driving (V. Von Helmolt).

Above: Freshie Queen, 1959 (P. LeBoldus). Opposite: Premier Duff Roblin at the Beaux Arts Ball, 1962 (UMA).

for higher education. The premier saw public expenditures as part of a social investment in the future of the province, and he governed in an era that encouraged a greatly enhanced role for the state in almost all aspects of life. "Catching up" was the name of the game. Roblin, who had attended the U of M in the 1930s, remained at the helm until 1967, when he resigned the premiership to run unsuccessfully as the leader of the national Progressive Conservative Party.

The "long decade" from 1958 to 1970, usually known as the "Sixties," was in many ways the "golden decade" at the U of M. It was a period of rapid growth—of buildings, of enrolment, of faculty, of budgets. Everywhere in Canada, there existed a psychology of growth, with precious few concerned about what would happen if the conditions that fuelled growth ever disappeared. The world of higher education was especially susceptible, as in every province new universities and colleges were being constructed and old ones being expanded. The changes were not merely in size and scope. Everywhere, the old ways were being cast aside and replaced by new ones supposedly more appropriate to the second half of the twentieth century. In terms of the University of Manitoba, this meant the complete acceptance of international academic standards, with their emphasis on disciplines, research, graduate degrees, professional training, centralization, and faculty organizations, as well as on tenure and academic freedom. The new ways also meant changing standards of manners and morals. Liquor, for example, was first legally served on the Fort Garry campus in September of 1960. Periods of rapid change are always accompanied by tensions, strains, and problems, which are often not properly understood by those involved in them. In retrospect, we can sense some of the tensions at the U of M in the 1960s, which were mixed with the excitement of—and more than occasionally created by—growth.

As the fifties ended, two areas of the university were in the spotlight: the colleges and failure rates. The troubles at United College had begun over the spring of 1958 with the dismissal by its board of history professor Harry Crowe for comments about the college administration he had made in a private letter to a colleague. This letter had somehow made its way to the desk of President Lockhart. Several of Crowe's colleagues resigned in sympathy over what they regarded as Crowe's "arbitrary" dismissal, and a number of students did not re-register at United, many moving to the main campus of the university. The Canadian Association of University Teachers was called into the case, and later issued a report highly critical of the college administration. The "Crowe Affair" did not have much direct impact on the main campus of the university; United College was located downtown and—although officially a part of the University of Manitoba—had long been virtually autonomous. United saw

itself as equal to or even better than the university in those fields, mainly in the undergraduate arts and humanities, in which it had specialized. The shock waves from the Crowe incident had a substantial effect on United for many years to come, and may well have weakened its momentum as it moved into the period of growth of the sixties.

On the Fort Garry campus as well as downtown, the college system was also in the news. In 1959 the Senate had debated a request from St.

By the 1960s, the only remnant of the old Broadway site was the School of Art, which remained in the old Law Courts Building until 1965 (UMA).

Andrew's College for formal affiliation with the university, but that body chose not to alter the existing requirement that an affiliated college offer all the courses for a bachelor's degree. Since St. Andrew's felt unable to meet such a requirement, its admission to the university community was delayed for more than two decades, although it built new buildings on Dysart Road in 1964. By 1959 both St. Paul's and St. John's had moved to the main campus, had opened impressive new physical facilities there, and had begun periods of substantial enrolment growth, aided by federal government grants. Moreover, despite four building extensions at St. Paul's in the early 1960s, the teaching facilities continued to be overcrowded. Classrooms built to accommodate 137 classes a week held 183, by scheduling over lunch hours and teaching from 4:30 to 6:00 p.m. St. John's also experienced an enrolment boom. For both

colleges, the expansion of numbers was very much a mixed blessing. Not only were physical facilities stretched to the limit, teaching staffs had to be greatly increased to accommodate the additional numbers. In the case of both colleges, most of the new faculty came in the form of lay instructors. St. Paul's, particularly, had operated by making extensive use of clerical faculty whose financial expectations were minimal. In 1960 more than half the fifteen professors were members of the Jesuit order. The warden at St. John's actually calculated the "profitability" of courses, measuring student enrolments against the federal grant per student to the college. Obviously, the new situation stretched budgets to the utmost.

On 13 October 1959, Professor Meredith Jones, chair of the Arts Building Committee, reported that the committee was recommending creation of a new college to accommodate a total of 750 students, 250 of whom would be housed in its own residence. The committee agreed that the college would not be autonomous or have its own curriculum, and therefore would not be like St. John's or St. Paul's. It would be under the jurisdiction of the Dean of Arts, and would form its own society and community. The report of the Arts Building Committee was debated at two special meetings of faculty council held in October. The faculty was evenly divided between those in favour of the committee's recommendation and those opposed. In the end, the Dean of Arts had to cast the deciding vote to proceed, and was able to do so only because one professor who was opposed had retired to his office during the vote, which was taken in his absence. Whether a

A "sing-in" on the steps of the Administration Building, 1960 (UMA).

college that was not autonomous, and which would have neither its own staff nor its own teaching programme, could be made viable was another matter entirely.

Apart from the colleges, the form in which growth became publicly controversial in the late 1950s was over failure rates, a matter that had been simmering throughout the decade. In his 1959 annual report, President Saunderson addressed the failure-rate problem, which had been discussed constantly in the local newspapers and at meetings of the Board of Governors. He admitted that the university was admitting far more students who had not been at the top of their secondary school classes, but added that Manitoba parents wanted their sons and daughters to be educated at their own provincial university. He noted that although American Ivy League universities like Harvard only failed 5 percent of their students, they only admitted the academically gifted. The U of M did have a higher failure rate in examinations, especially in first- and second-year courses in arts, sciences, and engineering. About 20 percent of the students were failing first year, and would have to repeat it or drop out.

Saunderson insisted that broader admissions standards did not fully explain the failure rate. He argued the major reason for failure was a lack of interest in the courses being studied. Saunderson's comments were, to some extent, belied by the comments of the Dean of Women in the 1959 *Annual Report*. She insisted that superior students registering for first year from grade

Pembina Hall cafeteria, early 1960s (UMA).

eleven did very well, while most of the failures came from a doubtful group with much lower averages. The dean insisted that more time should be spent with the good students and less with those "foredoomed to failure." As the dean's remarks suggested, lurking behind the failure-rate debate was the question of whether the university should continue to educate only the elite.

Whatever the rates of academic success (or failure), a feeling prevailed in the larger community that the university student body had changed virtually overnight in a variety of ways. Certainly, there had been a substantial shift in

student dress over the decade of the '50s. Before 1950, virtually every male university student dressed for school—as they had for many years—in white shirt, jacket and tie, and creased trousers, while females wore sweaters and skirts, saddle shoes and bobby sox. A few of the returning veterans had dressed casually, but most were prepared to accept the prevailing standards. Over the '50s, casual dressing had gradually increased, until by 1959 the typical university student of either sex dressed in dungarees (not yet called "jeans"), sweatshirts, windbreakers, and sack-like sweaters. The

Left: The Pony Corral, c. 1966 (UMA). This restaurant, originally built as a drive-in, was one of the most popular meeting places for U of M students in the 1960s. Below: the Freshie Week planning committee, 1959 (P. LeBoldus).

sporting of academic gowns, which had once been common at some of the colleges, also virtually disappeared in the '50s. Only St. John's College students still wore gowns—although University College students briefly did so as well later in the 1960s—and the editor of the 'Toban insisted that the Johnians were quite different in their attitude towards dress, being "always dressed to the teeth." The students themselves resolutely opposed any attempts to enforce dress regulations. Some saw the deterioration in dress somehow related to the growth of other sloppy behaviour. In January 1959, UMSU officials threatened to close its cafeteria if students continued to refuse to use the garbage cans for their litter. Students responded by setting fire to the garbage cans and eventually by organizing a strike to protest the quality of food in the university's cafeterias.

To escape the dreariness of campus food and brown-bag lunches, many U of M students (especially those with cars) ate at the Pony Corral, located at 1919 Pembina Highway, just north of University Crescent. The Pony Corral had started in 1956 as one of the earliest drive-in restaurants in

Winnipeg and flourished until it was destroyed by a fire in 1965. The restaurant seated thirty-two diners in steer-hide booths. The walls were decorated in discreet knotty pine and there was a large jukebox which played three numbers for a quarter. Diners enjoyed Chicken Pickin' chicken and the latest Elvis or Jack Scott record.

Dress, mess, and consumption of finger-lickin' chicken (and other fast food) were

leaders continued to be active in debating, in the annual mock parliament, and in battling with the university administration over a variety of issues. On 3 November 1959, a Manitoba team of Roland Penner and Frank Lamont debated at the Uptown Theatre the topic, "Resolved that the Western World Is Losing the Battle for Men's Minds." As if to challenge the *Tribune* story, a large number of students, in the

In the early 1960s, the *Manitoban* was often controversial. In this period, its editors included Peter Herrndorf, Heather Robertson, and Jim Lorimer. In early 1962, Robertson and Lorimer were burned in effigy (far right) by the football team and its supporters over their criticism of funding for campus sports. All three editors went on to careers in the media: Herrndorf as a producer and executive at CBC TV, and editor of *Toronto Life* magazine; Robertson as the author of important books on social issues and politics; and Lorimer as one of the country's leading book publishers.

only some of the perceived changes in student behaviour. In December of 1959, the *Tribune* reported that the current generation of students at the university was less political than its predecessors. One professor interviewed by the paper talked about a "fuzzy kind of conservativism, an indifference—a sort of dull satisfaction with things as they are." Most of the faculty, reported the *Trib*, did not find the student body less creative, simply less overtly political. Measuring this sort of attitudinal change was no easy matter. Certainly, student

late winter of 1960, staged a silent protest against early closing hours at the university library. They remained in their seats when the closing bell rang and lit candles. A petition of 518 names asked for the library to remain open until 11:00 p.m., instead of the 10:00 p.m. closing, which the administration insisted was common across North America. In the 1960 mock

parliament, Roland Penner—sitting as a Communist—introduced a motion censuring the government for not ousting Nazis from positions of authority in West Germany. The parliament also gave second reading to a private member's bill calling for a Canadian national flag. Those active in student affairs in the late 1950s and early 1960s agree almost unanimously that there was plenty of scope for political involvement, if one sought it out. Certainly, the number of federal, provincial, and municipal political figures who apprenticed in these years at the U of M is impressive.

The student newspaper, *The Manitoban*, was always ready to stir things up. In the autumn of 1960, '*Toban* editor Peter Herrndorf published an article copied from the Laval University student newspaper. A number of parents complained about its obscenity. The piece, "I'm All Alone—by Dora," was about a prostitute and a professor and was described by President Saunderson as "literary garbage." Herrndorf pointed out that Laval students had been expelled over the publication, and argued he was reprinting the article so that his student readers could judge the justice of the expulsions. The 1961 mock parliamentary elections were held in the middle of complaints that the *Manitoban* was partial to the NDP, particularly because of a 21 November editorial by associate editor James Lorimer. The UMSU president, Bill Neville, thought the matter had been blown out of all proportion. '*Toban* editor Heather Roberson supported Lorimer without reservations. "Anyone who wishes to limit the scope of the *Manitoban* in order to keep it 'fair and unbiased' does not want a newspaper but a publicity sheet," she insisted.

Not all students were serious all the time. In March of 1959, forty male students who had participated in a raid on the women's rez were fined $5.00 each by the university administration. Less than a year later, St. John's College students were fined for water damage caused with fire hoses in the college residence. Unfortunately, a caretaker who had tried to prevent trouble had been struck on the head in the course of the fray. Panty raids and other student hijinks were fairly common occurrences across North America at the end of the '50s, and probably did not lead to more trouble at the U of M than they did because the residences were normally emptied of students before warm spring weather arrived and the pranks could move outside. There was also a resurgence of stunts such as goldfish swallowing. Another popular activity was to fill one of the new Volkswagon Beetles with as many student bodies as could be crushed inside it. The local record was alleged to be twenty-six. Taché Hall rooms were regularly stuffed with newspaper, and some time during the '60s a student's tiny Italian car was carried into the residence dining hall, where he drove it through the dinner line to collect his meal.

The university administration did its best to curb student foolishness by organizing "approved" student activities such as freshie week. By the early 1960s this week had been arranged to coincide with registration. Booths in the UMSU cafeteria advertised social and other extracurricular activities for students old and new. In 1961, for example, these included a fashion show in the UMSU lounge and a men's reception in St. Paul's College, followed by a dance in UMSU. A bonfire and songfest was held on the riverbank behind the residence. A series of faculty receptions was held to choose the candidates for freshie queen, and the

Main cafeteria, Taché Hall, 1960 (UMA).

candidates for queen were announced at an informal dance on Saturday night at the UMSU gym. Beginning in 1960, Freshie Queen candidates were required to have an average of at least 70 percent in their matriculation examinations. The freshie parade, consisting of bands, floats, and marching students, was held in downtown Winnipeg on the following Friday

evening, followed by the Royal Premier, the biggest formal dance of the year, held in the civic auditorium on Vaughan Street.

The 1962 *Annual Report* noted a continual increase in enrolment, with students in regular courses reaching 7500. In the early 1960s, the number of foreign students greatly increased, chiefly at the postgraduate level. Both graduate student and foreign student numbers went up over the next few years. By 1961 there were 325 overseas students enrolled at the university, and by 1963, 730 students were enrolled in graduate studies.

The increased number of students put considerable pressure on the university plant, and there was an obvious need for an enhanced building programme. As Harry Duckworth has pointed out in his autobiography, one of the unexpected results of the enrolment boom was that arts subjects (the humanities and social sciences) returned to popularity, no doubt encouraged by the ethos of the '60s that later helped to create the counterculture. The university faculty and administration both subsequently resisted a move to a year-round academic system such as the trimester system announced with much fanfare in early 1964 by the not-yet-completed Simon Fraser University. The University of Manitoba claimed that the increased staff costs would be more than the advantages of space utilization. Whether the tried-and-true method of financing construction—by a combination of capital fund campaigns and matching provincial funds— would continue to prove adequate was another matter entirely.

The construction of a new college, the result

Premier Duff Roblin laying
the cornerstone for
University College, 1963
(UMA).

of the recommendations of the Arts Building
Committee in 1959, actually began in 1963,
although drawings and plans had been
generated several years before. In April 1963,
the distinguished historian W.L. Morton was
selected as provost of University College, which
was scheduled to open its doors in the autumn
of 1964. One of Morton's tasks was to create a
sense of identity for the new college. He chose
to do this by incorporating a variety of features
from a number of colleges and universities in
Britain and Canada. "Traditionally, science
men have all worked together in the past, but
arts men have always worked alone," he insisted.
"This college is an attempt to create a society
within a society without attempting to create a
super college which admits students of genius
level only." Morton, who had been a member of
the student commission of 1932, was finally
getting a chance to put some of the
recommendations of that commission into

practice. But what the public heard most about
were Morton's various attempts to replicate
"Oxford on the Red." Students who were
members of the college would wear burgundy
gowns, while those only attending classes there
would not. Each student would have his own
tutor. There would be a "high table" at
mealtime, and all members of the college would
be required to eat a set number of meals each
term in the college dining room. When CBC's
Rawhide (Max Ferguson) heard about this
requirement, it presented a satirical radio skit
in which a fictional member of college came to
the eve of graduation without having eaten his
mandatory meals, forcing him to consume a
large number of dinners within a very brief
time span—with predictable results.

From the beginning, University College had
trouble with its Oxford-like "innovations."
Students did not like wearing gowns, not even
burgundy ones. A glitch at registration in

University College students' lounge, c. 1965. Note the gowns (UMA).

September of 1964 did not add the cost of the required meals to the registration fee for UC students. Provost Morton was forced to write to 159 day students who had not bought meal tickets that they would have to pay for them or withdraw from the college. The students understandably objected to the whole business. The well-advertised tutor system did not work very well, since the tutors had no academic authority or standing. At the same time, University College quickly attracted a number of very bright students and acquired a reputation as the home of student radicalism on the campus. These students clustered for complex political debate by sitting on the radiators in the corridors of the college, where they became known as the "radiator radicals." This contingent was probably the least likely group of the college to be attracted to the traditional Oxford features.

Athletics at both intramural and inter-varsity level continued to flourish. The university began the decade as an independent, but was able to join the Western Canadian Inter-collegiate Athletic Association (WCIAA) in 1962, when the mounting of a football team gave it teams in all core sports. The decision to reintroduce varsity football was taken by UMSU on 30 November 1961, although the *Manitoban* had mounted a campaign against it. A crowd of 100 students, including a squad of cheerleaders, demonstrated in favour of football outside the meeting room. Later that night, the demonstrators burned *'Toban* editors Heather Robertson and Jim Lorimer in effigy. The student newspaper had opposed the reintroduction of football, chiefly because of its cost. The following autumn, nearly 800 students accompanied the Bisons on a "Seagram's Special" to watch the team play in Saskatoon, and, despite a defeat, snake-danced down Main Street on Sunday upon their return at CP Station. That first team had a record of

1–5. But the Bisons football team ultimately became WCIAA champs in 1968, and won the College Bowl (later named the Vanier Cup) in 1969, defeating the McGill Redmen 24–15. The hockey team, having been Canadian champions in 1965, went on to represent Canada at the World University Games in 1966. Other national championships came in cross-country and track.

On the intramural level, male participation ran high through the decade, although female participation declined precipitously (to around 20 percent) by 1970. According to its historian, United College dominated many intramural sports in its last years before becoming the University of Winnipeg. The 1960s were marked by several other developments in athletics. One

U of M Bisons football team, 1962 (UMA).

The Glee Club Shows

No Glee Club show this year [1971]? Its demise seemed imminent even ten
years ago. The shows annually lost a fortune. Winnipeggers' continuous
exposure to professional excellence through MTC, Rainbow Stage, and the
ballet has made them more sophisticated and demanding, less willing to
endure the foibles of the enthusiastic but inexperienced amateur performer.
Glee Club was really an anachronism. It reached its zenith box-office-wise
in the '50s, when it was practically the only show in town, and when
university students projected a lovable, innocent (and totally false) image
now to be seen only on late, late shows.

Yes, it probably makes sense. Suitable Glee Club vehicles aren't being
written very much now. The shows traditionally featured big production
numbers, so lots of people could participate (sometimes the multitudes on
stage made Ben Hur look like Two for the Seesaw). More important, the
irresistible enthusiasm of those same multitudes was what carried the
shows, since the leads could vary in quality from brilliant to something
less.

Why it was called the "Glee Club" is to me a mystery. The title is
unfortunate, summoning as it does images of resolutely cheery middle
Canadians. The first event of a typical Glee Club year was the Choosing of
the Show. At the innumerable conferences, each in his turn one-upped his
fellows by bringing forth for consideration an obscure item that only he
had ever heard of: "It ran for one week in 1934, but the critics didn't
understand it--it was way ahead of its time." Perusal of the script
usually revealed that indeed the critics hadn't understood. It was really
much worse than they had thought. The actual season began in late
September with "auditions." Ominous word! Performers hate auditions because
they don't know what's expected of them, and soul-destroying failure is a
very real possibility. Producers hate auditions because watching fifty
girls in succession sing "Ah can't say no!" with stupefying coyness is a
numbing, mind-boggling experience. Still, you have to have auditions. Even
though by show time about 50 percent of the chosen elite would have
dropped out, to be replaced by somebody's cousin who was pressed into
service, and who could almost hold a tune if the wind was blowing the
right way, and if somebody goosed him on the high notes.

Sure there were bad things about Glee Club. At times, and
indefensibly, talented "imports" (non-students) were used to upgrade
the shows' qualities (I counted ten imports in one show). Sure, it
gave a totally false picture of what a career in theatre is really like.
Many stage-struck Glee Clubbers who went expecting more of the same found
instead that the business is about as much fun as ditch-digging, and most
of the people you meet as likable as wolverines. Maybe (heresy!) the shows
weren't even that great. Maybe if I saw a Glee Club production now, from a
more jaded perspective, I'd hate it. But I doubt it.

  Jack ("Jock") Abra graduated from the university in 1964.
  Excerpt from Alumni Journal (1971).

Two of the Glee Club musicals of the 1960s: *Kiss Me Kate* (1962), top, and *South Pacific* (1965) (UMA).

Barney Charach

A controversial medical students' float in the freshie parade in the early 1960s. People were still uneasy talking about "the pill" (UMA/T).

was a substantial improvement in sports facilities, including a swimming pool building completed in 1965, and capped by the Pan American Games outdoor stadium and track, the first in the world to use artificial material (tartanturf) for its track. The second was the

establishment in 1964 of a degree programme in physical education, which became a faculty in 1965. Finally, in 1968, the university itself accepted full financial responsibility for intramural and inter-varsity athletics. For the first time, the students were not themselves the principal sponsors of the athletics programmes.

By the middle of the 1960s, there was considerable evidence of a new student ferment on the campus. The student body became slightly older, as the university for the first time imposed a compulsory grade twelve entrance requirement. For the most part, the U of M student body shied away from the publicly political side of the campus unrest experienced everywhere in North American during the decade. There was the occasional local incident, however. On 7 November 1968, a number of engineering students were barred by protesters from meeting with recruiters from the Dow Chemical Company (the makers of napalm and Agent Orange), and a few weeks later there were clashes over interviews with the Hawker-Siddley aircraft manufacturers.

But the relative lack of student involvement in public politics did not necessarily mean that the students were apathetic. In November 1964, UMSU did vote to boycott South Africa, but, for the most part, put its weight behind questions of immediate interest to students on the campus. In early 1965, UMSU backed a boycott of classes to protest a proposed fee increase, and 1200 students marched to the legislature in support. The daughter of education minister George Johnson stood outside the demo with a placard reading "I like Daddy." An informal debate occurred at the autumn convocation in 1965 between President Saunderson and the president of UMSU, Winston Dookeran. Saunderson insisted that there was no "free lunch" for students and that tuition fees would therefore have to be raised, and Dookeran riposted with talk of "undeniable

Cafeteria scene, Pembina Hall, c. 1965 (UMA).

student rights." These included the right for students to be represented on the Board of Governors.

By the mid-1960s, the university administration was having considerable trouble with its efforts to protect the student body from the new morality. In 1965 President Saunderson

The Founding of University College

To some [Provost] Bill Morton seemed a man of excessive dignity, even pompousness, and he often gave cause for such assessment. But as this writer knows, he could knock back his Scotch and tell stories with the best. His anecdotal knowledge of the more colourful characters in the fur trade was unrivalled. But perhaps his prime social characteristic was a belief in a social order characterized by rank, authority, civility and obedience.

Soon after his appointment as Provost, he presented the Advisory Committee with a draft of "provisional regulations" to be valid for a period of five years beginning in November 1962. One section read: The purpose of the College is to provide a fellowship devoted to a life of study and discussion; to see to it that numbers and busyness do not separate students from students and diminish the companionship of study; to provide for the mastery of symbols, evidence and ideas; to provide at all levels of study and at all convenient times, opportunity for the discussion and refinement of ideas tested by formal discourse and conversation; to cultivate a sense of the wholeness of knowledge in all the arts and sciences; to bring together a company, men and women from diverse fields of scholarship and walks of life. While no one on the Advisory Committee was ready to oppose this statement, some felt it sounded more like a description of a monastery than a College; others felt it was expressed in pompous language, and almost everyone agreed it was too idealistic.

One part of the provisional regulations did cause open and vigorously expressed objection. It stated that only those: of professional rank of at least three years standing . . . shall be Fellows of the College. This group would be the governing body, and all others would have to earn their way on. One assistant professor wrote a very strong letter of protest, stating that if this was the way things were to be, he wanted no part of it. The Provost threatened to resign but was talked out of it. The offending clause was deleted. The draft also provided for Honorary Fellows who would be distinguished citizens of the community, and Associate Fellows from among the faculty. Both groups, the rules said, would be expected to dine in Hall whenever invited. Some members of the committee wondered what would happen if anyone failed to dine as prescribed; the answer was that they would cease to be Fellows of the College. News of this plan for force-fed students and honorary fellows reached Max Ferguson of the CBC in Toronto, and he turned it into an amusing skit. Morton got a copy of the tape and played it back one night at dinner. He seemed to enjoy it as much as anyone.

Morton was often accused of attempting to create "Oxford on the Red," and there was some truth to the charge. He denied it with some heat and he once said to the writer (who never knew what he meant): "It will be no more mock Oxford than mock turtle is turtle."

Murray Donnelly was Provost of University College from 1966 to 1978. Excerpt taken from his University College: A Personal History (1989).

VW bug going through the
new U of M gates, 1964
(UMA).

was forced to deny that he had "banned" *Playboy Magazine* from the campus. He claimed that there simply was not room for it on the shelves in the bookstore, in competition with "important" journals such as *Atlantic Monthly, Harper's,* and *U.S. News and World Report.* To prove his point that he had nothing against *Playboy,* the magazine's Miss September appeared on campus in 1966 as the freshie week mascot, escorted around campus by the president himself.

The 1966 UMSU presidential campaign was fought partly over student criticism of the university food service, and the UMSU council in March of 1966 approved an anti-calendar to evaluate faculty members and courses. UMSU subsequently mounted a major campaign to be represented on all decision-making bodies of the university, arguing that this was a better use of UMSU time than the sponsorship of social activities, many of which were being taken over by individual faculties.

Early in 1967, the *Manitoban* called the office of the Dean of Women Students "one of those quaint hangovers from the Victorian era," and an insult to female students. The student newspaper, a few weeks earlier, had run into trouble over editorials about Remembrance Day, which it called "quite a bit like Victoria Day. At one time it had a great deal of

Opposite: The cover of the
1968 *Student Guide* (UMA).
Right: Winnipeg dance party,
1965 (UMA/T).

significance. Today the meaning has long disappeared and only the firecrackers remain." These comments brought charges of insensitivity and talk of freedom of the press.

The older generation of taxpayers did not always understand the student perspective, even and perhaps especially when it was devoted to such issues as the defence of free speech and freedom of the press. Unfortunately, the students did not always occupy the high ground.

Early in 1964, UMSU received a bill for $1100 for damage done to a CPR train during a football excursion to Regina in the autumn of 1963. The 1964 freshie parade was severely criticized by Winnipeg's acting police chief, who cited "disorganization, grabbing of policemen's hats, the possibilities of injuries to students riding on the lowbeds used to carry the flats, the horsing around, the sometimes ungentlemanly language, the jostling of the crowd and the grabbing of girls from the streets to put them on floats." He also complained about the excessive consumption of liquor by the student revellers.

Thanks to a study headed by sociologist William Pickering, released in 1965 as *Religion and the Undergraduate: A Study of Changes in the Religious Faith and Practice of Students in the University of Manitoba*, we have an useful picture of undergraduate life and values in the middle of the decade of the sixties. The study, organized by the university chaplains, was considerably broader in scope than its title might suggest, since it was necessary to establish a general context for the data collected (in February 1964) and the conclusions reached. Pickering began by setting the scene, writing:

> The vast majority of the students—about 9 out of 10—live in accommodation off the campus, two, three, or more miles away. About one out of every two students lives at home. These sorts of facts, plus the way in which the timetable is arranged, means that in practice university life on the campus quietens down about 3 or 4 p.m., and becomes completely dead after 5 p.m.... It is hardly surprising that Manitoba is nicknamed a 'car-pool' university where the students' lives are centered on transportation.... It is little wonder ... that student clubs and societies ... receive minimal support.

The authors noted that the entire ethos and tradition of the Fort Garry campus worked against extracurricular activities. There was no set lunch hour, for example, and students could

Above: The early
introduction of televised
classrooms, c. 1965 (UMA).
Opposite: Exams in the old
Bison Gym, 1960s (UMA).

select courses in which all classes were held in the morning. For such students, the report claimed, university was less a way of life than a place to attend lectures. The fraternities and sororities were downtown, and the authors suspected that Greek membership exceeded that of membership in all on-campus clubs and societies. The affiliated colleges were different, but many students found them cliquish.

The survey was restricted to senior undergraduates, although 1044 of 1291 potentials responded. Of the respondents, more than one-half lived at home. Many students saw university as an extension of high school rather than as a distinctive way of life, reported the sociologists, who noted that the registrar in 1963–64 reported that 56 percent of U of M students had home addresses in Winnipeg. In all, eight out of ten students had addresses in Manitoba, and 86 percent lived in the prairie provinces. Nearly half the student body was of British origin (44 percent), with the percentage

considerably higher in the affiliated colleges (as much as 76 percent at St. John's College). The Franco-Manitoban population was under-represented in the student population, while Germans (at 14 percent) were over-represented. Students of Polish and Russian origins totalled 11 percent, and 8 percent were of Ukrainian background. Only three of every ten senior undergraduates were women.

A number of significant academic developments occurred at mid-decade, most of them well in line with general trends across North America. Teacher training was transferred to the university for the fall of 1965, part of an ongoing effort by the province to upgrade the credentials of its teachers. Experiments carried out with closed-circuit television as a regular teaching device, beginning in 1965, led the university administration to embrace the concept as a way of dealing with the increasing enrolments. Television teaching proved quite successful in zoology, once the problems of poor equipment were overcome. In 1966 the university spent $150,000 on a television control room, studios, and four receiving theatres in the Armes Building and one in the Isbister Building. By 1967 a number of first-year courses were being offered via television to students in the specially equipped classrooms. Many students grumbled about TV teaching.

Several other important developments of mid-decade also looked to the future. In 1964 the university library introduced a photocopying service, and, in its first year of operation, 43,356 exposures were made, an average of over 160 per working day. The

Student Political Action in the 1960s

The new act University of Manitoba Act [1968] included an innocent-looking
clause that proved to be a "sleeper," namely that the act would come into
effect when all bodies had named their representatives to the Board and the
Senate. I believe this clause was introduced by government lawyers at the
drafting stage as a standard pro forma provision. But the students, who are
always one step ahead of university administrators, seized upon it as a means
of blackmail. They could delay naming their representatives to the Senate
until certain "non-negotiable" demands were met. The fun had just begun.

The student union demanded that it conduct the elections of students to
the Senate, that one of the student representatives on the board be a
student, and that meetings of the Board and Senate be open to the public.
Viewed in retrospect, these were pretty tame demands. I had no difficulty
with the first and strongly favoured the other three, provided that
confidential matters could be discussed in closed session at the Board and
Senate. As yet, however, the students were unwilling to settle for
anything but full and open meetings. At this point, I suggested to
President Saunderson that he might solve the impasse by soliciting the
help of the senior sticks, who, as a group, were inclined to be
conservative in their views. A meeting was called, but each senior stick
brought with him or her the representative on the student union of that
faculty. Before Saunderson could introduce the subject, all sticks
announced that they would be represented by their student union
representatives. Thus, in a twinkling of an eye, Saunderson found himself
facing the same implacable group he had been trying to bypass. The meeting
was a fiasco, but Saunderson never reproached me for my bad advice.

Gradually, the student union agreed that certain matters could be decided in
camera, and the Senate agreed to open meetings and to reserve one of its
places on the Board for a student. After the student union conducted
elections to the Senate and the Senate elected its representatives to the
Board, the Board agreed to debate the subject of open meetings for itself. I
had been elected to the Board from the Senate, as had Lloyd Dulmage, dean of
the Faculty of Arts. The Board agreed on the following procedure: to debate
the subject of open meetings at an open meeting and then move into closed
session to reach its decision. Scarcely had the debate begun, when Dulmage
moved and someone seconded that board meetings be open. The many students in
the gallery erupted into cheers, and the chair had no choice but to put the
question. I voted against, because we had agreed to hold the vote in camera
but, under pressure of the cheers, the motion passed. Thus, I was perceived
as opposing open meetings (which I favoured) and Dulmage became the darling
of the gallery by breaking the agreement. The Manitoban later reported "that
this senior administrator [Duckworth] could not be trusted."

The student leaders who led the campaign included Chris Westdal, later
Canadian ambassador to Ukraine, Janice Johnson, who sits in the Senate of
Canada, Thomas Traves, currently president of Dalhousie University, and
Nelson Wiseman, who became a well-known political scientist. No wonder
they outsmarted the rest of us.

Henry (Harry) Duckworth graduated from the university in 1936, and was
later its vice-president (1965 to 1970) and chancellor (1986 to 1992).
Excerpt from his One Version of the Facts (2000).

photocopying machine, which, like most such technology, was in the process of getting more portable and less expensive almost by the day, revolutionized university administration, and not for the better. No longer did copying involve messy carbon paper and place a premium on accurate typing. Within a few years, every unit on campus had at least one machine, and the quantity of paperwork generated increased exponentially and continually. Everything could be saved and produced in multiple copies, and usually was. Unnecessary and useless paperwork became one of the least attractive (if most enduring) characteristics of the university bureaucracy.

Increased enrolments and expanded numbers of automobiles on campus created enormous pressure on parking, which seemed likely only to get worse. In November of 1966, the university threatened to withhold the marks of students who did not pay parking fines. At that point, the parking system was collecting $3500 in parking fines every year, and many of the huge parking lots of the modern campus were still but a dream in the planners' eyes.

By mid-decade, the days in which the university's administrators (on behalf of the Board of Governors) would negotiate directly and informally about funding with the Manitoba government, and receive numbers-driven financial grants from the federal government, were clearly over. Several Dominion-wide committees investigated university financing (the Bladen Committee, for example) and the administration of Canadian universities (the Duff-Berdahl Commission). There were a few key questions in Manitoba. One was the extent

An open meeting of the Board of Governors, November 1969 (UMA).

to which the BoG should be totally in charge of the financial side of the university administration, especially since it was in no sense a representative body. Another was continuation of the traditional concept of a single university for the entire province. Moreover, the province clearly wanted decisions about higher education made in a different manner from the informal negotiations of the past. In October of 1966, the federal government announced it would change its funding policies for higher education. In place of a direct per-capita student grant to each institution, federal aid would take the form of block grants to the provincial governments. This decision placed the responsibility for higher education almost completely in the hands of the province. For its part, Manitoba had already established a seven-member Council of Higher Learning, which would permit recommendations on policy to be made outside the corridors of power in the legislature.

Right: One of the university's first computers (UMA). Above: Televised classroom console (UMA).

Over the course of 1966, the Council of Higher Learning proposed major changes to the university system in the province, most of them connected with the colleges. The college situation had been the cause of much discontent for years, of course. Brandon and United colleges, and to some extent Collége St. Boniface, chafed under University of Manitoba tutelage. For their part, administrators at the University of Manitoba, led by William Sibley, the Dean of the Faculty of Arts and Science, chafed at the autonomy of the affiliated colleges on the Fort Garry campus. Sibley insisted that the colleges made it impossible to conduct rational academic planning, claiming that what was needed was "one Board, one President, one Dean, one Department head." St. John's and St. Paul's were extremely worried about finances, particularly given the announcement of the termination of federal per-capita grants. The Council of Higher Learning responded to the college by proposing to detach Brandon and United colleges as separate universities, to continue St. Boniface as a teaching centre in French, and to produce a new, closer relationship with the University of Manitoba for St. John's and St. Paul's, probably along the lines of that already prevailing at University College. The new order on the Fort Garry campus would be determined in the spring of 1967 by a special committee on college structure, chaired by Lionel Funt.

Independently of the actions of the Council of Higher Learning, although doubtless influenced by the spirit of consolidation, the University of Manitoba and the Law Society of Manitoba (which, since 1914, had enjoyed joint responsibility for the Manitoba Law School) signed an agreement for the university to take over responsibility for the law faculty in a new building to be erected on the Fort Garry campus. The Law Society acted reluctantly, pleased to be rid of a financial burden but unhappy that the school should become isolated from the law courts, which were downtown. Despite much good will, the new building (Robson Hall) was not ready for opening until 1969.

The University Committee on College Structure (the Funt committee) met often in the spring of 1967. Its final report addressed the questions of programmes of studies, the status of teaching staffs, and the working relationships between colleges and their individual departments. Although never mentioned by name, the University College model was the one recommended by the committee. The colleges would have their courses, their faculties, and their libraries integrated into those of the university, would be encouraged to maintain certain areas of "emphasis and excellence," and would remain autonomous only in an administrative and a social sense. In return for their surrender of autonomy, the colleges would receive the provision of "ancillary services" by the university. Such were the recommendations of the committee, not immediately accepted by St. Paul's and St. John's colleges.

On 1 July 1967, the University Grants Commission (UGC) succeeded the Council of Higher Learning, with, among other responsibilities, a mandate to administer the block grant Manitoba would receive from the Dominion. It was not clear at the beginning

whether the UGC would continue a direct per-capita granting system or would go to an omnibus budget for the universities. The U of M wanted the colleges to submit budgets to it in August of 1967, but the colleges decided to submit their financial requests directly to the UGC instead. This attempt by the colleges to preserve their autonomy led to considerable behind-the-scenes manoeuvring. A compromise eventually was worked out whereby

Very informative lecture today...... I counted 8,654,302 holes in the ceiling tiles.

the university assumed responsibility for the academic budget of the colleges and the colleges' budget requests became part of the university's. Several years of further negotiations were required before the colleges and the university—in 1970—reached a final satisfactory working arrangement, embodied in separate agreements between the university and each college. With St. John's and St. Paul's

Even after University College abandoned the wearing of gowns, the college was still considered elitist in some circles, as this 1968 cartoon from the *Manitoban* reveals.

Work done at the U of M Department of Plant Science resulted in the creation of triticale, the first man-made cereal, in the 1960s. Above: (left to right) : the U of M's E.N. Larter and L.H. Shebeski inspect a field of triticale with F.J. Zillinsky at the CIMMYT research centre in Mexico, c. 1970 (UMA). Shebeski, as head of Plant Science, and Larter, as the Rosner research chair, were instrumental in the development of triticale.

thoroughly integrated into the university, they ceased to be—if ever they had been—important autonomous players on the campus scene.

Over the decade, both the size and composition of the faculty and the nature of its work altered considerably. Numbers of faculty had, of course, increased and stood at 880 by 1969. Many of the new appointments came toward the end of the decade, especially in the basic undergraduate faculties. In 1970, for example, the Faculty of Arts made seventy-five new appointments and had thirty resignations and deaths, while the Faculty of Science made twenty-seven new appointments and had seven deaths and resignations. Most of these appointments were given at the junior level to scholars around thirty years of age. Because of the volatility of the job market during the decade, nobody expected these faculty members to grow old together and come up for retirement at the same time, around the end of the century. The university was forced to recruit this new faculty internationally, for there simply

were not enough qualified Canadian academics to meet the national demand.

Not only were numbers increased, but the composition of the new faculty was different as well. Before 1960, the typical U of M faculty appointment was British- or Canadian-born, educated at first-degree level at a small number of colleges and universities in Britain and Canada, and trained professionally in Canada, the United States, or Great Britain. The new faculty was a much more international lot, with a much higher proportion born and educated in the United States and with members from all parts of the world. The Americans were particularly well represented in the arts departments, especially in the social sciences, where the United States had taken the lead after the war. The new faculty had lighter teaching loads and expected—and were expected—to be far more heavily involved in research than had been their predecessors. Canada had experienced a virtual revolution in funding for research in the late 1950s and 1960s, with the creation of the Canada Council in 1957 and the Medical Research Council in 1960, and the expansion of the National Research Council in 1962. After these agencies were established, few well-conceived research projects went unfunded, and major shifts in ancillary support for research (the introduction of computers, photocopiers, and cheap airfares, for example) made research much easier than ever before. Canadian research funding was one of the attractions for many of the new appointments.

No faculty was changed more profoundly during the '60s than the medical faculty. Major overhauls in curriculum and admissions

Aerial view of campus, 1965 (UMA).

procedures came only as the decade came to an end, but three important developments had already occurred by that point. One was the extension of medical training beyond the first degree, involving residency programmes increasingly centrally administered by the faculty. Another was an increased emphasis on the needs of the population of the northern part of the province, through the Northern Medical Unit (NMU), founded by J.A. Hildes in 1969. The NMU provided physician services to 25,000 inhabitants of the remote north in Manitoba, and fostered much useful research on the medical problems of the northern inhabitants. The final and most important was a substantial increase in research, which ceased to be conducted by individual researchers assisted by a few technicians, and became well-funded

multidisciplinary team research, employing large numbers of postgraduates and non-medical scientists. Funding came from the Medical Research Council and a variety of other organizations, such as the National Cancer Institute of Canada. Competition for funding was substantial, and a series of important medical advances in several fields (such as the treatment of cancer and heart disease) was announced by the medical school over the decade. In the 1970–71 *Annual Report* of the university, listing the publications by the medical faculty required thirty pages. By that time, write Ian Carr and Robert Beamish in their history, *Manitoba Medicine,* "research, and the promotion and organization of research, was now the Manitoba medical school way of life." So it was in its own way at most units of the university.

The university itself made a contribution to the shift to research, establishing a number of research institutes over the course of the decade. Northern Studies flourished at the medical school, and a Centre for Settlement Studies was created with Central Mortgage and Housing Corporation money at the main campus. At the end of the decade, an Institute for Transportation Studies joined the Natural Resources Institute, founded in 1968 with money from the Ford Foundation. Other research institutes established in the late 1960s included the Legal Research Institute (1968) and the Manitoba Institute of Cell Biology (1969). As early as 1965, the university had established a research board to coordinate and oversee research, thus recognizing its importance apart from teaching.

Manitoba researchers made a number of well-publicized breakthroughs over the course of the decade. The *Saturday Evening Post* on 1 July 1967 (and subsequently the *Reader's Digest*) featured a lead story about triticale ("the first crop species man has ever created"), one of several new grain plants developed in the Plant Science Department of the Faculty of Agriculture.

The lengthy process of developing triticale as a cereal crop began in the mid-1950s. The development process involved crossing wheat with rye, and then treating the hybrid (and sterile) plant with chemicals to restore its fertility. Compared with wheat, triticale grain contains a higher percentage of lysine, a protein component required in the human and animal diet for growth. It was thus ideally suited for agriculture in third-world countries that got most of their protein from cereal crops. By the

Excavation of the site for the new University Centre, 1968 (UMA), the largest of the many new buildings that transformed the look of the Fort Garry campus in the 1960s.

This 1965 cartoon from the *Manitoban* captures the mood of excitement and confusion created by the construction boom on campus in the 1960s.

mid-1990s, triticale was grown on more than 2.4 million hectares worldwide, and contributed more than 6 million metric tons per year to global cereal production. The Manitoba plant scientists were also active in developing new strains of grain that were resistant to rust, a major blight on grain crops.

Early in 1968, a story in the *Manitoban* exploded like a bombshell across the campus and the city of Winnipeg. The student newspaper reported that four faculty members openly acknowledged their use of marijuana and that two heads of departments at University College were also smokers of the dreaded weed. Perhaps half the student body at the university, the newspaper added, were indulgers. President Saunderson vehemently denied the charges, responding with threats of a lawsuit. The

Mounties launched an investigation into the drug culture of the university, and the editor of the newspaper backed down from his charges in the very next issue. Nevertheless, as Saunderson acknowledged in his memoirs, he had already informally begun investigating on-campus use of drugs when the *'Toban* story appeared. The *Alumni Journal* later reported that while most students denied using the drugs themselves, "they say they could get it if they wanted to." Moreover, none of those interviewed by the *AJ* "seemed surprised at the original stories in the Manitoban." Stories about extensive soft drug use on the campus circulated widely on an anecdotal level in the late 1960s, but little concrete information ever emerged in this regard. Only those who were on the scene at the time know the truth.

In 1968, the university also adopted a tenure system for professors. It included a bylaw that said that in the absence of a negative decision within three and one half years from appointment to a tenure-track position, a faculty member automatically achieved tenure. Many pointed out that this system had no goals, no standards, and no procedures to be followed in tenure decisions, essentially leaving policy in the hands of departmental heads and deans. But it brought the U of M's practices in line with those of all other major universities in North America. In theory, tenure protected academics from capricious dismissals, sometimes for political reasons, and was associated by its supporters with academic freedom.

In the same year, the long-simmering conflict between the university administration and the student leadership over representation on university governing bodies heated up. The students, led by UMSU president Chris Westdal and vice-president Janice Johnson, took advantage of a clause in the newly amended University of Manitoba Act, which revised membership on the BoG and Senate to reflect the concern for broader representation. At first, the students delayed naming their representatives to the Senate until a number of other demands were met. At the next Senate meeting, they then outmanoeuvred the administration on a vote to ensure that all subsequent meetings would be open.

Enrolment, of course, continued to increase constantly during the sixties. Numbers reached 11,750 in regular winter daytime courses in 1965 (an increase of 20 percent over 1964), 13,000 in 1966, and 14,575 in regular winter daytime courses, and an overall total of 24,658 in 1970. By the latter date, a Planning Secretariat, in consultation with a Senate committee, was studying the limitation of enrolment to 18,000 full-time equivalent students.

The enormous expansion of enrolment inevitably led to a commensurate expansion of new buildings on the Fort Garry campus. Mary Speechly and Pembina halls were begun in 1963 and completed in 1964. The Allen Physics Building, the Parker Chemistry Building, the Engineering Building, and the library were all expanded. A new Engineering Building, erected in 1967, got a computer centre on the top floor, where the university's new IBM 360/65, delivered in 1966, was permanently installed. A Cyclotron was begun in 1961, the first in western Canada. Art, Pharmacy, Architecture, and Music all got their own buildings. The new Art Building brought the Arts faculty and its students from downtown. The Fletcher Argue Building, the Education Building (with two additions), the Robson Hall law building, and the UMSU building were all completed before the end of the decade. A similar expansion occurred at the medical complex at the downtown campus with additions to the old buildings, the completion of the five-storey Chown Building in 1965, an expansion to the dental building, and the construction of the Immunology Building in 1969. A visitor in 1970 who had not seen either the Fort Garry or downtown medical campuses for ten years would hardly have recognized them.

Chapter 7 ↝ *1970—1977*

At the end of the 1960s, the University of Manitoba was affected by the confluence of developments that created a much more confrontational public atmosphere than had ever existed before on the campus. These developments were simultaneously international, national, and local. Internationally, the growing American involvement in the war in Vietnam was affecting politics across the continent and, indeed, around the world. Vietnam protest led to a fatal confrontation between soldiers and students at Kent State University in Ohio at the beginning of the new decade. In Canada, the separatist movement in Quebec would soon explode into its own violence and the Parti Quebecois would come to power in Quebec. The decision of oil cartel producers (OPEC) to cease exporting would raise the price of oil (and energy) considerably, and help ignite a major period of inflation. Watergate would eventually lead to the resignation of the American president.

Within the province of Manitoba, its first NDP government struggled to free itself from the dead hand of the past. Its leader, Ed Schreyer, was young, still in his early thirties. A graduate of the U of M, he had been a lecturer in political science at St. Paul's College, and had won the New Democratic nomination only days before the election in 1969. Most of the new cabinet came from Winnipeg's North End and was of non-British origin. The NDP, which governed Manitoba for most of the 1970s, had ended

Opposite: U of M students listening in 1972 to scientist and broadcaster David Suzuki, a popular guest speaker at many universities during this period (UMA/T).

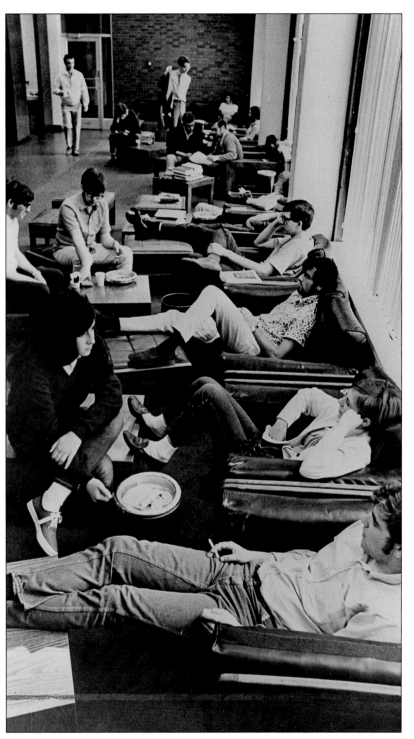

the Anglo-Scottish ascendancy that had ruled the province since its Red River days.

Locally, the students were agitating on several fronts. In addition to their continuing demand for involvement in the decision-making bodies of the university, students became involved in the radical student politics and counterculture of the time in North America. The political integration was particularly powerful and vociferous among the editorial staff of the *Manitoban*. A part-time involvement in the counterculture, particularly its emphasis on "sex, drugs, and rock'n'roll," may have been more general among the student body.

Students were not the only people chafing under the old spirit of paternalism of the university. Both the faculty and the support staff decided to organize labour unions at about the same time. Although faculty and staff were organizing for quite different reasons, the end result in both cases was the negotiation of collective bargaining and collective agreements that limited the university's earlier ability to behave and spend its money pretty much as it pleased.

Around 1970, moreover, the halcyon days of 10 percent enrolment increases and constant economic growth suddenly ended. Growth curves no longer automatically continued upwards. The new and energetic NDP government began to hold the university administration more accountable for its stewardship, through the University Grants Commission (UGC). These developments further limited the fiscal flexibility of the university. The resultant decline in revenue and distinct tightening of the purse strings was also influenced by the new collective agreements.

In 1969 Hugh Saunderson, who had been president since 1954, announced his retirement. His successor, Ernest Sirluck, was one of the university's own graduates and a respected scholar. He had spent his entire academic career in well-funded major universities to the east—the University of Chicago and the University of Toronto—and had achieved his main administrative reputation as a dean who was willing to stand up to student protestors. Sirluck's advance billing as a confrontationalist with students was perhaps more than a bit undeserved, but he was not a man who was likely to work quietly behind the scenes.

Ernest Sirluck arrived on the campus on 1 July 1970 as president designate but did not actually take office until September. By his own account, he was in trouble before he had even officially taken office. To deal with the student demands for more representation on the BoG and the Senate, he suggested appointing student "assessors" without votes or the right to make motions until the University Act of 1968 could be amended to allow formally for more student governors and senators. Although the president-designate viewed the offer as a major concession, the students were understandably suspicious that the proposal was nothing more than a way to appear to satisfy their demands without actually sharing power. As a result of these "concessions," Sirluck actually took office on 1 September 1970 with many student leaders hostile to him.

If the university as a whole was in a state of transition, at least one institution's views were crystal clear. In its issue of 21 July 1970, the student newspaper, *The Manitoban*, left no doubt

WOLF HECK

where it stood. The newspaper reviewed the film *Woodstock*, emphasizing that while the movie was great, "our culture is being ripped off, packaged, and sold back to us." This one issue carried feature stories on the political science, sociology, and anthropology departments at Simon Fraser University (which was involved in a major governance controversy with the university administration), on the Kent State massacres, and on the Black Panthers. It even provided a two-page chart entitled "Here is the dope on dope." In short, the *Manitoban* spoke for an internationally oriented and highly politicized student left and counterculture, and it continued to do so throughout the early 1970s. The result was a student newspaper that was often a bit short on campus news that did not fit into its larger ideology, but that provided its

Opposite: Student lounge in Fletcher Argue Building, 1969 (UMA). Above: Prince Charles visits the campus as part of the Manitoba centennial celebrations in 1970. He is accompanied by his official student escort (W.Heck).

Lecture hall, Fletcher Argue
Building, c. 1970 (UMA).

readership week after week with access to the best of radical journalism from across the continent. It got its Canadian content chiefly from *The Last Post* and the *Georgia Strait* in Vancouver.

In October of 1970, the FLQ in Quebec kidnapped James Cross and Pierre Laporte. Prime Minister Pierre Trudeau responded to the crisis by introducing the War Measures Act in Parliament and sending the Canadian military into Quebec. The *'Toban* not only carried the national story of the War Measures

Act but also a local story about one U of M sociology professor who had cancelled his classes until the War Measures Act was revoked. The newspaper subsequently reported in detail on a well-attended Teach-in on the issue held at University Centre, which had finally opened a few weeks earlier. The *'Toban*'s proudest moment probably came late in 1970, when a story on the concessions made by the Manitoba government to Churchill Forest Industries (CFI) was published and subsequently distributed across the province in 50,000 leaflets. The provincial legislature debated the story at length. The CFI claimed it was defamatory. Premier Ed Schreyer eventually admitted the province had made a bad deal, but he blamed the previous administration. *Manitoban* lawyers did battle with the paper corporation in the courts, but the whole business fizzled out without much result.

Over the next few years, the *'Toban* carried regular stories attacking the educational system for its top-down authoritarian character and encouraging various forms of alternate structures. It also reported with enthusiasm any suggestion of discussion of educational reform within the university structure itself, such as a committee recommendation in 1971 for credit-evaluation grading, with a pass grade backed by a written evaluation in place of the usual marking system. Much cynicism about the educational system was mixed into these discussions. In its 1974 convocation issue, the *Manitoban* described the university as a "MULTIVERSITY," adding, "an even more accurate term might be TRADE SCHOOL, differing from other trade schools in that the courses are longer, luxuries more abundant, and those trades offered are higher paying." A "free university"—an alternate teaching experience staffed by volunteers outside the system—existed on campus and in Winnipeg in the early '70s, and struggled to find students.

Shortly after taking office, the new president had learned privately that the university had a huge $3.8 million deficit, which was buried in the books, and that the new government would be less generous than it had been in the past. Combined with a shortfall in enrolments, this meant that the new administration would have

to pinch pennies from the outset. Nobody entirely understood what had happened to enrolment. It was projected at 10 percent for 1970–71 (and had exceeded that figure in each of the last four years of the 1960s), but it suddenly fell off and never did recover its momentum. There were many possible explanations. The growth at Red River Community College and the University of Winnipeg might have been at U of M expense, thought some observers. Others blamed the economic slowdown and the reduced job opportunities of the early 1970s. Many blamed the increased cost of attending university, particularly for students from socio-economic classes who had never come to university before. Some thought the political problems on campuses across North America were responsible for the downturn, and a few even blamed it on the disenchantment of both the high school and university-level student with traditional education.

The new need for financial restraint soon conflicted with the double-digit inflation of the 1970s that followed in the wake of quadrupling oil prices in 1973. At the same time that the university was receiving less money, it was finding the cost of almost everything it paid for (from library books to salaries) constantly increasing. Until 1977 the university held the line on tuition

In 1970, the *Manitoban* joined forces with *Omphalos*, a Winnipeg underground newspaper, to produce a joint issue that "broke" the story of the provincial government's deal with Churchill Forest Industries.

Fort Garry campus, looking north toward the new University Centre and the Administration Building, 1975 (UMA).

increases, although it passed on the costs to students in most other areas such as room and board, food services, and parking. By the 1970s, the great shift in family financing of higher education in Canada was completed. Most Canadian parents no longer felt fully responsible for sending their children to university, and now expected that the students themselves would finance the bulk of their costs through work and loans. Despite increasing sophistication in the elaboration of financial aid programmes for students, particularly in the form of student loans, the cost of higher education to students (and their families) kept going up and up.

President Sirluck was also informed in his first days at the helm that the deal over a pension plan agreed to by the BoG in the dying days of his predecessor's administration, although completing a negotiation that had begun before the creation of the UGC and had dragged on for years, was not acceptable to the UGC (and presumably the new NDP government). The politicians thought that the university's contribution was too high. Renegotiations were necessary to reduce the university's contribution by 2 percent from 8 percent to 6 percent, to reduce the limit on equity investment, and to increase the government representation on the investment committee. Despite these changes, the pension plan was accepted by 75 percent of those voting in a referendum, with the faculty by far the least enthusiastic.

When, within weeks of his assumption of authority, Sirluck had started red-pencilling budgets and renegotiating the pension plan, he had completed the alienation of practically everybody on the campus. As he wrote in his autobiography, "It is hard to see how I could have had a more unpopular start. I had barely arrived from hated Toronto when I snatched away a treasured new pension plan, cut staff, and imposed unfamiliar restraints on government spending." His insistence on a rent-free house away from the campus, instead of the on-campus house that previous presidents had used since the 1930s, did not contribute to his popularity. The *Manitoban* front page that carried the story of Sirluck's installation also carried the news that the Minister of Education for the Black Panther Party had failed for the second time to show up on campus, a story the newspaper obviously thought deserved equal attention.

In January 1971, the student newspaper published a narrative offering "the inside story of how Ernest Sirluck was selected administration president." The author seemed to feel that an account of normal administrative politics was a sensational revelation, and made much out of such points as the fact that almost all the short-listed candidates had university administrative experience.

A few months later, on 2 April 1971, the *Manitoban* published a three-page "play for

radio, stage, film, comic-strip or animated cartoon." Entitled "The continuing story of Peter the Teenage Prick or the Ingenue and the Engineers," it featured a good deal of vulgar and obscene language but no graphic descriptions of either sex or violence. The language employed was no worse than can be heard on most television sitcoms today, but at the time it was quite scandalous. Public criticism of "Pete the Teenage Prick" was led by cabinet minister Joe Borowski, who, in the House of Assembly, as well as in interviews and letters to the local newspapers, made clear how shocked he was by the language. The anonymous author was doubtless quite pleased at the sensation that was created. When the *'Toban* later editorialized on President Sirluck's first year in office, it commented that "Old Saunderson had to deal consistently with dope busts, student radicals and demonstrations, the Canadian Union of Students, right wing demands, left wing demands, moratoriums and border blockades. About the most volatile issue Sirluck has had to face has been 'Pete the Teenage Prick' from last year's *Manitoban,* which was hardly more than a piquant example of the types of things which emerge when there are no more pressing issues

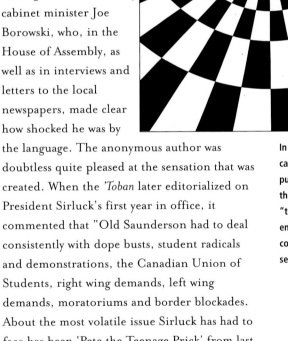

In 1971, the *Manitoban* caused a furor when it published a "play for radio" that featured the story of "the ingenue and the engineers." Its psychedelic cover (above) gives a good sense of the times.

presenting themselves for journalistic analysis."

In the autumn of 1971, the management of food services at the university was transferred to an outside company (it was Saga Food Services from 1973), the first of a long series of privatizations involving this sector of ancillary services and, arguably, the first anywhere at the university. It was certainly the case that the provision of on-campus food had been the object of student criticism for many years. Campus radio surveyed 2000 customers in the University Centre between the hours of 8:00 and 6:00 p.m., discovering that most students did not know who was running food services—and didn't care—although 94 percent thought food prices at the university were too high. The survey also disclosed that students spent an average of $1.50 a day on food in the cafeteria. Half of those surveyed thought the food was good, the other half thought it was bad. The 'Toban reported in October 1971 that the University Centre cafeteria had been overcharging for soft drinks for over a month and nobody had noticed—or complained.

The new fiscal and financial policies of restraint gradually brought the BoG and the

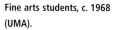
Fine arts students, c. 1968 (UMA).

university administration into conflict with the Faculty Association (UMFA). The president of UMFA told the organization's general meeting in December 1971 that "it is becoming clear that as the economic situation deteriorates, the Faculty Association has diminishing leverage." Both the Faculty Association and the professoriate complained that the budget-cutting was affecting the university's ability to deliver its programmes, pointing out that the number of administrators only grew as the faculty and staff numbers were cut. The Faculty Association demanded more representation on the BoG, the Executive of Senate, and the Dean's Council; these demands were rejected. The association also pressed for an opt-out system for membership dues, which was refused by the BoG on the grounds that it would change retroactively the terms of employment. The concept of retroactivity to employment terms never bothered the university when, in this

decade, it first began allowing tickets for overdue parking to be issued to faculty members or when it introduced library fines for faculty. The university administration professed to believe that UMFA was quite wrong in its perception that the BoG was dragging its feet on granting legal status to the association. But whatever the attitude toward UMFA, it was becoming increasingly clear that the university administration and its faculty and staff were now in an adversarial relationship. A return to the "Good Old Days" when harmony and cooperation had been achieved by allowing the university to be run as a feudal fiefdom (or, perhaps better, a concentric series of feudal fiefdoms) was quite impossible. The Faculty Association began to think about recognition as a collective bargaining agent under the Labour Relations Act (i.e., becoming a union). So, too, did various segments of the support staff, including maintenance workers and clerical

Student-faculty hockey game, c. 1970 (UMA).

people. The UMFA applied for certification as a union early in 1973, the first university faculty group to do so in English Canada.

Financial constraints also led to new concerns about the historic systems of decentralization carried over from the earlier days of the university. The U of M's library, for example, had continued throughout the 1960s to rank near the bottom of libraries of major universities in Canada, and, indeed, fell steadily behind those of other established institutions of higher learning in the nation. In a 1972 report, the university librarian blamed this situation in large part on the multiple-library system in effect at the university. He noted that the U of M library system in 1972 had twelve libraries and three reading rooms, one of the most complex systems west of the Lakehead. He observed that the new universities had universally eschewed a multiple system, although he did not add that the new universities of the 1960s had also avoided the college system and branch campuses. (They would later discover that student demand made branch campuses necessary.) The bottom line in 1972 was that a multiple-unit system appeared extremely cost-ineffective, and the units found themselves under increasing pressure to consolidate.

A number of important new student institutions were transformed or first emerged in the early years of the decade. In 1970 the first Festival of Life and Learning, sponsored by UMSU, the administration, and various other organizations, appeared for an entire week in February. The festival was a continuation of an annual celebration that went back to the 1950s, called the Festival of the Arts, but it was now

Ernest Sirluck

A native of Winkler, Manitoba, Sirluck graduated from the U of M in 1940. After serving overseas with the Canadian army, he obtained his MA and PhD from the University of Toronto. A respected Milton scholar, he taught at the University of Chicago and was vice-president of the University of Toronto before becoming president of the U of M in 1970.

Opposite: President Ernest Sirluck faces a crowd of student demonstrators during the CAIMAW strike in 1973 (photo: W. Heck).

considerably enlarged and broadened. It featured art, drama, music—especially rock music—movies, and invited outside speakers, often Americans, who were currently in the news. Some of the celebrity speakers and performers, such as Betty Friedan or Germaine Greer, drew huge crowds. For years, the festival was a rather heady week (or two) at the University Centre.

In early July of 1971, a student pub finally opened in University Centre, and a few days later the first UMSU alternate course guide, a supposedly critical look at the course offerings of the university, based on student questionnaires, was published. There had been earlier guides (the *Scoop* in 1962, edited by Melinda McCracken, or the *Score* in 1968) but this was the first publication to name names, actually identifying the professor whose course was being evaluated. These guides lasted until

Above: In the early 1970s, the *Manitoban* and much of UMSU took on the look of the international youth revolt. In 1972, for instance, as a protest against segregating the sexes in the student naprooms in University Centre, staff from the *Manitoban* and UMSU posed for this photo, which then appeared on the front page of the student newspaper (complete with black bars for modesty). Right: The cover of UMSU's 1972 student guide, *Tales of Terror*.

1976, and in their last years there was always a question as to whether they would be funded. They were perhaps less successful than those at some other universities, since most students at the U of M gave most professors reasonably good evaluations. A few months later, the Campus Gay Lib Club was formed as a social and cultural centre for male and female students at the university. In March 1972, the first president of FREE Gay Liberation of Minnesota spoke to a crowd of over 2000 in Campo in University Centre on "The Right to be Gay."

At the same time that new student institutions were appearing, many of the older student traditions appeared to be wasting away. In 1967 UMSU had stopped producing the annual yearbook, *The Brown and Gold*, ostensibly because nobody could be found to edit it, and

publication thereafter was irregular until the last issue appeared for 1975. There was no operetta/musical production by the Glee Club in 1970, ending an almost continuous run of production that had begun in 1927. The reason given was "lack of student interest." The musicals were never revived. Formal and semi-formal dances virtually vanished, except at graduation, replaced by the "social." Public debating by students ceased to be a popular spectator sport, as it had been since the beginning of the century. Debates became a purely rhetorical device, as was the case in 1971 when Cy Gonick and Ruben Bellan (both faculty members in the economics department) debated the Gray report on American ownership in Canada before a capacity crowd in the Multi-Purpose Room of University Centre. Gonick was also editor of *Canadian Dimension* and later an MLA with the NDP government. The issue of foreign ownership was an important one in Canada at the time, particularly among left-wing nationalists.

Student participation in intramural sports also continued to fade; in 1970–71, male participation was only 38 percent of total enrolment, and many of those who played were involved in more than one sport, thus being double-counted. Whether the situation with varsity athletics represented a decline from earlier times was arguable. The U of M fielded both men's and women's teams in most major sports in the 1970s, and each year brought home two or three regional or national championships. In the 1971–72 academic year, for example, Bisons teams won WCIAA championships in men's soccer, women's volleyball, and women's field hockey, and the women's volleyball team went to the national finals. Support for these teams was confined largely to the physical education complex. Spectator attendance at varsity games was generally low. Teams heading off to regional or national tournaments were not sent off by campus-wide pep rallies, or greeted upon their return (even if triumphant) by large numbers of students. From 1971 to 1974 the

student body could not even read about these teams in the pages of the student newspaper, which deliberately ignored competitive sports. No U of M athlete or athletic team in this period captured the fancy of either the outside or the student public. As budget cutting increased, there were ever louder mutterings to be heard about the amounts of money being spent on varsity athletics.

In September of 1972, the *'Toban* reported that UMSU "has hit the national news again" by releasing the highly confidential U of M annual budget in its 1972–73 student handbook, *Tales of Terror*. The source of the leak was not known, and various members of the BoG and Senate blustered about the breach of confidentiality to no avail. The newspaper had great fun comparing the salary and perks of President Sirluck with those of the prime minister of Canada, the premier of Manitoba, and other leading politicians, pointing out how much more remuneration Sirluck was receiving than the various elected officials. It managed to suggest that an unwillingness to make such information public was behind the budget secrecy.

A month later *The Manitoban* itself became the news. The newspaper, under editor Maria Horvath, had begun a series of changes in policy in the autumn of 1972. On 10 October 1972, for example, the paper announced a new sports-reporting policy, under which no article or feature

Student protester, 1976, (UMA).

promoting the competitive aspects of sports, including scores, would be published. The policy notice, presumably written by Horvath, emphasized that "the 'Toban will feature the recreational aspects of sports, hopefully encouraging those of us less skilled students who have been too timid to participate. Articles will deal with the sports facilities on campus, all the various participatory sports (play just for the fun of it), some of the more exotic forms of recreation such as sky diving and yoga, and analyses of the politics of sports." For several years thereafter, a highly successful series of U of M varsity teams won national championships without being mentioned in the campus newspaper. The 'Toban shortly thereafter dropped its twice-weekly edition and moved to one issue a week. It also began a new advertising policy, under which it would not accept ads that the editorial staff deemed offensive. At the same time, the newspaper remained resolutely focussed beyond the campus, running stories on Vietnam, American foreign policy, women's liberation, the growth of international agribusiness, and the Churchill Falls diversions and their threats to Aboriginal people. The newspaper soon found itself being heavily criticized by UMSU, which controlled the purse strings of the paper.

There were two issues between UMSU and the newspaper. One was that the *Manitoban* was not adequately covering campus events. The other concern between UMSU and the newspaper was that the 'Toban's editorial policies were leading the newspaper into financial difficulties. According to the *Tribune*, the *Manitoban* required advertising representing one-third of its space in order to break even, and it was running at a steady 28 percent. In February 1973, editor Horvath was impeached by UMSU but later reinstated. The reinstatement was followed by the resignation of UMSU president Bill Balan and an announcement by Horvath that she was resigning as editor in order to work toward a true editorial collective. That there was not more pressure on the *Manitoban* in the early 1970s to moderate or cease its radical ideology suggests that many students, while not sharing the newspaper's politics, were probably pleased enough to have access to its perspective. That point of view, which they could not get anywhere else in the community, certainly was student-oriented.

In the meantime, while certification of the Faculty Association worked its way slowly through the bureaucratic machinery, AESES (Association of Employees Supporting Education Services) became quickly certified in May 1973 to represent all employees at the university except academic staff, those employed in academic capacities, and those covered by other unions. It was hardly the first bargaining unit on campus, but AESES was easily the biggest, encompassing 1200 workers in all corners of the university. One of the reasons that so many workers unionized in the early 1970s was the double-digit inflation that characterized the Canadian economy in those years. Subsequent 1973 BoG negotiations with AESES led to a collective agreement, but the university was unable to reach a similar agreement with the Canadian Association of Industrial Mechanical and Allied Workers

(CAIMAW, local 9), representing the Operations and Maintenance and Food Service people. In October 1973, local 9 walked off the job, beginning a twenty-two-day strike, which disrupted the campus and caused both controversy and demonstrations. This first major strike at the university came as a shock to many.

Soon after the settlement of the CAIMAW strike, the university's professoriate voted in favour of unionization. The vote, announced on 6 December 1973, was 562 in favour and 415 against. Eighty-five percent of those eligible to vote had cast a ballot, and 57 percent of those

voting were in favour of unionization. Unionization had been hotly contested, with the anti-union faction led by Professor Brian Scarfe of Economics. The university agreed to drop the legal question of whether the Faculty Association was really a union, and Senate subsequently recommended to the BoG that a joint committee be established to settle the status of the statutory powers of Senate, should UMFA become certified. The Labour Board announced in November of 1974 that UMFA was granted its certification.

Opposite: By the 1970s, only engineering students continued the tradition of student pranks. In 1976, for example, they assembled a small car inside the office of the Dean of Engineering. This tradition continued into the 1980s, when, for instance, students somehow placed a car on top of the Tier Building (WFP). Below: Protest in support of the AESES strike, 1975 (UMA).

Baldur Stefansson, whose work in the Department of Plant Science was instrumental in the development of canola, now one of Canada's most important crops (photo: Department of Plant Science).

Amid the changes and reorganization that the university experienced during this period, important research developments continued to take place. At the medical school, a team led by Dr. Henry Friesen continued work on hormone research. A graduate of the university, Friesen had discovered the protein prolactin while doing post-graduate work in the 1960s. After returning to the university as professor of physiology in 1973, his research team continued its work on prolactin, which has been instrumental in helping men and women with reproductive problems, and includes the development of a simple blood test to identify high levels of this hormone. This same research laboratory has investigated and provided care for people with pituitary deficiencies. Friesen also discovered two other hormones, one of which has been identified and is now synthetically reproduced to help short-statured children.

Starting in the late 1960s, a research team led by Dr. Baldur Stefansson in the Department of Plant Sciences, Faculty of Agriculture, had been working with other researchers to develop rapeseed to make it more useful and accepted. Stefansson's team increased the oil and meal protein content of rapeseed, and, by 1974, had produced a new variant of rapeseed, which has subsequently been trademarked as "canola." Canola is now the most valuable crop grown in Manitoba, and over five million hectares are cultivated annually throughout the world.

Early in 1974, a university Centennial Committee was established under co-chairs Professor Murray Donnelly of University College and James Burns of Great West Life to

plan the celebrations for the 100th anniversary of the establishment of the university. The centennial subcommittee considered as possible centennial edifices a winter sports complex, a performing arts theatre, and library expansion to be financed through a capital fundraising campaign. The student newspaper reported in November that the subcommittee had rejected a performing arts theatre, partly because nobody

Fort Garry campus, facing west from the Administration Building, winter 1975 (UMA).

on the committee championed it, partly because it would be hard to raise money for such a project in the Winnipeg cultural community. The Centennial Committee itself recommended the sports project to Senate, which supported the recommendation but added that the university should ask the government to commemorate the anniversary with a major capital project specifically designed as a centennial project. While the committee discussed these important matters, the university experienced its first streakers when three male students rushed through the Commerce Lounge dressed only in sneakers and hoods.

The centennial celebrations were still under discussion while the appointment of physicist Donald Wells as a university vice-president created a brief diversion at Senate. Wells was American-born and a landed immigrant. An undercurrent of concern had long existed about the number of Americans brought to the university in the period of expansion, but had never before surfaced. In response to questions about the proportion of Canadians at the U of M, President Sirluck reported to Senate that 83 percent of the senior administration were Canadian, 84 percent of the deans and assistant deans were Canadian, and 70 percent of the

The Festival of Life and Learning was an important event in the 1970s. Guest speakers included David Suzuki, seen visiting the Department of Botany in 1977 (W. Heck).

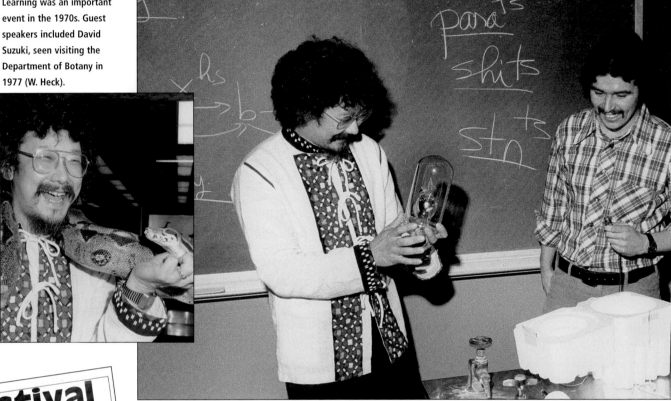

WOLF HECK

professoriate were Canadian. He added that 95 percent of the non-Canadians on faculty had landed immigrant status. Sirluck refused to consider the possibility of a minimum quota system, saying, "Quotas are harmful and restrictive."

As the campus grew and more students used their own cars to get to school, parking became a major issue. The beginning of the academic year 1974–75 saw significant changes to parking enforcement on the campus. The police force was raised to eighteen members, and, more significantly, for the first time the parking tickets were made legal summonses instead of informal demands for payment not enforceable in the courts. The police were also given the power to tow cars illegally parked, and the cost of recovery of the vehicle was set at $15. For the first time, ticketing was done in faculty lots as well as in student and staff lots.

The matter of centennial buildings was considered in the midst of well-publicized concerns over shortages of space at the university and the ongoing saga of fiscal restraints in the province and at the university. In January 1975, the Senate Planning and Priorities Committee forecast a shortage of over 400,000 square feet at the university by 1978, with the biggest problems in dentistry, administrative studies, and education.

Student registration, c. 1975 (UMA).

Commerce prof E.R. Vogt attempted to run for senior stick in his faculty to publicize its financial and space shortages. The university was also being pressed to renovate Taché Hall by an otherwise unsung student organization named the Resident Students Association (RSA), which had spent much labour preparing a brief to the administration in the autumn of 1974. Taché was in sad shape in the early 1970s, the home of radiator pipes that clanked, rattled, and burst. Many rooms, it was rumoured, still contained the original furniture of World War II (or was it 1912?).

The RSA was actually one of the success stories of the student movement for self-government.

Formed out of independent house councils in the 1960s, the RSA took over the government and discipline of the residence halls (Taché and Mary Speechly) in the early 1970s, and in the process acquired considerable freedom in social matters. It organized social activities (including a Sunday night movie), initiated the construction of the Condo Lounge, and lobbied for a coeducational section of Taché Hall. The RSA members were nothing if not bold. At one point, the famous international photographer Yosef Karsh was invited to judge the residence's photo competition. Surprisingly, he accepted, and donated to the residence a print of one of his photographs of

Researching the University's Centennial

As a research assistant for the University Centennial Committee, I had the marvelous opportunity--unique perhaps in the University's first century-- to learn more about this institution than any previous student, for I was hired to produce a variety of historical and contemporary information on the University for use in its centennial year, 1977.

For instance, I plotted the University's revenues and grants from 83 years of financial records and Council Minutes (a fire destroyed records previous to 1898); I counted 79,641 degrees granted in 75 years of Convocation Books. To produce these and other facts and figures I checked stories in 520 issues of the Bulletin, consulted innumerable Alumni Journals, reports, studies, manuals and minutes, words without end! I visited the vaults and the rare books room, the inner sanctums of the University's might and any back corners or hidden lofts where records are sometimes stored.

Plotting University grants and revenues caused the grey hairs on my head to multiply. How, I asked, does one show, on a single graph, the rise in the provincial government grant from $250--yes, two hundred and fifty dollars--in 1878, to $50 million in 1975? I worked valiantly and produced a strident graph 12 feet long! A graph, twelve feet long? I am keeping it as a souvenir while the Centennial Committee records contain a very demure and controllable 16-inch effort! In the course of this exercise I came across some unusual sources of University revenue. Did you know that in 1903 permits to cut hay on University premises yielded $275.55 to campus coffers, or that provincial marriage licence fees, in 1884, contributed $3,756.49? And that in 1975, the sale of University ice-cream and dairy products produced $266,098 for these erudite halls of learning, and parking fees another $297,080?

Working with graphs and statistics, however, was not the major part of my assignment. I interviewed exactly 116 deans, directors, department heads, professors and administrators, to "document and determine"--the wording of my official directive--the activities and achievements of the University. And was I impressed. This University had produced so many outstanding graduates, household names like Marshall McLuhan, or J.W. Pickersgill, Margaret Laurence or John Hirsch, to mention only a few. It has on its faculty academics like historian W.L. Morton or mathematician George Gratzer, scholars who are internationally recognized and respected as authorities in their disciplines. But most of all, it was the accomplishments of the University during its first century which excited me the most. Indeed, they are something to be proud of, achievements to boast about which would require volumes to audit fully.

Vera Fast graduated from the university with a PhD in 1984, and was a research assistant to its Centennial Committee. Excerpt from the Alumni Journal (1976).

Winston Churchill. After much delay, the province finally agreed in 1977 to renovate Taché.

Through the UGC, on 27 February 1975, the Manitoba government refused to give firm assurances of special consideration for the university, including any money for the construction of new buildings. The UGC projected no new construction in its grants for the next two years. The BoG in turn accepted the president's recommendations for financial restraint, especially in staff replacement. The university had once again run up a large deficit, which stood at $3,835,492 as of 31 March 1975. The province had announced partial relief on the deficit under stringent conditions. The university would have to liquidate its deficit in five years (later increased to ten) and would have to strike a balanced budget for fiscal

University of Manitoba
UM100
1877-1977

In 1977, the university's centennial logo appeared in many guises, including flower beds (above) and a bumper sticker (left) (UMA).

1975–76. The operating grant announced the same day was calculated as a 25 percent increase, but the university claimed it was really only 20 percent. *The Manitoban* headline on this story was "U of M Shafted!"

Labour problems soon were once again added to the mix of public controversy. In early March 1975, AESES took a strike vote and was on the picket lines by 20 March. This strike of 1100 support workers—clerical, technical, administrative, and computer personnel—bit deeply into the operations of the university as it

WOLF HECK

was coming up to final examinations and convocation. Many students were conflicted. UMSU announced that it supported the demands of the union but not the work stoppage. The issues were mainly over money, as the workers continued to chase inflation. This strike was a nasty one, including the arrest of nine people at a mass picket on University Crescent on 2 April. Winnipeg Transit drivers honoured the strike and refused to drive buses past the picket lines. The examination period was completed with difficulty, but convocation had to be cancelled. Not until 10 May did the AESES workers return to the job. The strike also further delayed the publication of the president's annual report for 1973 to 1975, which did not appear until after the strike was settled. When the report finally appeared, it was quite different in form from its predecessors, which went back continuously to 1920. Instead of a short report by the president and longer ones by the various units, this one was "a comprehensive report of the University's activities written from a single perspective."

President Sirluck announced in July that he was stepping down, effective in 1976. The

WOLF HECK

Winnipeg press subsequently reported that he would receive an annual $36,000 pension upon his retirement, as well as other financial benefits he had negotiated at the time of his acceptance of the appointment. In August of 1975, the university and UMFA reached agreement on a first contract, a one-year agreement. One of the support unions, Services Employees International Union (SEIU), at about the same time, rejected an offer of a 22 percent salary increase in the first eight months and 6 percent thereafter. As for the UGC, it rejected outright in August a university budget request for a 33 percent increase. W.J. Condo (now of the UGC) claimed publicly that the university was overstaffed and proliferating courses. He said about 100 professors were currently on sabbatical leave and had not been replaced, indicating the extent of the overstaffing. Moreover, there were far too many courses with extremely low enrolments. In October the university scaled back its budget request to 20 percent.

By the mid-1970s, virtually the only faculty on campus that still engaged in communal pranks, some of them misguided, was the

Throughout the 1970s and into the 1980s, student involvement in politics remained high. During the 1980 federal election, Pierre Trudeau spoke to an overflow crowd at University Centre (W. Heck). During the same visit (opposite page), Trudeau was greeted on campus by President Ralph Campbell (W. Heck).

Right: A large crowd turns out for NDP leader Ed Broadbent at University Centre during the 1980 election (W. Heck). Opposite: Starting in the late 1960s and into the 1970s, many students began to frequent places like The Fireplace, a lounge just north of the university that featured live folk and rock music.

WOLF HECK

Faculty of Engineering. On 23 January 1976, the engineers created an extension of H-Lot on the third floor of the Engineering Building in front of the dean's office. A lime green Volkswagon convertible, licence number 4-ME, was delivered at night to the dean's door with a sign indicating that it was for the dean's use until Friday. The dean said he had planned to use it to ride the corridors, but "they flattened all the tires."

By the beginning of 1976, the plans for the centennial celebration in 1977 were well underway, less, of course, any new buildings. There were to be three special convocations, the first beginning on 28 February 1977, the actual birthday of the university. This special convocation would be attended by 100 of the university's most distinguished graduates, chosen by alumni and the Centennial Committee. Each guest would get a medal commemorating the event. This plan was subsequently abandoned, and a public evening and party (tickets $1.00 per person) were substituted for the convocation. A May convocation would be held on campus, and mini-convocations would also be held in Thompson, Dauphin, and Brandon. The homecoming convocation would be in October. The Centennial Committee planned special souvenir pamphlets showing the development of the university, and former president Hugh Saunderson was asked to prepare his memoirs. While the Centennial Committee felt obliged to defend spending $85,000 on the event, other observers expressed private surprise that so little had been organized, apart from the non-existent buildings.

In early February of 1976, Senate considered a report by Professor A.M.C. Waterman, chair of the committee, to re-examine the part played by student fees in the university's total revenue. The Waterman report called for an end to the de facto moratorium on tuition increases, which had existed for the past ten years. It insisted that in future the fee structure of faculties should reflect the relative cost of the education provided, which meant that expensive faculties like medicine should be charging higher fees. It also recommended that there be no differential fees set for out-of-province students. In a private working paper on university fees, not part of his report, which was leaked to the press, Waterman argued for the need eventually to set fees at full cost, subsidizing those who could not afford to pay them on the principle that consumers rather than producers should be subsidized. Waterman's report was highly controversial and fiercely debated in the Senate, which eventually, in a close vote, approved it.

A centennial building came closer to reality in April 1976. The government refused to provide the full cost of an addition to the Dafoe Library as a centennial project, but suggested it might be willing to cost-share the construction on the basis of $2 of provincial funding for every $1 raised by the university. A month later, the BoG agreed to the proposed cost-sharing arrangement. The new library addition would add 1700 square metres to the facility and cost about $3 million. BoG chair W.R. McQuade subsequently proposed, and the BoG accepted,

that there be a centennial project combining a sports complex and a library addition on a cost-sharing basis, with the government putting up $4 million and the university $2 million. The UGC recommended this arrangement to the cabinet in September. While the government sat on the recommendation over the early autumn of 1976, opposition grew to a proposal by the UMSU president that UMSU contribute half a million dollars to the university's share of the project.

The opposition emphasized that such a contribution would increase student fees for many years, and the debate was carried on in the context of a series of price increases announced by the university for the new academic year. Parking fees were raised, increasing for students to $55 with a plug. Parking fines increased from $2 to $5. Food prices in the university's facilities were increased an average of 15 percent. The NDP government decided late in October that it would fund a centennial building project only to a maximum of $2 million. If there were to be two buildings, the university would have to raise more money than it had previously anticipated. In early November, UMSU voted by secret ballot 13–7 against the half-million-dollar

BOB TALBOT

contribution to the centennial projects. Shortly thereafter, the NDP Provincial Council demonstrated its suspicions of the university's financial arrangements by passing resolutions calling for a full accounting of university spending and a more open budget.

While the debate raged over the centennial projects, Dr. Ralph Campbell assumed the helm as the new president of the university. Campbell was born on an Ontario dairy farm, served in the RAF and won two Distinguished Flying Crosses before studying agricultural economics and becoming Dean of Scarborough College at

the University of Toronto. One of the serious problems he had to face was that of organized labour on the campus. In September of 1976, eight of the nine support staff bargaining units had contracts about to expire. Later that month, UMFA was awarded a 9.25 percent salary increase by an arbitrator, and it ratified the contract early in October. But there were threatened strikes by Canadian Union of Public Employees (CUPE) workers at the Health Sciences Centre and by the Campus Police, members of CAIMAW. In January of 1977, AESES rejected the university's offer, and was subsequently angered by the employer's refusal to agree to arbitration. As 1977 opened, the university was still at loggerheads with three of the five major support staff unions—CUPE, SEIU, and AESES—whose contracts were still unsettled.

The publication in 1976 of a report on Canadian Studies by Professor Thomas Symons of Trent University, entitled *To Know Ourselves,* once again called attention to the special problems of curricula and staffing at Canadian universities. The report was concerned that not enough Canadian content was being taught in many courses, and worried that the appointment of non-Canadians contributed to this deficiency. In September of 1976, in a paper to Senate, President Campbell outlined a series of policies and procedures to fill academic positions at the university by Canadians, naturalized citizens, and landed immigrants. A non-Canadian would be considered only if no suitable Canadian applicant was available. Senate accepted this policy, and, subsequently, debated a recommendation that the university appoint a director of Canadian Studies with a sizeable budget of between $40,000 and $50,000. In his 1976–77 presidential report, Campbell noted with pride, "We have paid considerable attention to Canadian Studies and, not surprisingly, have discovered that the Canadian content of our curricula and our research is substantial." The "Canadian Question" emerged again late in 1977, when several members of the psychology department were publicly critical of the department's hiring policies, claiming that Canadians were disadvantaged in the process.

The engineering student band, c. 1975 (UMA).

In 1976, first-year enrolment fell from 3078 in 1973 to 2570 in 1976. This substantial decline would be felt through the entire university for several years to come.

In November UMSU passed a motion asking the university to enforce no-smoking areas, including classrooms. A chorus of student complaints emerged about the shortage of computer facilities on the campus. Most of the complaints came from the Computer Studies students and referred to the small number of computer terminals and line-ups at card readers and keypunchers. Major speakers at the 1977 Festival of Life and Learning included David Suzuki, Irving Layton, Judy Chicago (creator of *The Dinner Party*), Tom Symons, and Robin Mathews, the latter two both advocates of Canadian Studies. The same year, the CRTC turned down a request from CJUM-FM, the campus radio station founded in 1975, to relax its restrictions on advertising so that the station could obtain more revenue. In order to survive,

Ditchball game, c. 1980
(UMA).

increase in 1977, raising the students' cost for a space with a plug from $55 to $90. Some members of Senate stalled the fee increase in late February by successfully moving to table the motions, saying they wanted a clear notion of where the added revenue would go. As a symbol of its opposition to the increases, UMSU refused to participate in Centennial Day celebrations and cancelled its programme of student activities for the centennial. In March Senate finally approved the fee increase for 8000 students in fifteen faculties.

The actual centennial ceremony was held in University Centre on 28 February 1977 before "a surprisingly small crowd," reported the *Manitoban*. Conspicuous by their absence were Premier Schreyer, Mayor Juba, and the president of UMSU. University historian W.L. Morton presented an interesting account of the founding of the university in 1977, but because of a poor sound system, he was not audible in much of the room in which he spoke. The premier performance of the "University of Manitoba March 1877–1977," by composer John Greer, was given by the U of M Chorus and Symphony Orchestra. The formal programme was followed by a dance in the Multi-Purpose Room, with music provided by Jimmy King's Golden Boy Brass. Those in attendance agreed that the birthday cake and other goodies provided by Food Services were very good.

Subsequent centennial events were less fraught with trouble. The series of three centennial lectures in the spring of 1977, sponsored by IBM, were all attended by several thousand spectators each. One of the lectures was actually a panel discussion on "The Artist in

CJUM-FM mounted a public fundraising campaign and easily exceeded its target of $30,000. It closed a few years later, however.

After some delay, recommendations for tuition fee increases finally went to Senate in February of 1977. The increases were modest but were seen by opponents as the thin edge of the wedge. Several critics of tuition increases pointed to what had happened to parking as an illustration of the dangers. After the substantial increase in parking fees in 1976, the Parking Committee recommended another massive

Canada," featuring five of the university's more distinguished graduates: Adele Wiseman, Barry Broadfoot, John Hirsch, filmmaker Roman Kroiter, and Manitoba's deputy minister of culture, Mary Liz Baker. The May convocations, held at the university and, for the first time, in three communities outside Winnipeg (Thompson, Brandon, and Dauphin), were great successes. Isabel Auld was installed as the first female chancellor; she served three terms in the post. Born in Winnipeg, Auld was a graduate of the University of Saskatchewan (in biology) and for many years had been involved in volunteer activities in Winnipeg. The Homecoming Convocation in October also went well. A subsequent centennial symposium on "Values and Morals in Modern Life," sponsored by Great West Life, brought leading thinkers to talk to large audiences. Among the nine speakers were neurologist Sir Roger Bannister, broadcaster June Callwood, economist Robert Heilbroner, and author Jessica Mitford.

The Christmas holidays in the centennial year were marked by the first general closure of the entire university for the season. Many faculty and students complained that the closure, intended to save money in operating costs, had not been properly debated or publicized. On a less contentious front, over the winter of 1977, a new outdoor game was invented by a group of architecture students who found themselves in a ditch on Hecla Island on a field trip with nothing much to do. The game was called Ditchball, and the rules were quickly regularized. The ditch became a standard size of thirty metres in length, over

Ralph Campbell

A native of southern Ontario, Campbell studied at the University of Toronto and at Oxford as a Rhodes Scholar. An agricultural economist, before becoming the university's eighth president (1976 to 1981), he was principal of Scarborough College. Campbell has also been very active in international development, and has been an economic advisor to governments in Jordan and Kenya.

four metres in depth, with an ice-playing surface three metres wide by thirty metres long with a dog leg curve. The object was to get the ball into the opponent's goal by kicking or throwing, but not by carrying it. The size of teams varied, but could include up to 100 players. The ball became a uniform foam "rhombacubeoctahedron" of twenty-five sides, twenty centimetres in diameter. With the centennial sport invention of Ditchball, the first hundred years of the University of Manitoba drew to a close.

Epilogue

It is too early to write a proper or satisfactory history of the last twenty-five years of the University of Manitoba. It is difficult for any historian to have enough distance (or access to information) needed to deal with events that are often still in process in the life of an institution as large and as diverse as the University of Manitoba. Instead, this epilogue is devoted to describing a few of the major achievements and exciting developments at the university in the period since the centennial anniversary of 1977. Not intended as a history, it is, rather, an illustrative celebration of some of the wonderful things that can happen on a university campus.

The external and internal tensions that often beset the university during the 1970s were not, unfortunately, followed by easier times in the subsequent two decades. Those decades, the last two of the twentieth century, were difficult for most public institutions in all parts of the world. In North America, this was a period of prolonged, and sometimes extreme, financial restraint. For educational institutions, fiscal trials were only partially mitigated by new expectations, often led by dramatic changes in technology. The challenges, while in some ways exhilarating, were usually very hard to meet. The University of Manitoba was not spared many of the difficulties of the period. However, the university undertook a successful fundraising campaign, and the Centennial Campaign, launched in the university's centennial year of 1977, raised $8 million from

Opposite: The Administration Building (photo: Bob Tinker).

Students of the joint U of M and University of Zambia programme in agriculture, 1983 (UMA).

the private sector, matched by $4 million in government funding. After 1977, the university had to deal with cuts to funding coupled with the financial demands of an ageing infrastructure, both physical and human.

Despite these problems, the university did survive the pressures of the 1980s and early 1990s, and it did continue to grow and develop. If there is one theme that seems to predominate in these two decades, it may well be "outreach." Over the past quarter-century, the university and its people clearly have become increasingly aware of their social and educational responsibilities, not just to the student body, but also to the larger community at both the local and international levels.

In 1977, for example, through its Faculty of Agriculture, the university began one of its most successful collaborations with a university in the developing world when it was awarded a large Canadian International Development Agency (CIDA) grant to help "Zambianize" the University of Zambia's School of Agricultural Sciences. That collaboration ran from 1978 to 1982. A team of Canadians was sent to Lusaka to teach and to establish field trials in wheat, triticale, and animal science. Another part of the project involved bringing Zambian nationals to Canada for graduate training, and several of these students studied at the Fort Garry campus. In an effort to ensure that the students would not become estranged from their native land by their experience in Canada, the students were then financed to return to Zambia with their supervisors for field trials.

The university has continued this international outreach, both with CIDA and with other organizations. A recent major project has involved China. Since 1990, U of M professors have administered six major CIDA-supported projects in five Chinese universities. All these projects have provided educational and research skills for Chinese professors and students that increase their capacity to operate internationally. All have involved exchanges of faculty and students between Manitoba and China, a meeting process that occurs on and off the university campus and has benefitted both the Chinese and the Canadians.

Outreach has not been confined to the international level. One of the most important community outreach programmes of the university began in 1978, when Joyce Fromson of Physical Education started planning the outreach sports programme for children that would become the University of Manitoba Sports Camps (first opened in the summer of 1979) and the University of Manitoba Mini-University (first opened in the summer of 1981). These programmes have provided enjoyment for thousands of youngsters over the years, as well as summer employment for hundreds of U of M students. They have shown that recreational activity designed to be accessible to all can be "fun," and that children aged ten to fifteen years are extremely eager to gain exposure to the intellectual and academic life of the university. The Mini-University programme has combined recreation with access

Arnold Naimark

A native of Winnipeg, Naimark received his MD from the U of M, and served as head of the department of physiology and later as dean of the Faculty of Medicine before becoming the U of M's ninth president (1981 to 1996). He has also had a distinguished career in public service outside the university, and has been the chair of groups such as Winnipeg's North Portage Development Corporation and the Canadian Biotechnology Advisory Committee.

Rhodes Scholars

In the past 30 years, students from the U of M have won more Rhodes Scholarships than students from any other university in western Canada and the university ranks third in Canada. Through its history, U of M Rhodes Scholars have made their mark in Canada and the world. Here is just a sample of past U of M Rhodes Scholars:

1922	Graham Spry	one of the founders of the CBC
1931	W.L. Morton	one of Canada's best-known historians
1933	James Coyne	Governor, the Bank of Canada, 1958-1962
1950	Murray Smith	long-time Manitoba public educator
1951	Alan Gotlieb	civil servant and diplomat
1953	William Norrie	mayor of Winnipeg, 1979-1992
1966	Wilson Parasiuk	civil servant and cabinet minister

Mini-University students and teaching staff, summer 2000. Mini-University is a U of M innovation that has been imitated by many other universities in Canada and the U.S.

to a variety of university departments. These outreach programmes have served as the models for similar programmes across the continent, and are probably the U of M "innovations" that have been most copied by others in the United States and Canada.

In a different type of community responsibility and outreach, the university played a critical role in hosting the Pan American Games in 1999, as it had in 1967. The thirteenth Pan Am Games brought to Winnipeg

more than 5000 athletes from forty-one countries, participating in forty-one sports. Most of the competitors were housed in an Athletes Village set up on the Fort Garry campus, which included Taché Hall, Mary Speechly Hall, St. John's College, St. Andrew's College, and University College, as well as the recently completed Helen Glass Nursing Building. The Max Bell Centre was the site for roller sports (hockey and artistic); a new Investors Group Athletic Centre, constructed in preparation for the games, was used for volleyball, basketball, and rhythmic gymnastics; and University Stadium, constructed for the 1967 games, was pressed back into service, with an upgraded track. The indoor track at the Max Bell Fieldhouse was replaced, and more than a million dollars spent in upgrading university residence facilities. Despite tight security, a carnival atmosphere often prevailed throughout the campus as athletes from many countries mingled with university and public volunteers.

The Pan Am Games provide an excellent illustration of the way in which outreach can be beneficial to the institution extending the assistance, as the university received a considerable boost to its facilities in the process of hosting the event. But outreach can work in the reverse as well, and the university has been the direct, as well as the indirect, recipient of generosity. In 1951, through the efforts of Manitoba's Icelandic community, a chair of Icelandic was endowed. This long connection between the university, Iceland and Icelandic-Canadians was continued in 1999 when, as part of the Icelandic millennium celebrations, the Government of Iceland, the Eimskip Shipping Company, and the University of Iceland

Eimskip Fund announced a $1 million millennium gift to support the university's unique Icelandic library collection. Begun in 1936 with major donations of materials from Manitoba's own Icelandic community, the university library's Icelandic collection now contains nearly 27,000 volumes. It is the largest collection of printed Icelandic materials in Canada and the second in North America only to the 32,000-volume collection at Cornell University. The Icelandic gift, coupled with fundraising within the Icelandic-Canadian community, enabled the construction of a new reading room and study centre for Icelandic studies at the Elizabeth Dafoe Library, which was opened in October 2000 by Davíð Oddsson, the Prime Minister of Iceland.

The university's 1987 "Drive for Excellence" fundraising campaign was another example of being the direct recipient of generosity. That campaign was launched with a goal of $42 million, the largest of any fundraising campaign in western Canada at the time. The final achievement of the "Drive for Excellence" was

Some of the several thousand international athletes who enjoyed the hospitality of the U of M's Athletes Village during the 1999 Winnipeg Pan Am Games.

XIII Pan Am Games
Winnipeg '99

PAULA HORECZY

A ceremonial dancer at the annual Graduation Pow Wow, celebrating the achievement of U of M Aboriginal students.

spectrometry work at the U of M is helping researchers better understand large biological molecules. A continent away, groundbreaking research by the U of M's Dr. Frank Plummer at a clinic in Nairobi, Kenya, is leading the search for a possible vaccine against the HIV virus. Since the 1980s, Plummer, a U of M graduate and professor of microbiology and internal medicine, has been exploring the natural immunity a group of Nairobi prostitutes appear to have to HIV. The source of their immunity may hold the key to the development of an HIV vaccine.

Teaching, research, and outreach have all been combined in the creation of the university's Department of Native Studies. The genesis of the department and other programmes lay in the creation in 1970 of the Indian Metis Eskimo Students' Association (IMESA), whose first president was Ovide Mercredi. IMESA worked to increase awareness of the needs of the university's Aboriginal students, and eventually helped to lead to the creation of the Department of Native Studies in 1975. Only the third such department to be formed in a Canadian university, it now offers both undergraduate and graduate courses. The university itself has since developed many outreach programs to encourage and assist Aboriginal students, and hosts an annual Graduation Pow Wow for Aboriginal students. Since the early 1970s, many U of M graduates have become leaders in the First Nations community, including Mercredi and Phil Fontaine, both of whom were National Chiefs of the Assembly of First Nations; playwright Ian Ross; and Justice Murray Sinclair, co-chair of Manitoba's Aboriginal Justice Inquiry.

$55 million from the private sector and a grant of $13 million from the Province of Manitoba, for a total of $68 million.

In the last two decades, the university's tradition of research has also continued in many fields. Faculty from the Department of Physics and Astronomy, for instance, now operate the world's most accurate and highest resolution deflection type mass spectrometer. Mass

The university has also felt its responsibility to the rest of the Canadian university community. In 1986, it hosted the two-week annual meeting of Canada's learned societies. Under the direction of Professor Ed Rea, the university prepared for an ongoing meeting of more than 5000 delegates, about half of whom opted for on-campus accommodation, as well as displays by forty-nine scholarly publishers. More than fifty students volunteered to assist, many of whom wore a bilingual T-shirt that read "I told 2500 learneds where to go." Food services organized a staff of 300 to deal with ordinary meals and 114 special functions. A large beer tent set up between Robson Hall and

University College was a great success, particularly appreciated because of a heat wave (with temperatures over 30 degrees Celsius) for the first week of the meetings. Less appreciated, of course, was the infestation of mosquitoes brought on by the hot weather. A fifteen-day meeting with a few minor glitches but no major disasters was a triumph for both the university and the local organizers.

On another national front, in 1987 Senate established the Centre for Higher Education Research and Development (CHERD). Among a variety of responsibilities, CHERD expanded a range of management development programmes that had been created earlier by the Office of

A strikers' march during the U of M Faculty Association strike in 1996. This bitter confrontation was the longest faculty strike in English-speaking Canada to that time (UMFA).

Award-Winning Authors

Over the years, U of M faculty and alumni have won many literary awards. W.O. Mitchell and Paul Hiebert, for instance, won the Leacock Award for Humour. U of M faculty and graduates have won many Governor General Awards, beginning with Bertram Brooker in 1934, who was then teaching at what would become the university's School of Art.

1934	Think of the Earth	Bertram Brooker
1946	Colony to Nation	A.R.M. Lower
1947	The Tin Flute (translation)	Gabrielle Roy
1949	The Red Heart	James Reaney
1950	The Progressive Party in Canada	W.L. Morton
1956	The Sacrifice	Adele Wiseman
1957	Street of Riches (translation)	Gabrielle Roy
1958	A Suit of Nettles	James Reaney
1962	The Gutenberg Galaxy	Marshall McLuhan
1962	Twelve Letters to a Small Town	James Reaney
1966	A Jest of God	Margaret Laurence
1974	The Diviners	Margaret Laurence
1977	Ces enfants de ma vie	Gabrielle Roy
1987	A Dream Like Mine	M.T. Kelly
1993	The Stone Diaries*	Carol Shields
1997	fareWel	Ian Ross

*also won the Pulitzer Prize

Above right: Carol Shields, just one of the many award-winning writers who have studied or taught at the U of M. Shields, author of the Pulitzer Prize-winning novel *The Stone Diaries*, taught for many years in the university's English department (MWG).

Higher Education Management. These courses included the Senior University Administrators Course and the University Management Course, which were and are still recognized as the nation's principal training programmes for senior and middle-level university administrators. These programmes have also been offered internationally and widely copied.

CHERD's other activities have included an instructional development unit directed at the U of M, and an active research and publications section.

Outreach in its various guises has been important. But so too has been the creation of innovative academic infrastructures. The U of M Libraries acquired its first manuscript collection in 1960. In 1978 Richard Bennett joined the university library staff and began the development of the university's Archives & Special Collections. The Archives have since become an important repository of several types of historical records. It is the official keeper of the university's records, a documentary record that, particularly since 1945, is absolutely massive; it sits in the Archives, waiting for

someone to produce a full-scale university history. In 1981 the Archives also became the home of the records, or "morgue files," of the *Winnipeg Tribune,* which had ceased publication abruptly in 1980. Founded in 1890, the *Tribune* had long been Manitoba's second-largest newspaper, and its archives provide an invaluable record of the province's history. With over 150,000 photographs and over 2.5 million clippings, the *Tribune* collection keeps a major source of Winnipeg and Manitoba history accessible to the public. In 1992 the Archives also established an archives of the agricultural experience, intended to record the many roles that agriculture has played in the history of the Prairie West. This collection includes the papers of corporate giants such as United Grain Growers and Ogilvie Grain, along with donations from individuals and families that include diaries, letters, and other records of the small family farm. The acquisition of the Frederick Philip Grove papers in 1960 formed the nucleus of the Archives' specialized collection of writers' manuscripts. Today, it is one of the major archival sources for prairie literature, holding the papers of more than fifty authors. Included in this collection are the papers of poet and social activist Dorothy Livesay, poet and critic Eli Mandel, and bestselling writer Ralph Connor (the Reverend C.W. Gordon), and of contemporary writers such as David Arnason, Heather Robertson, and Carol Matas. Over time, the presence of the university Archives actually helped generate a teaching programme, and in 1990 the History Department set up the first history-based training programme for archivists in Canada.

Emőke Szathmáry

Born in Hungary, Szathmáry came to Canada as a child. Educated at the University of Toronto, she taught at Trent University, McMaster University, and the University of Western Ontario. Before coming to the U of M as its tenth president in 1996, she had been vice-president of McMaster University. An anthropologist, she has focussed her research on the genetics of Aboriginal peoples in North America.

The new Icelandic Reading Room in the U of M Elizabeth Dafoe Library, opened in 2000 as part of the Icelandic Millennium celebrations (Photo: Henry Kalen).

Another example of constructive infrastructure has been the development of the University Teaching Services (UTS) at the university. Created in 1972, the growth of UTS

The U of M Archives holds many important collections, including over 150,000 photographs and 2.5 million clippings from the *Winnipeg Tribune*.

has been most rapid since the mid-1980s. It expanded largely in response to a sense that good teaching was not sufficiently recognized and that there was little opportunity to learn how to be a more effective teacher. The UTS objective, therefore, has been "to assist faculty members and graduate students who teach courses to experience greater success in their teaching and teaching related responsibilities." Much of the assistance has been in the form of workshops, the publication of a newsletter, the establishment of a new faculty orientation programme, and a one-on-one peer consultation programme. The programme has also developed a system for recognizing teaching award-winners (the Wall of Recognition) and a special reception where graduating students honour teachers who have been especially influential in their lives.

Obviously, a good many new programmes and courses have been introduced at the U of M since 1977. Probably the academic programme that has had the greatest general impact is

University 1. By the late 1980s, the university became concerned that many first-year students were not adequately prepared, either academically or emotionally, for their university experience, resulting in both high attrition rates and a high utilization of student services. Clearly, a programme was needed that would improve retention rates and emotional satisfaction among first-year students. An "Introduction to University" course, a three-credit-hour course for first-year students, was first offered in 1992-93. By 1995 Senate had decided that most students entering university directly from secondary school should enrol in a single organizational entity, which would be called "University 1" and which would be independent of any single faculty or school. University 1 was first mounted as a programme in the summer of 1998. Students could select from more than 200 first-year courses in twelve faculties and schools to fulfil their first-year requirements. This wide range of choice allowed students to try out courses in several disciplines while taking prerequisites to qualify for one or more programmes in second year. Course choice, coupled with extensive advising and programming, has helped students make a successful academic and personal transition to the university.

While many of the events of the last twenty-five years at the university have been innovations, others represent continuations of long and proud University of Manitoba traditions. Sports have been an important part of the university since its earliest days, and this tradition has been maintained with many individual and team achievements. As just one example, in one weekend in early March of 2001, the men's and women's Bisons volleyball teams pulled off a rare double, winning both the CIAU men's and women's national volleyball titles. The U of M has been producing winning volleyball teams for many years, based on a provincial high school volleyball programme that has to be one of the best in the nation. The records speak for themselves. The women's team has been to the national tournament every season for the past fifteen years, winning gold in 1990, 1991, 1992, and 2001. This year's team, a collection of Manitoba players, started slowly, and was the underdog throughout the tournament. The men's team has

been to the last seventeen national tournaments, winning in 1984 and 1985, 1995 and 1996, and 2000 and 2001. The Bisons men had a 17–1 conference record and a seventeen-match winning streak during the season.

Some of the good things that have happened at the university have been one-time-only or simply fun projects. On 18 March 1991, one of the largest ditchball tournaments in the world was held on the Fort Garry campus. Twelve teams of eleven students each competed. Three of the students on each team had to be female. All teams came from the Faculty of

The U of M was part of the community effort that fought Manitoba's 1997 Flood of the Century. While faculty from the department of engineering helped to plan the province's flood defences, UMinfo's website (below) provided up-to-the-minute information and communication for both a local and international audience.

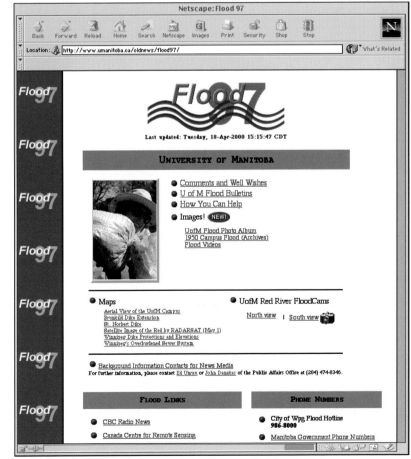

Architecture, because, for some unknown reason, ditchball had neither caught on across the campus, nor beyond it. The ditch used in 1991 was constructed of snow to a depth of four metres and was more than fourteen metres long. It was shaped like a boomerang and had an ice floor and walls. Points were scored by throwing the ditchball up the ditch to the team's goalie at one end. A team from Environmental Studies III was the eventual winner.

One of Winnipeg's most enduring social institutions (although scarcely unique to the city) is the "garage sale," in which people sell their unwanted goods, usually from their garages on Saturday morning. Attending garage sales has become a Saturday morning activity for many Winnipeggers. On 24 October 1983, the university held the "world's largest garage sale" at Taché Hall, as every unit cleaned out its closets and donated surplus material to be recycled through the community. The mountain of goods filled two floors in the hall, and consisted of everything from old books to old computers to old agricultural implements. By the time the doors opened at 1:00 p.m. on the day of the well-publicized sale, a huge crowd had assembled outside the building. People purchased everything in sight, including 6000 old library books for $15,144. This writer

The University of Manitoba crest, approved by the BoG in 1956. The crest's four quarters represent the founding constituents of the university. Clockwise from top left they are: the province of Manitoba; St. Boniface College; Manitoba College and United College; and St. John's College.

remembers obtaining a complete twelve-volume set (somewhat out of date) of the *Encyclopedia Canadiana* at the sale for the bargain price of $5.00, and proudly staggering through the hordes of shoppers to his car (parked miles away) with his haul. Estimates of attendance at the garage sale were in excess of 15,000 people.

■   ■   ■

Founded just seven years after the founding of the province itself, the University of Manitoba has grown and matured along with its community. Begun—as George Bryce suggested—with the precocious optimism of a booming frontier society, the university has grown from a federation of small denominational colleges with a few dozen students to one with two significant campuses with more than 19,000 undergraduate students, 2600 graduate students, 1900 faculty, and 2000 support staff and an annual budget of $323 million. In its 125 years, the University of Manitoba has educated generations of students, and now has more than 110,000 alumni internationally. It has been home to research that has both saved and enriched lives around the world. Although the University of Manitoba's first 125 years have not been without trials, for every trial and challenge there have been many triumphs as well.

Appendix

**CHANCELLORS OF
THE UNIVERSITY OF MANITOBA**

Archbishop Robert Machray	1877-1904
Archbishop Samuel Matheson	1908-1934
John Dafoe	1934-1944
Justice Andrew Dysart	1944-1952
Victor Sifton	1952-1959
Justice Samuel Freedman	1959-1968
Peter Curry	1968-1974
Richard Bowles	1974-1977
Isabel Auld	1977-1986
Henry Duckworth	1986-1992
Arthur Mauro	1992-2001
William Norrie	2001-

**PRESIDENTS OF THE
UNIVERSITY OF MANITOBA**

James MacLean	1913-1934
Sidney E. Smith	1934-1944
Henry Armes	1944-1945
Albert W. Trueman	1945-1948
Albert Henry S. Gillson	1948-1954
Hugh Hamilton Saunderson	1954-1970
Ernest Sirluck	1970-1977
Ralph Campbell	1977-1982
Arnold Naimark	1982-1996
Emőke Szathmáry	1996-

**CHAIRS OF THE
BOARD OF GOVERNORS**

Isaac Pitblado	1917-1924
John A. Machray	1924-1932
Dalton C. Coleman	1933-1934
Justice Andrew K. Dysart	1934-1944
Justice H.A. Bergman	1944-1946
W.J. Parker	1947-1950
Victor Sifton	1950-1952
Justice Paul G. DuVal	1952-1955
A.R. Tucker	1955-1960
George T. Richardson	1960-1964
Peter D. Curry	1964-1968
F.O. Meighen	1968-1969
M.J. Arpin	1969-1971
Justice Brian Dickson	1971-1973
Peter A. Cain	1973-1975
Sol Kanee	1975
W. Raymond McQuade	1975-1980
Dr. Louie C. Melosky	1980-1983
Alexander M. Runciman	1983-1988
David Malaher	1988-1991
William H. Mitchell	1991-1994
Keith Findlay	1994-1995
Pamela LeBoldus	1995-1997
Paul M. Soubry	1997-

**UNIVERSITY OF MANITOBA
DISTINGUISHED PROFESSORS**

H.G. Friesen Physiology	1981
J.C. Gilson Agricultural Economics	1981
N.S. Mendelsohn Mathematics and Astronomy	1981
T.P. Schaefer Chemistry	1982
A. Sehon Immunology	1982
H. Cohen Applied Mathematics	1983
L.G. Israels Medicine	1983
D. Gibson Law	1984
A. Morrish Physics	1984
R. Stanton Computer Sciences	1984
J.M. Bowman Pediatrics	1985
G. Gratzer Mathematics	1985
R.P. Kroetsch English	1985
N. Anthonisen Medicine	1986
K.K. Klostermaier Religion	1986
A.R. Ronald Medicine	1986

J.L. Hamerton
Human Genetics 1987

J.G. Eales
Zoology........................ 1989

N.S. Dhalla
Physiology 1990

H.C. Card
Electrical and
Computer Engineering 1990

H.C. Wolfart
Linguistics 1993

E.J. Hinz
English 1993

P. Fortier
French and Spanish 1993

T. Anna
History 1997

N. Gupta
Mathematics and
Astronomy.................... 1997

F. Hawthorne
Geological Sciences......... 1997

Arnold Greenberg
Pediatrics and
Child Health 1998

John Nichols
Linguistics and
Native Studies................ 1998

Vaclav Smil
Geography 1998

Madgy Younes
Internal Medicine........... 1999

Willem T.H. van Oers
Physics and Astronomy..... 1999

**UNIVERSITY OF MANITOBA
MEMBERS OF THE
ROYAL SOCIETY OF CANADA**

ACADEMY II: ACADEMY
OF HUMANITIES AND SOCIAL SCIENCE

Anna, Timothy
History 1995

Barber, Clarence
Economics.................... 1977

Berry, E.G.
Classics 1971

Donnelly, Murray S.
Political Studies 1973

Driedger, Leo
Sociology...................... 1997

Friesen, Gerald
History 2001

Kinnear, E. Mary
History 2001

Klostermaier, Klaus
Religion 1997

Kroetsch, Robert
English 1986

Martin, Garry L.
Psychology 2001

Nichols, John D.
Linguistics 1997

Shields, Carol
English 1996

Wolfart, H. Chris
Linguistics 1995

ACADEMY III: ACADEMY OF SCIENCE

Anthonisen, Nicholas
Internal Medicine........... 1989

Bowman, John
Pediatrics 1986

Bushuk, Walter
Food Science 1986

Cerny, Petr
Geological Sciences......... 1991

Dhalla, Naranjan
Physiology 2000

Duckworth, H.E.
Physics........................ 1954

Eales, Geoffrey J.
Zoology........................ 1988

Ferguson, Robert B.
Geological Sciences......... 1961

Friesen, Henry G.
Physiology 1978

Gratzer, George
Mathematics and
Astronomy.................... 1973

Gupta, C. Kanta
Mathematics and
Astronomy.................... 1990

Gupta, Narain
Mathematics and
Astronomy.................... 1985

Hamerton, John L.
Human Genetics 1997

Hawthorne, Frank C.
Geological Sciences......... 1990

Lewis, Marion
Pediatrics and
Child Health 1993

Mendelsohn, Nathan S.
Mathematics and
Astronomy.................... 1957

Morrish, Allan H.
Physics........................ 1969

Naimark, Arnold
Past President
(Physiology) 1987

Ronald, Allan
Internal Medicine........... 2000

Schaefer, Theodore
Chemistry.................... 1973

Sehon, Alec
Immunology 1969

Shafai, Lotfollah
Electrical and Computer
Engineering 1998

Shebeski, L.H.
Agriculture 1968

Waygood, E.R.
Botany........................ 1971

Wilson, H.D.B.
Geological Sciences......... 1960

SPECIALLY ELECTED FELLOWS

Smil, Vaclav
Geography 1997

**UNIVERSITY OF MANITOBA
3M TEACHING AWARDS**

Jack London
(Law) 1987

Beverly J. Cameron
(Economics) 1991

Norman E. Cameron
(Economics) 1994

M.G. (Ron) Britton
(Biosystems Engineering). 1995
Donald Trim
(Applied Mathematics) 1997

PRESIDENTS OF UMSU

George H. Lee	1914
Rod K. Finlayson	1915
W.T. Straith	1916
U.D. Clark	1917
Eileen Bulman	1918
A.A. McCoubrey	1919
George H. Lee	1920
H. Bruce Chown	1921
C. Dick	1922
D. Black	1923
E.C. Corrigan	1924
F.W. Bamford	1925
Harry Moss	1926
T.E. Holland	1927
J.N. Crawford	1928
L. Adamson	1929
C.H.A. Walton	1930
W.L. Morton	1931
John S. Anderson	1932
W.M. Bendickson	1933
Hector J. Craig	1934
W. Donald Ross	1935
J.M. Robinson	1936
W.R.O. Turner	1937
William T. Cave	1938
R.O.A. Hunter	1939
G.R. Hunter	1940
John H. Halin	1941
Fred Tallman	1942
A.C. Hamilton	1943
Monte R. Halperin	1944
David S. Robertson	1945
Lynn A.K. Watt	1946
Peyton V. Lyon	1947
Fred R. Bicken	1948
William A. Appleby	1949

Arthur V. Mauro	1950
William Norrie	1951
Conrad Wyrzykowski	1952
Richard Bocking	1953
Scott Wright	1954
Miles Pepper	1955
Julius M. Koteles	1956
Charles Anderson	1957
Biran Knapheis	1958
James E. Foran	1959
Roy MacKenzie	1960
Linly G. Abdulah	
William Neville	1961
Marshall Rothstein	1962
Bruce Doern	1963
Richard Good	1964
Winston Dookeran	1965
David Sanders	1966
Chris Westdal	1967
Horace Paterson	1968
Alan L. Bodie	1969
Israel Lyon	1970
Roy Hamm	1971
Bill Balan	1972
John D. Perrin	1973
Robert M. Setters	1974
Victoria E. Lehman	1975
James F. Snidal	1976
Roger E. Nelson	1977
Caroline M. Dabrus	
Steven J. Ashton	1978
Debra Slade	1979
James Egan	1980
Timothy Rigby	1981
Eric Tatarchuk	1982
Michael Young	1983
Carol Manson	1984
Jeffrey Kushner	1985
Mark Rogers	1986
Kevin Janzen	1987
Robert A.M. Cielen	1988
Karen Taraska	1989

Adam DiCarlo	1990
Paul Kemp	1991
Paul Kemp	1992
Cory Pollock	1993
Blessing Rugara	1994
David Gratzer	1995
Trevor Lines	1996
Katherine Kowalchuk	1997
Christopher Kozier	1998
Steven Fletcher	1999
Steven Fletcher	2000

EDITORS OF THE MANITOBAN

Alex Sinclair	1916-1917
Graham Spry	1919-1920
	1920-1921
G. Hasted Dowker	1921-1922
Cecil Drew	1922-1923
David A. Maclennan	1923-1924
James Prendergast	1924-1925
Leonard L. Knott	1925-1926
T.R. Lancaster	1926-1927
J.A. MacKay	1927-1928
R.M. Macdonnell	1928-1929
C.H. Cowperthwaite	1929-1930
W.L. Morton	1930-1931
E. Maxwell Cohen	1931-1932
John E. Thompson	1932-1933
John C. Birt	1933-1934
John W. McInnis	1934-1935
Gordon W. Leckie	1935-1936
D'Arcy Dolan	1936-1937
Charles Mackenzie	1937-1938
James E. Wilson	1938-1939
Edward Parker	1939-1940
Sylvan F. Sommerfeld	1940-1941
Harvey Dryden	(Sept.-Feb.)
	1941-1942
Earle J. Beattie	(Feb.-Sept.)
	1941-1942
Bob Tivy	1942-1943

Ken Williamson........	1943-1944
Don Smith	1944-1945
Dave McQueen........	1945-1946
Chris Young	1946-1947
Max Haskell	1947-1948
Jack Madden	1948-1949
Murray Smith	1949-1950
Harold Buchwald	1950-1951
Joe Gelmon	1951-1952
Clare Irwin..............	1952-1953
Milton Orris............	1953-1954

Clare Irwin,
  Avonne Horkoff,
  Charles Huband,
  Frank Muldoon
  (editorial board) ....
	1954-1955

Ron Kinney.............	1955-1956
Reg Skene	1956-1957
Brian Knapheis	1957-1958
Lyon Weidman	1958-1959
Dave Humphreys.......	1959-1960
Peter Herrndorf	1960-1961
Heather Robertson	1961-1962
Robert McKenzie......	1962-1963
Martin Knelman.......	1963-1964
Michael P. Moore......	1964-1965
Carol Schollie	1965-1966
Eugen Weiss.............	1966-1967
Brian Gory..............	1967-1968
Sheila Moore	1968-1969
Alvin Finkel.............	1969-1970
Ed Reed	1970-1971
Paul Sullivan............	1971-1972
Maria Horvath..........	1972-1973
after February 1973 the paper worked as a collective	
Bob Harrison, Nick Smirnow........	1973-1974
no editor in chief stated...........	1974-1975
Noelle Boughton	1975-1976

Steve Lobay,
  Garth Cramer,
  Daly deGagne,
  Doug Smith...........
	1976-1977

Doug Smith.............	1977-1978
Brock McGinnis	1978-1979
Bryan Dewatt	1979-1980
Andrew Coyne	1980-1981
Jon Penner.............	1981-1982
Shelley Kowalchuk (News/Features)	
Danielle Comeau (News/Copy)	1982-1983
Bill Swift................	1983-1984
Kevin Russell, Michael Malegus.....	1984-1985
no editor in chief......	1985-1986
no editor in chief......	1986-1987
Angela Heck, Elizabeth Bricknell..	1987-1988
Eric Bertram...........	1989-1990
Paul Hayward	1990-1991
Alayne Armstrong	1991-1992
Jeff Zuk.................	1992-1993
Michelle Paquette	1993-1994
Chris Zuk	1994-1995
Jeff Oliver	1995-1996
Matt Lazowski	1996-1997
Ed Danzen..............	1997-1998
Ed Danzen...............	1998-1999
Kevin Matthews.........	1999-2000
Phil Koch................	2000-2001
Bernice Pontanillia	2001-2002

RECIPIENTS OF THE DISTINGUISHED ALUMNI AWARD (FORMERLY THE ALUMNI JUBILEE AWARD)

Hon. Mitchell Sharp	1959
Dr. Joseph Doupe............	1960
Dr. Henry Duckworth........	1961
Dr. William Allen	1962
Richard Hunter, QC	1963

Hon. Alfred Monnin	1964
Dr. David Golden............	1965
Dr. Leonard Shebeski	1966
Prof. Gordon Donaldson....	1967
Dr. John Parkin	1968
Simma Holt	1969
Dr. Wallace Grant............	1970
Dr. John Page	1971
Mary Elizabeth Bayer	1972
Hon. William John McKeag	1973
Dr. Morley Cohen	1974
William Kurelek/ Kathleen Richardson.......	1975
Dr. Robert Anderson.........	1976
Dr. James Burns..............	1977
Dr. Walter Bushuk	1978
Israel Asper	1979
Prof. Grant Marshall	1980
Esmond Jarvis.................	1981
Ivan Eyre	1982
Beverly Bajus	1983
Dr. Cameron Jay	1984
Margaret Storey...............	1985
Dr. Percy Barsky	1986
Monty Hall	1987
Gail Watson....................	1988
Betty Jane Wylie	1989
Dr. Allan Ronald..............	1990
Leslie Hughes	1991
Jean Carson	1992
Barry Broadfoot	1993
Susan Lewis....................	1994
Dr. Henry Friesen	1995
Chief Justice Richard Scott..	1996
Dr. John M. Bowman	1997
Dr. Peter Kondra	1998
R.W. (Bill) Pollock / Marion Vasey-Genser	1999
Robert Silver	2000
Dr. Jarislaw Barwinsky........	2001

Selected Reading

This bibliography is intended neither as a complete guide to the published and unpublished material available on the history of the University of Manitoba, nor as a listing of the materials used in the preparation of this work. It represents, instead, a brief listing of published work on the history of the U of M, intended for the use of readers.

AUTOBIOGRAPHY AND MEMOIRS:

Broadfoot, Barry, *My Own Years* (New York, 1983)

Camsell, Charles, *Son of the North* (Toronto, 1954)

Duckworth, Henry E., *One Version of the Facts: My Life in the Ivory Tower* (Winnipeg, 2000)

Eccles, W.J. "Introduction," *Essays on New France* (Toronto, 1989)

Kirkconnell, Watson, *A Slice of Canada: A Memoir* (Toronto, 1967)

Lower, A.R.M., *My First Seventy-Five Years* (Toronto, 1967)

Saunderson, Hugh H., *The Saunderson Years* (Winnipeg, 1981)

Sirluck, Ernest, *First Generation: An Autobiography* (Toronto, 1996)

Trueman, Albert W., *A Second View of Things: A Memoir* (Toronto, 1982)

Walton, Charles H.A., *A Medical Odyssey: Vignettes of People and Events at Home and Abroad* (Winnipeg, 1980)

Wright, Eric, *Always Give a Penny to the Blind Man* (Toronto, 2000)

COMMISSIONS AND REPORTS:

Report of the Royal Commission on the University of Manitoba (Winnipeg, 1910).

Report of the Royal Commission on the Possibility of Readjusting the Relations of the Higher Institutions of Learning so as to Provide for Their Support and Increase Their Service to the Province (Winnipeg, 1924)

Report of the Royal Commission on Impairment of the University of Manitoba Trust Funds, 1932-33 (Winnipeg, 1933)

GENERAL:

Axelrod, Paul, *Making a Middle Class: Student Life in English Canada during the Thirties* (Montreal and London, 1990)

Cameron, D.M., *More than an Academic Question: Universities, Government, and Public Policy in Canada* (1991)

Masters, Donald C., *Protestant Church Colleges in Canada: A History* (Toronto, 1966)

Shook, Lawrence K., *Catholic Post-Secondary Education in English-Speaking Canada: A History* (Toronto, 1971)

BRANDON COLLEGE:

McKenzie, A.E., *History of Brandon College Inc.* (1962)

Stone, C.G., and F. J. Carnett, *Brandon College: A History, 1899-1967* (Brandon, 1969)

MANITOBA COLLEGE:

Edwards, J.A.M., *Andrew Baird of Manitoba College* (Winnipeg, 1972)

Mackay, J., et al., eds., *Manitoba College* (Winnipeg, 1921)

Rumball, W.G., and D.A. MacLennan, *Manitoba College: An Account of Her Achievements, Past and Present, and of Her Contribution to the Growth and Development of Western Canada and to the Progress of Presbyterianism* (Winnipeg, 1921)

MANITOBA LAW SCHOOL:

Edwards, Clifford H.C., and Jack R. London, "The University of Manitoba Faculty of Law 1966-1984," *Dalhousie Law Journal*, 9,1 (1984): 166-180

Legal Education in Manitoba (Winnipeg, 1970)

MANITOBA MEDICAL SCHOOL:

Carr, Ian, and Robert E. Beamish, *Manitoba Medicine: A Brief History* (Winnipeg, 1999)

PHARMACY, FACULTY OF:

Steele, John W., *The History of the Faculty of Pharmacy, University of Manitoba 1899-1999* (Winnipeg, 1999)

ST. BONIFACE COLLEGE:

Regnier, P.R., "A History of St. Boniface College," unpublished MEd thesis (University of Manitoba, 1964)

ST. JOHN'S COLLEGE:

Fraser, William J., *St. John's College, Winnipeg 1866-1966: A History of the First Hundred Years of the College* (Winnipeg, 1966)

ST. MARY'S ACADEMY AND COLLEGE:

Malloy, M., "A History of St. Mary's Academy and College and its Times," unpublished MEd thesis (University of Manitoba, 1952)

ST. PAUL'S COLLEGE:

Friesen, Gerald, and Richard Lebrun, eds., *St. Paul's College: University of Manitoba: Memories and Histories* (Winnipeg, 1999)

Laping, N., "A History of St. Paul's College," unpublished MEd thesis (University of Manitoba, 1972)

UNITED COLLEGE:

Bedford, Allen Gerald, *The University of Winnipeg: A History of the Founding Colleges* (Toronto, 1976)

UNIVERSITY COLLEGE:

Donnelly, Murray, *University College: A Personal History* (Winnipeg, 1989)

UNIVERSITY OF MANITOBA:

Bennett, Richard, "It Gathers Strength as It Goes: A Brief History of the Alumni Association of the University of Manitoba," *Alumni Review* (summer 1982)

Corbett, E.A., *Sidney Earle Smith* (Toronto, 1961)

Glenn, A.L., "A History of the University of Manitoba, to 1927," unpublished MA thesis (University of Manitoba, 1927)

Gregor, Alexander Douglas, "The Federated University Structure in Manitoba," unpublished PhD dissertation (Michigan State University, 1974)

Machray, Robert, *Life of Robert Machray* (Toronto, 1909)

Morton, W.L. *One University: A History of the University of Manitoba, 1877-1952* (Toronto, 1957)

WESLEY COLLEGE:

Kirkconnell, Watson, *The Golden Jubilee of Wesley College, Winnipeg, 1888-1938* (Winnipeg, 1938)

Wilson, N.R., *The Case for Wesley College* (Winnipeg, 1910)

COLLEGE AND UNIVERSITY PUBLICATIONS:

a. Student Newspapers and Yearbooks:

   The Brown and Gold, 1915-1976

   The Gleam, 1913-1914

   The Johnian, 1931 ff.

   Le Bonifacien

   M.A.C. Gazette, 1908-

   Manitoba College Journal, 1887-1913 (scattered issues)

   The Manitoban, 1917-

   The Uniter, 1948-

   Vox Wesleyana, 1897-1938

b. Other Student Publications:

   Report of the Student Commission of the University of Manitoba (Winnipeg, 1932)

   UMSU Alternate Course Guide, 1971-1976

c. University Publications:

   U of M Alumni Journal, 1936-

   U of M Bulletin, 1968-

   U of M Calendars

   Report of the President of the U of M, 1920-